4100/1057: ...ght
C0-AQZ-421

Sol Darrel (P294)
(Uncle Jim Shires)

P. 50
P154
P173
P222

THE WHITE ROSE GARLAND

OF YORKSHIRE DIALECT VERSE AND LOCAL AND FOLK-LORE RHYMES

THE WHITE ROSE GARLAND

OF YORKSHIRE DIALECT VERSE AND LOCAL AND FOLK-LORE RHYMES

Chosen and Edited with Notes

by

W. J. HALLIDAY, M.A., Ph.D.
Chairman of Council, Yorkshire Dialect Society

and

ARTHUR STANLEY UMPLEBY
Honorary Secretary, Yorkshire Dialect Society

LONDON
J. M. DENT AND SONS LTD

This book is copyright. It may not be reproduced whole or in part by any method without written permission. Application should be made to the publishers:

J. M. DENT & SONS LTD
Aldine House · Bedford St. · London

Made in Great Britain
by
Richard Clay and Company, Ltd.,
Bungay, Suffolk

First published 1949

TO

DOROTHY UNA RATCLIFFE

PRESIDENT OF THE YORKSHIRE DIALECT SOCIETY,

LOVER OF THE YORKSHIRE DIALECT,

POET OF THE YORKSHIRE DALES

PREFACE

This collection of Yorkshire Dialect Verse and Local and Folklore Rhymes celebrates the fiftieth anniversary of the founding of the Yorkshire Dialect Society. The success attending the publication by the Society of small collections of dialect verse and of prose during the War has encouraged the Society to issue this new collection. Professor Moorman's anthology, published in 1916, has gained for itself a secure place in the affections of all Yorkshire-dialect lovers. Its introduction is beyond praise, and the selection of the poems was made with discrimination and skill. But much good dialect verse has been written since those days, and this anthology includes the best of contemporary verse.

To make sure that the field of new dialect verse was well covered, the Council of the Yorkshire Dialect Society appointed three sub-committees to make a preliminary survey of available recent verse, each sub-committee confining itself to the verse of one Riding. For the East Riding the members were Messrs C. H. Drewry, F. Austin Hyde, and R. M. Wilson; for the North Riding, the President (Mrs McGrigor Phillips), Messrs F. W. Dowson, and A. Stanley Umpleby; for the West Riding, Messrs E. G. Bayford, F. A. Carter, and B. R. Dyson. It is with much regret that we have to record the death of Mr Drewry and Mr Dowson, soon after the committees had completed their task. The collating of the reports of these sub-committees has been done by the two editors, who are solely responsible for the final selection of poems. It is pleasing here to acknowledge with a deep sense of gratitude the labours of these members.

The best and most effective order in which these poems could be presented was a matter of long consideration. Should they be separated into Ridings? There was much to be said in favour of such an order, but the editors felt there was one considerable drawback. The topographical boundaries of the Ridings are not the dialectal ones. Thomas Blackah, Tom Twisleton, David Lewis, and Miss May Yorke write in the West Riding administrative area, but use a dialect that is northern in form. It was decided, therefore, to print the poems in strict alphabetical order of authorship. This obscures historical development (if there is such a thing), but adds to the facility with which authors may be traced and read. The collection, after all, is intended primarily for literary interest and enjoyment.

This brings us to the question of dialect. The editors accept no responsibility for the linguistic accuracy of the dialect forms in these poems. Dialects are subject to movement and flux, and in some places the dialect student will find a word or expression which has been introduced from another area, or developed on alien lines. The author is judge, jury, and defendant in every such case. We are not compiling a dialect atlas, nor presenting a dialect thesis. The dialect is always accurate in the sense that it represents the speech of some person in some particular area. No attempt has been made to normalize spelling. This would indeed be a gigantic labour. The shades of sound are so fine in the dialects that anything short of phonetic transcription is bound to contain errors and inconsistencies. And even phonetic transcription does not give those subtle nuances of accentuation and intonation which are among the characteristic features of the spoken dialect.

A glossary has been added to the collection to assist the reader. In giving modern equivalents for the dialect words and expressions, we have confined ourselves to the meanings which the words and expressions carry in their particular context. It is important to recognize this, as every user of Wright's great Dialect Dictionary will testify.

We have excluded from the collection long narrative poems like Richard Blakeborough's 'T' Hunt o' Yatton Brigg', J. S. Fletcher's 'Leet Livvy', 'The York Minster Screen', and others. These poems have great literary merits, but they would be out of place in a collection that is predominantly lyrical in character. They should be brought together in a single volume, a task the Society may well be advised to undertake in the future. But, whilst excluding these longer poems, we have taken the liberty of giving a few stanzas from Castillo's long poem, 'Awd Isaac'. This long poem, in its analysis of religious experience, has the subjectivity of lyrical verse, and is, in the second place, so characteristic of its author's method and technique that we have abstracted a few stanzas. We hope that this show of violence does not do it wrong. We have taken an extract also from the 1683 'A Yorkshire Dialogue'. Historically the poem is too important to be omitted, but its length and its difficult early dialect led us to take this course. With these (and one or two minor exceptions, like Tom Twisleton's 'The Christmas Party') the poems are presented as they left the authors' hands. Moorman altered many of the poems in spelling and in length to obtain a greater uniformity. We have preferred the author's version in every instance where it could be checked.

We hope the annotation will not be considered excessive. It has been our aim in the notes to give only such associated items of interest in connection with the poem or rhyme as will increase the reader's appreciation of its matter and art. Besides, much of the material which we have used is not now readily accessible, and is in danger of being lost or forgotten.

But we are anxious to avoid a merely antiquarian approach. These poems are to be read as literature, and not as quaint survivals of an outmoded and inferior form of speech. Dialect has long been under the scalpel of the linguistic 'autopsist': here we present it as a body of England's, breathing English air—or at any rate that part of it that blows over Yorkshire. For here you will find poets of varied backgrounds and from many walks of life: the peasant poet, the artisan poet, the scholar poet, the town poet, the country poet, all expressing themselves, their loves, their hates, their hopes, their fears, their humour, their melancholy in the homely folk-speech of the people. There is a chapter of the social history of England here, a chapter that tells of the slow emergence of a social conscience in English industry and politics. The great revival of romance in English poetry at the close of the nineteenth century was ushered in by (among other things) a return to nature; the rise of dialect verse (the voice of the people) in the middle of the nineteenth century was the direct outcome of that negation of nature which we call the Industrial Revolution. It was an indictment of the ills and miseries that followed in the wake of expanding trade and a machinery-dominated economy. Many of the songs of Ben Preston, John Hartley, and Samuel Laycock, and of the compilers of Annuals and Almanacks, are links with those of Hood and Elliott (himself a Yorkshireman) in the ceaseless (and eventually successful) campaign for cheaper food, the emancipation of the sweated labourer, better wages, and a higher standard of living. It is significant that some half-dozen of the poets represented in this anthology began working before the age of ten. They were educated in the hard school of experience, and they wrote with burning sincerity of ills they themselves had felt and seen: it was a fierce resentment that made their verses. Yet it was not satire they wrote. Satire implies a degree of sophistication they never acquired. They released their cabin'd, ample spirits in simple realistic narrative or poignant lyrical cry. It is noteworthy that most of this verse had reference to the textile industry. Incidentally, it is curious that the great coal-mining industry (the core of the revolution) seems to have inspired no one in Yorkshire to sing either its hazards or its rewards. In Northumberland the ex-miner, Joseph Skipsey, wrote, but not in dialect, of the perils and sorrows of his craft.

But of course our dialect poetry is wider in theme and scope than this. The writers we have just mentioned were not always complaining of their lot. Indeed, this represents but a small fraction of their verse. They belonged in the main to the industrial West Riding, but the dales and the wolds and the moors have produced their singing birds as well. And here we leave the loom and the mule and the stithy and the flat-backs for the curlew, the purple ling, the laverock, and the lillilow. The pipes play a milder air, a sweeter note, and even if the moil and toil of a farmer's life is the theme, there is a softer approach and a kindlier tone.

But although tragedy lurks sometimes in the background, it is the humour of Yorkshire dialect verse that is its most priceless possession. There might be thoughts that occasionally lay too deep for tears, but there are never thoughts that lie too deep for laughter. And this rich humour is an attitude to life, an attitude of glad acceptance of the joys of life, and a recognition that these, on balance, are more numerous than the ills. It is more than the mere Herrickian grace after meat, the satisfaction of thanking God for a good dinner. It is the faculty of seeing into the heart of things, of separating the genuine from the spurious, of judging character, and of having a balanced sense of values. The poet can laugh at the world because he has learnt to laugh at himself.

Side by side with this humour—perhaps, indeed, one facet of it—there is found in much of the verse a real sympathy with misfortune, a sense of the tears in mortal things. Yet it never degenerates into pessimism. What man has made of man never makes the poet bitter: much more often it is the gratitude of men, their nobility under suffering, their nameless unremembered acts of kindness and of love that inspire his highest flights.

You will find all these qualities, and more, in these poems. But there is one other noteworthy feature. In the last few years there has been a revival of interest in dialect poetry, and a new dialect verse has arisen, written, not by those who now habitually speak the dialect, but by those who were familiar with that atmosphere in early life, or have been drawn to it by temperament and inclination, or have been impressed (to use the jargon of the day) by its literary potentialities, in the course of their reading and study. You might think that the resulting product would be a spurious artificial thing, but you would be wrong. Instead, the movement has enriched our dialect verse, for it has led to experimentation in verse forms, and to a less narrow conception of the function and scope of dialect literature. Dialect verse need not be written solely in Quince's 'eight and six' or Bottom's 'eight and eight', or, for that matter, in Burns' 'Mouse' stanza. It can be moulded into sonnet or sestina without loss of naturalness or simplicity. But here the reader must judge for himself.

The other sections of this anthology call for briefer comment. The local and folk-lore rhymes represent a selection—and that only a small one—from a large mass which we have gathered in a life-time's reading. Our aim has been to be as representative as possible, to include as many places and show as many sides of the folk-lore as we can within the narrow compass of a single volume. But there can never be any finality in this section: the line has to be drawn somewhere, and readers, we hope, will be induced to add to and supplement our researches by their own experience and reading. This is our excuse, also, for the fulness of the references in the notes to these sections. There are customs and rhymes which have a wider provenance than the county of Yorkshire. Obviously a county boundary bounds nothing but administrative details. But we have taken pains to attest their specific associations with our county, and in order to prove their (and our) *bona fides*, we have always quoted the source or the authority.

The biographical notes are inserted to acquaint readers, not so much with the facts of the writers' lives, as with their published works. The lists of works are not complete, but they show, we think, what are the most important of their writings. Dates, except of publications, are not given in the notes on living writers. Diligent search has failed to find details of one or two of the contributors. Perhaps, through the goodwill of some of our readers, this can be rectified in a future edition.

We give separately a list of those to whom we are under many obligations for help whilst we have been engaged on the work. But it is fitting to make special reference here to our President, Dorothy Una Ratcliffe. The book owes much to the inspiration of her own enthusiasm and her love for all things Yorkshire. It is with more than formal gratitude that we formally inscribe the anthology to her.

W. J. H.

May, 1949. A. S. U.

MOTTOES

'You shall therefore understand: That the Countie of Yorke was in the Saxon tongue called Evona-ycyne, and now commonly Yorkshire farre greater and more numerous in the Circuit of her miles than any Shire of England. Shee is much bound to the singular love and motherly care of Nature, in placing her under so temperate a clime, that in every measure she is indifferently fruitfull. If one part of her be stony, and a sandy barren ground: another is fertile and richly adorned with Corne-fields. If you here finde it naked and destitute of Woods, you shall see it there shadowed with Forrests full of trees, that have very thicke bodies, sending forth many fruitfull and profitable branches. If one place of it be Moorish, Mirie, and unpleasant, another makes a free tender of delight, and presents it selfe to the eye, full of beautie and contentive varietie.'

John Speed. 1627.

'I will prove, in the teeth of a parcel of brokers and retailers of ancient rhapsodies, and such mouldy trash, that our vulgar tongue is not so mean, silly, inept, poor, barren, and contemptible, as they pretend.'

Heroic Deeds and Sayings of the Good Pantagruel. 1532.

'Every province loves its dialect: for it is, properly speaking, the element in which the soul draws its breath.'

Goethe's *Autobiography.* 1831.

'He spoke the King's English in one circle, and the King's Yorkshire in another.'

Southey: *The Doctor.* 1834–47.

'It was a great Answer of the Shunamite Woman, *I dwell among my own People.*'

William Penn: *Some Fruits of Solitude.* 1693.

'Let them record them, that are better skild,
And know the moniments of passed times:
Onely what needeth shall be here fulfild,
T'express some part of that great equipage.'

Spenser: *Faerie Queene.* 1589–96.

'And I come after, glenyng here and there,
And am ful glad yf I may fynde an ere.'

Chaucer: *Prologue to the Legende of Goode Women.* 1380–86.

Ther nys no man that may reporten al.

Chaucer: *The Squire's Tale.* 1386.

CONTENTS

ACKNOWLEDGMENTS

ON behalf of the Yorkshire Dialect Society we desire to express our grateful thanks to all those who have contributed poems to this collection. Their ready co-operation has alone made possible this up-to-date assembly of dialect verse. They are William Beaumont, Geraldine Binnell, Henrietta Blakeston, Fred Brown, F. A. Carter, W. Cowley, C. W. Eastwood, Brenda English, Elsie A. Grassby, James R. Gregson, George Hardwick, Ruth Hedger, Florence May Hopper, Robert Horspool, F. Austin Hyde, Letitia Langstaff, Fred Lawton, Wilson Midgley, E. Irene Myers, Q. Nicholas, George Allen North, A. Irving Parke, Irene Petch, Dorothy Una Ratcliffe, Irene Sutcliffe, Ethel Walter, May Yorke.

To the following holders of copyright we extend our gratitude for permission to publish copyright poems: Mr J. Fairfax Blakeborough, M.C. (Richard Blakeborough), Miss Carlill (J. A. Carlill), Mrs Charlesworth (Douglas Charlesworth), Mrs Cowling (George H. Cowling), Mrs Elgee (Frank Elgee), Mr Herbert Hampson (Walter Hampson), Messrs Watmough (John Hartley), Mr H. E. Hatton (Edmund Hatton), Mrs Moorman (F. W. Moorman), Mr N. Thwaite (John Thwaite), Miss Turner (Sir Ben Turner), Mrs A. Seville (Ammon Wrigley). If we have omitted to obtain permission for any poems still in copyright, we offer our apologies.

To Mr E. G. Bayford, Mr B. R. Dyson, and Mr O. B. Stokes, who have helped in the compilation of the biographical notes, we are much indebted.

Our obligations to certain standard publications will be obvious. Especially, with gratitude, we single out that Yorkshire classic, Richard Blakeborough's *Yorkshire Wit, Character, Folk-lore, and Customs*, and F. W. Moorman's *Anthology of Yorkshire Dialect Poems.* To Mr J. Fairfax Blakeborough, M.C., we are greatly indebted for the privilege of making use of the very valuable George Calvert–M. Stapylton manuscript book in his possession; and to the Chief Librarian of Leeds, Mr F. G. B. Hutchings, who readily placed the resources of his Library's fine collection of Yorkshire books at our disposal and gave us special facilities for using it; and to Mrs M. Lowther and the staff of the Darlington Public Library for similar help.

W. J. H.
A. S. U.

INDEX OF AUTHORS

YORKSHIRE DIALECT VERSE, 1673—1947

ANONYMOUS

I

A Yorkshire Dialogue between an Awd Wife, a Lass, and a Butcher

(1673)

AWD WIFE. Pretha now, lass, gang into t'hurn
An' fetch me heame a skeel o' burn;
Na, pretha, barn, mak heaste an' gang,
I's mar my deagh, thou stays sae lang.

LASS. Why, Gom, I's gea, bud, for my pains,
You's gie me a frundel o' your grains.

AWD WIFE. My grains, my barn! Marry! not I,
My draugh's for t'gilts an' galts i' t'sty.
Than, pretha, look i' t'garth and see
What owsen i' the stand-hecks be.

LASS. Blukrins! they'll put, I dare not gang
Oute'en you'll len' me t'great leap-stang.

AWD WIFE. Tak t'frugan, or t'awd maulin-shaft,
Coom tite agean an' be not daft.

LASS. Gom, t'great bull-segg he's brokken lowse,
An' he, he's hiked your broad-horned owse;
An' t'owse is fall'n into t'swine-trough,
I think he's brokken his cameril-hough.

AWD WIFE. Whaw! Whaw! lass, mak heaste to t'smedy,
He's noo dead, for he rowts already;
He's boun; oh! how it bauks an' stangs!
His lisk e'en bumps an' bobs wi' pangs.

His weazen-pipe's as dry as dust,
His dew-lap's swelled, he cannot hoast.
He beals; tak t'barghams off o' t'beams
An' fetch some breckons frae the clames.
Frae t'banks go fetch me a weam-tow,
My nowt's e'en wrecken'd, he'll not dow.
E'en wellanerin! for my nowt,
For syke a musan ne'er was wrowt.
Put t'wyes amell yon stirks an' steers
I' t'owmer, an' sneck the lear-deers.
See if Goff Hyldroth be gain-hand,
Thou helterful, how dares ta stand!

LASS. He'll coom belive, or aibles titter,
For when he hard i' what a twitter
Your poor owse lay, he took his flail
An' hang'd 't by t'swipple on a nail;
An' teuk a mell fra t'top o' t'wharns
An' sware he'd ding your owse i' t'harns.
He stack his shak-fork up i' t'esins
An' teuk his jerkin off o' t'gresins.
Then teuk his mittens, reached his bill,
An' off o' t'yune-head teuk a swill
To kep t'owse blude in. Leuk, he's coom.

AWD WIFE. Than reach a thivel or a strum
To stir his blude; stand not to tauk.
Hing t'reckans up o' t'rannel-bauk.
God ye good-morn, Goff; I's e'en fain
You'll put my owse out o' his pain.

BUTCHER. Hough-band him, tak thir weevils hine
Frae t'rape's end; this is not a swine
We kill, where ilkane hauds a fooit.
I's ready now, ilkane leuk to it.
Then 'Beef!' i' God's name I now cry.
Stretch out his legs an' let him lie
Till I coom stick him. Where's my swill?
Come hither, lass; haud, haud, haud still.

LASS. What mun I do wi' t'blude?

BUTCHER. Thou fool,
Teem 't down i' t'garth, i' t'midden-pool.
Good beef, by t'mass! an' when 'tis hung
I's roll it down wi' tooth an' tongue,
An' gobble 't down e'en till I worry.
An' whan neist mell we mak a lurry
A piece o' this frae t'kimlin browt
By t'Rood! 't will be as good as owt.

AWD WIFE. Maut-hearted fool, I e'en could greet
To see my owse dead at my feet.
I thank you, Goff; I's wipe my een
An', please, you too.

BUTCHER. Why, Gom Green?

2

A Yorkshire Dialogue

(1683)

F. Mack hast good Pegg, sweep th'house and don the seaun,
Our Land-Lord, woman, will be here by Neaun.
I had an Inklin on't at th'Arvall Feast,
Methinks he macks deevlish stickle but hast.

M. It's time for me about the House to Tripp,
Hee's be as welcome as watter into a Shipp.
It's nut aboon Three weeks gane sin th'Rent day,
Husband, what have you gitten upp to pay?

F. I've five Nobles, Pegg, and some odd money,
Thou seld some Cheeses, hes thou onny?

M. Seaven groats and a penny is all my Stock.
Thou knows whore it liggs, I've nowther Key nor Lock.

F. Pray thee, tell truly, hes thou neay mayer?
Did thou nut sell some Garne at our last Faire?

M. What if I did, heve I nut mayer to pay
Then I can mack of Trouts, Kirne Milke, and Whey?

F. Thou Snoutbands me sayer may I nut jest?
I seaur I ment neay harm to thee i' th'least;
Come hither, Hobb, what little stock hes Thou?
I knawe Thou's Addle some, with driving Plewe.

S. The small stock I've gitten up togeather
Is Twelve Bodles, a Groate and six pence, Fatther.

F. I mun borrow 't, Hobb; what, ista willing?
When I git money Thou's have a Shilling.

S. Ise gang and fetch it hard fest in a Cloote;
You may seaun lows't yoursell, and tack it out.

F. Here's Three and Three pence in odd Money, Pegg,
That macks Forty Shillings, Reet as my Legg;
Passions a Life, heer'st' Land-Lord just at Deaur,
Stand you by, Ise speak to him, doe nut feare.

L. Ise come to see Thee, how dusta, Billy?
What macks Thee hustle, thou's mayr fawse than silly.
Thou Glincks and Glimes seay I'd misken'd thy face,
If thou had wont at onny other place:
Ist God Moarn or God Deen, what saysta, Will?
I think you heve nut dyn'd, here's a good smell.

F. Leet pray you Land-Lord, and you then will knawe,
I think my wife hes Pyes i' th'Ewn to draw.

L. How now, Peggy, methinks thou's varra fine,
Have you some Guests to come to day, to dyne?

M. Wellaneering! we'd need have every Neaun
Something that's good, to keep our Hearts aboon.

L. But courser Fair I think, might you content,
You tack neay thought, how to pay me my Rent.

F. Weese pay you as we mack't, and as't comes in,
And you can have neay mayer o'th'Catt but th'Skin.
Here's Forty Shillings, we heve neay mayer,
Weese have a Cow to sell at our Neest Fair.

L. What can I deau with this? It will nut clear,
And pay seay Mickle as streights your awd Arreare.

F. Here's bad times. Pray you, Land-Lord, be content,
Forbear us but and you's heve all your Rent.

L. But it will be a lang time first Ise feard,
And whiles th'girse growes, th'Horse Starves as I've heard.
Next time I come, you mun clear off, I leauke:
Thur Driblets mack me scrat, where duz nut yeauke.

F. But you mun Let us Rive up some fresh grund,
Or else wee'l turn your Farme into your hand.

L. Wad yee'd gane titter, I had been neay warse.
For you'r not worth the warst Fart of mine A——
You may gang when you will, Ise never Care,
Ise get another Tenant I neer fear.

F. Wee'r sattl'd here: and sea to stir wee'r laith,
But weel I wait weese gether here nea Graith.

L. You ill my Farm for you have said to some,
You'r quite undone and beggar'd sin you com.

F. Some Pikethanks for ill hes teld you that,
An uncouth Dog hes manny Barkers at.
Ise Sackless on't, Sir, by this fire that Reeks,
Ile Swear't upon all Beauks that opens and stecks.

L. Away, away! If I sud let you Sitt
Rent free, I see you cud nut Live on it.
Your Corn's as Rank as ever it can stand.
There's sike a wreck, it liggs all down o' th'Land:
And yet you say your Farme is starke att th'Rent,
And you for Tennants give me nea Content.
You can nut pay nor I can nut forbear,
Provide seay for your selves another Yeare.

F. Wee'r nut seay browden on't, as you suppose,
I thinck langer we stay, the mayer weese lose.
Wad wee'd neer kend your Farme, nor had come here,
But bowght what's best, if it cost nut ore dear.

There's neay Feaul like to th'awd Feaul, I may say;
They that are bund, I see they mun obey.
The time that we com here, wee've cause to curse;
A tumbling stone, I see, neer gathers Moss.
We war ore weel before and did not waite,
And now we may the time rue when 't's ore late.

L. Come, come, for all your goodly Cracks and Braggs,
Ill Husbands and Sluggards mun gang in Raggs.
If you ow'd money when you com tu th' Farme,
Your Creditors, not it, have deaun you harme.
If all your stock be gaen, lean to your Kin;
Near is my Sarke, but nearer is my Skin.
Charity begins at hame: Ise nut bund
To let you Live Rent free upon my grund.
There's neay Sell like to th'awne Sell. You've Farmes anew
Offer'd, you say; God speed you, Ise ne'er Rue.
A weaud Horse I've heard it oft Reported
And a Rotten Harrowe are seaun parted.
Fareweele, Ise weay to find th'awd saying true,
It's an ill made Bargain whore beath Parties Rue.

(lines 275–380)

3

The Yorkshire Horse-dealers

Bane ta Claapam town-gate lived an oud Yorkshire tike,
Who i' dealing i' horseflesh hed ne'er met his like;
'Twor his pride that i' aw the hard bargains he'd hit,
He'd bit a girt monny, but nivver bin bit.

This oud Tommy Towers (bi that naam he wor knaan),
Hed an oud carrion tit that wor sheer skin an' baan;
Ta hev killed him for t'curs wad hev bin quite as well,
But 'twor Tommy opinion he'd dee on himsel!

Well! yan Abey Muggins, a neighborin cheat,
Thowt ta diddle oud Tommy wad be a girt treat;
He'd a horse, too, 'twor war than oud Tommy's, ye see,
For t'neet afore that he'd thowt proper ta dee!

Thinks Abey, t'oud codger 'll nivver smoak t'trick,
I'll swop wi' him my poor deead horse for his wick,
An' if Tommy I nobbut can happen ta trap,
'Twill be a fine feather i' Aberram cap!

Soa to Tommy he goas, an' the question he pops:
'Betwin thy horse and mine, prithee, Tommy, what swops?
What wilt gi' me ta boot? for mine's t'better horse still!'
'Nout', says Tommy, 'I'll swop ivven hands, an' ye will.'

Abey preeached a lang time about summat ta boot,
Insistin' that his war the liveliest brute;
But Tommy stuck fast where he first had begun,
Till Abey shook hands, and sed, 'Well, Tommy, done!'

'O! Tommy,' sed Abey, 'I'ze sorry for thee,
I thowt thou'd a hadden mair white i' thy ee;
Good luck's wi' thy bargin, for my horse is deead.'
'Hey!' says Tommy, 'my lad, soa is min, an' it's fleead!'

Soa Tommy got t'better of t'bargain, a vast,
An' cam off wi' a Yorkshireman's triumph at last;
For thof 'twixt deead horses there's not mitch to choose
Yet Tommy war richer by t'hide an' fower shooes.

4

The Dead Pig

T'owd pig's got mezzles an' she's deead, poor thing.
An' what will you mak o' her poor awd heead?
'Twill mak as good a yune as iver baked breead.
An' what will you mak o' her poor awd legs?
As good a set o' bed-props as iver propped beds.
An' what will you mak' o' her poor awd skin?
'Twill mak as good a blanket as iver man lay in.
An' what will you mak o' her poor awd tail?
'Twill mak as good a hammer-shaft as iver drove a nail.
An' what will you mak of her poor awd lugs?
As good a pair o' bed-flops as iver flopped bugs.

5

A Fragment: On the Witch, Molly Cass

Foor seear sha wor a queer au'd lass,
Ez meean ez muck, ez bou'd ez brass;
Ah meean t'au'd witch, au'd Molly Cass,
'At lived nigh t'mill at Leeming.
Noo fooak will clack, Ah've heeard 'em saay,
At t'dark o' neet, when pass't that waay,
Tha fan' it ommaist leet ez daay,
Sike leets war awlus gleaming;
An' sum held ti 't 'at mair 'an yance
Wiv her feet fra t'grund they'd seean her prance,
Loup hoos heigh up, wi' t'Divil dance.

6

Willie' Waggin

Rummle, rattle, creeak an' greean,
Willie' waggin's heeam ageean:
Jow't an' joggle, slaw an' sure,
Yance ageean he's weather'd t'moor.
Weather'd t'moor seea cawd an' bleeak,
Ti arn a bit o' honest ceeak.
Crowlin', crowlin', creep an' crowl,
Whether t'weather's fair or foul:
Week bi week he gans his roond
Coverin' t'seeam awd bit o' grund.
Takkin' here an' liverin' there
Givin' ivv'ry yan the'r share
O' what belangs 'em. Ah've neea doot
He'll sumtahmes give 'em t'wrang un oot,
Fer mem'ry's bud a wankle stick,
An' offen plays us all t'seeam thrick
O' snappin' when upo' 't wa leean,
Or just as offen finnd it geean.
A seet o' years poor 'Farmer' went,
An' hoss an' maisther seeamed content
Wi' t'other's company. Ah've heeard
Beeath maisther an' his steed appeared

Ti hev an understannin' clear,
Bud whether't is seea Ah's nut seear,
'Tis sartin summat roond 'em hung
At soonded like an unknawn tongue
For stoppin', startin', 'gee' or 'harve'
'Twas onnly t'maisther him could drahve.
What teeals t'awd waggin could let oot
If't could bud talk! for monny a bout
We've hed, as rahdin' heeam fra t'toon
We yan wad talk another doon.
An' frinnd wad nod across ti frinnd
An' talk thersels reet oot o' wind;
Hoo seea an' seea did sike an' sike,
An' sike a yan his drops did like,
An' teeals o' love went slyly roond
Wi' spicey bits in. Ah'll be boond
At sumtahmes yan mud catch a waff
O' summat droll at meead us laugh.
An' sumtahmes things was whispered law
At t'rist o' t'waggin munnot knaw.
Theease tahmes hev geean an' weean't reto'n
For tahme an' tahde keeps rowlin' on.
An' noo it's varry sad ti pen,
Poor Willie rahdes heeam biv his sen.
Rummle, rattle, creeak an' greean,
Willie' waggin's heeam ageean:
Jow't an' joggle, slaw an' sure,
Yance ageean he's weather'd t'moor.

7

Johnny Clagclod

The call ma Johnny Clagclod,
    Ah cums fra Danby Deeal;
Ah's i' pleeace wiv a farmer,
    Ti plew an' swing a fleeal.
Ti tent his flocks, an' leeak ti t'kye,
    Ti hedge, an' theeak, an' stack,
Ti be a handy farmer's lad
    At any kin o' mak.

Chorus

Bud Ah deean't knaw what's cum'd ti me,
    Ah reetlins cannot say,
Fer soond asleep er wide awake,
    Be Ah warkin' er at play,
Ah deea nowt bud think o' Polly Peeat,
    God bless her breet blue een,
Ah's daffled an' daazed,
Ah's sackless, Ah's craazed,
    Fer sha licks owt at ivver Ah've seen.

Sha oft wad saay 'Thoo's daft, John,'
    Said Ah 'Poll, thoo's ti bleeam,
Thoo's fairly to'nd mah heead, Poll,
    An' set mah heart afleeam:
Neea lass Ah've ivver seen, Poll,
    Seea snod an' feck ez thoo,
Ther's neean can scrub a skeeal wi' thee,
    Wi' me neean ho'd a plew.'

Chorus: Bud Ah deean't knaw, etc.

When t'sheep Ah gans ti scoore 'em
    Mah wits runs all askeeat,
I'steead o' reck'nin' scoore by scoore,
    Ah mumm'ls Polly Peeat,
Yan, tweea, three, Polly Peeat, Ah coonts,
    Go rabbit! hoo that lass,
Diz mak mah wits gan laatin' doon
    Fra thissel heeads i' t'grass.

Chorus: Bud Ah deean't knaw, etc.

Yah daay oor parson says ti me,
    'Wha deean't ya cum ti chu'ch?'
Fer answer Ah just splatthered oot,
    'There's neea lass theear can tu'ch
Mah Poll, says Ah, fer cumliness,
    Can onny match her airms?
Ya ha'en't a wench at cums ti chu'ch
    Wheeas tucker hides sike chairms.'

Chorus: Bud Ah deean't knaw, etc.

When Polly's marked her bridal bands,
  Ah'll bet Ah teeghs 'em on;
Ah've whispered at Ah've bowten t'ring
  Seea sha'll ha'e ti sattle on
Her weddin' daay: Ah've kelter enew
  Sha s'lack nowt o' graith an' gear,
Ah'll bet Ah walks ti chu'ch wiv her
  Afoore this tahm t'next 'eear.

Chorus: Bud Ah deean't knaw, etc.

8

A Dree Neet

'T war a dree neet, a dree neet,
  As t'squire's end drew nigh,
A dree neet, a dree neet
  Ti watch an' pray an' sigh.

When t'streeam runs dry, an' t'deead leeaves fall,
  An' t'ripe ear bends it' heead,
An' t'blood wi' lithin seeams fair clogg'd,
  Yan kens yan's neeam'd wi' t'deead.

When t'een grows dim, an' fau'k draw nigh,
  Fra t'other sahde o' t'graave,
It's laate ti square up au'd accoonts,
  A gannin' sowl ti saave.

T'priest ma' cum, an' t'priest ma' gan,
  His weel woorn taal ti chant,
When t'deeath smeear clems a wrinkled broo,
  Sike disn't fet yan's want.

Neea beeak, neea cann'l, bell ner mass,
  Neea priest iv onny lan'
When t'dree neet cums can patch a sowl
  Er t'totterin' mak ti stan'.

'T war a dree neet, a dree neet
  Fer a sowl ti gan awaay;
A dree neet, a dree neet,
  Bud a gannin' sowl caan't staay.

An' t'winner shuts tha rattled sair,
  An' t'mad, wild wind did shill,
An' t'Gabriel ratchets yelp'd aboon
  A gannin' sowl ti chill.

'T war a dree neet, a dree neet,
  Fer deeath ti don his cowl,
Ti staup abrooad wi' whimly tread,
  Ti claam a gannin' sowl.

Bud lahle deeath recks hoo dree t'neet be,
  Er hoo a sowl ma' praay:
When t'sand runs oot, his sickle reeaps,
  A gannin' sowl caan't staay.

'T war a dree neet, a dree neet
  Ower Whinney Moor ti traake,
Wi' sheeanless feet ower flinty steeans,
  Thruff monny a thoorny braake.

A dree neet, a dree neet,
  Wi' nowt neeawaays ti mark,
T'gainest trod ti t'Brigg o' dreead
  A lane lost sowl i' t'dark.

A dree neet, a dree neet,
  At t'Brigg foot theear ti meet
Lahle sowls at he war fatther on,
  Wi' neea good deeam i' seet.

At t'altar steps he nivver stead
  Thoff monny a voo he maade;
Noo t'debt he awes ti monny a lass,
  At t'Brigg foot mun be paad.

Tha feeace him noo wiv other deeds,
  Leyke black spots on a sheet,
Tha noo unscaape tha egg him on,
  O' t'Brigg his doom ti meet.

Neea dove hes sattled on his sill,
  Bud a flittermoos that neet
Cam' thrice tahmes thruff his casement
  An' flacker'd roond his feet,

An' thrice tahmes did a raaven croak,
  An' t'seeam leyke thrice cam' t'hoot
Fra t'ullots three; doon chimlas three
  Ther cam' a shrood o' soot.

An' roond t'cann'l tweea tahmes ther cam
  A dark wing'd moth ti t'leet,
Bud t'thod it swirled reet inti t'fleeam
  Wheear gans his sowl this neet.

'T war a dree neet, a dree neet
  Fer yan ti laate ti pray;
A dree neet, a dree neet,
  Bud a gannin' sowl caan't staay.

9

The Gleaner's Lament

T'poor fawk noo is daily robbed
Ov all the'r reets which t'scriptures ho'd
Has been the'r due daays oot o' coont:
Bud t'rich 'a'e noo lahl fear o' God.
T'yat's noo slammed i' t'gleaner' feeace
Neean noo maay gleean a winter's keeak;
Neea thresho'd noo is cleeaner swept
'An t'harvest field wiv a hoss reeak.
God's smile weean't favour sike a gam'
O' greedy brossen-gutted gaain.
Maay harvestin' be lang on t'waay,
An' maay ther' fall a seeght o' raain.

10

A Yorkshire Farmer's Lament

Rainin' ageean Ah deea declare;
It's twaa days wet for yah day fair:
Warse tahmes than theease was nivver seen,
Us farmers 'll be beggar'd clean.

Crops is seea bad Ah's varra flay'd,
Rents, rates, an' taxes caan't be paid:
Harvest foaks' wages gannin' on,
An' there tha stand an' nowt is done.

What a sad mess o' mouldy hay,
An' taaties rottin' all awaa:
Wheeat thin o' t'grund, an' small a t'ear,
It caan't yield weel Ah's varra seear.

Wots 'll be leet, seea leet Ah say,
At t'better hoaf 'll blaw awaa;
Beeans hez neea swads, tha've nowt bud top,
An' barley isn't hoaf a crop.

Fog disn't grow as weel as't owt,
An' tonnaps 'll be good for nowt;
Pasturs is nobbut varra bare,
An' stock cums doun at ivvery fair.

There's nowt te eeat for milkin' kye,
An' meeast on 'em 'll seean be dry;
Tahmes noo for farmers is seea bad,
You'll see next spring they'll breeak loike mad.

II

Song: Drink to the Bridal Garter

Nance is wed timorn at morn,
High doon a derry O,
Monny a lad's this daay forlorn,
High doon a derry O;
Bud cheer up, lads, yer glasses fill,
Fer ivvery Jack ther' is a Jill,
Sup off, my bucks, an' divn't spill,
An' maay Ah win her garter O.

Neea prude is Nance; they saay sha's maade,
High doon a derry O,
Her brahdal bands ov gowden braad,
High doon a derry O,

Noo fer a ribbon Ah weean't run,
It gi'es neea luck, an' stops wer fun,
Sike nimmy nammy waays ez sum;
Cum drink ti bridal garter O.

Here's health an' luck ti t'bride at darr,
High doon a derry O,
Her bridal bands baith stitch an' wear,
High doon a derry O;
Ti them at ho'ds a ribbon up
Neean on uz here'll drain a cup,
Sike healths wa hevn't time ti sup,
Ov slipshod, undarned stockins O.

T'bride at darn't her skets pull up,
High doon a derry O,
Maist leykly is a mucky slut,
High doon a derry O.
Yan best can tell a lass's waays,
Biv what sha wears, an' what sha saays;
A ribbon gi'en o' weddin' daays
Screens mucky undarned stockins O.

Maay ivvery bonny blushin' bride,
High doon a derry O,
Hev nowther muck ner hooals ti hide,
High doon a derry O,
An' maay sha on her bridal daay
Pull up her skets, an' smilin' saay,
'Mah garter's thine, tak it, Ah praay,
An' gi'e 't ti thi triew lovey O!'

Afoor wa pairt fill up each glass,
High doon a derry O,
Let each yan drink tiv his awn lass,
High doon a derry O,
Ti Bessy, Sally, Sue, an' Peg,
Ti Martha, Mary, Maud, an' Meg;
An' here's ti ivvery shap'ly leg
Roond which a brahdal band diz go

12

Song : Nance and Tom

I' t'merry tahm o' harvestin',
  Lang sen, Aye well a daay!
Oor Nancy, t'bonniest lass i' t'field,
  Hed varra lahl ti saay.
An' Tom wheea foller'd, foller'd her
  An' neegh ez dumb war he,
An' thoff he wark'd hard wiv his han's,
  He harder wark'd his e'e.

Fer Nan war buxom, Nan war fair,
  Her lilt war leet an' free;
An' Tom c'u'd hardlin's ho'd his wits
  He c'u'dn't ho'd his e'e
Fra Nance's feeace; an' her breet smahl
  Maade Tom's heart loup an' thump,
When fo'st he bussed her, Nancy awnd
  Sha felt her corsets jump.

Bud o' yah neet, Tom set her yam,
  'Noo Nance,' said he, 'Ah've gitten
A cauvin' coo, an' tweea fat pigs;
  An' wi' thi chairms Ah's smitten;
Thoo kens Ah hev a theeak mah lass,
  An' gear baith gert an' small,
Ah've fo'tty pund ligg'd by at yam,
  Tak me an' tak it all.'

Nance hing'd her heead, an' dropped her een,
  An' then sha sighed 'Aa dear!
Noo ho'd thi whisht, thoo's tell'd t'saame taal
  Ti monny a lass Ah fear.'
Bud Tom just bowldly sleeaved her waast,
  An' chuck'd her unner t'chin.
'O' Sunda' neet,' said he, 'Ah'll cum
  Ti hug thi milk skeeals in.'

. . . . . verse missing from ms.

Sha bun' aboot her matchless cauf,
   Four cletchin' streeahs did Nan,
Tweea wheaten an' tweea oaten streeahs,
   Bud nivver tell'd her man.
Sha platted 'em when t'harvest meean
   Her culler'd cheek maade paal;
Fer neea lass platts her band fer bairns
   An' then blirts oot her taal.

An' t'meean fer sham ahint a clood
   Her smahlin' feeace did hide;
Seea neea hedge skulker gat a peep
   At Nan's leg when t'war tahd.
An' neean i' t'village wad ha'e knawn
   'At roond her leg, leyke thack,
Sha'd bun a band ti gi'e her bairns;
   Bud sha tumm'ld off'n t'stack.

An'deeased sha ligg'd; her shap'ly limb
   Laad oot fer all ti see;
An' roond her leg a platted band
   War bun' belaw her knee.
Then up sha loup'd, an' laughin' said,
   'Noo, Tom warn't here ti see;
An' neean can saay Ah's scrawmy cauf'd
   An' t'band still guards mi knee.'

13

T'Au'd Parson

T'au'd parson's deead,
God rest his heead,
      He prayed an' preeach'd an' sang;
An' in a bridal race an' band
      He nivver see'd nowt wrang.
At monny a bridal don he stood
      When t'winner claimed his prize,
And monny a bridal leg he see'd
      Which gladdened his au'd eyes.
Bud noo he's deead,
God rest his heead,
      An' t'new cumd's ta'en his place:

We're teeached it's wrang
Fer t'bride to shew
Her leg at t'bridal race.
His au'd dame she
Says it maunt be,
Sha's sham'd a bride 'll stand
I' front o' folk an' lift her goon
While sha gi'es up her band.
Ti siken a farce
I say my harse
An' at all sike clack fart:
Oor mothers stitched an' ware ther band
An' wi' lifted goon ivvery yan did stand
An' was all triew maids at heart.

14

Cleveland Lyke-wake Dirge

This ean night, this ean night,
Every night and awle:
Fire and Fleet and Candle-light,
And Christ receive thy Sawle.

When thou from hence doest pass away,
Every night and awle:
To Whinny-moor thou comest at last,
And Christ receive thy Sawle.

If ever thou gave either hosen or shoon,
Every night and awle,
Sitt thee downe and putt them on,
And Christ receive thy Sawle.

But if hosen nor shoon thou never gave nean,
Every night and awle,
The Whinnes shall prick thee to the bare beane,
And Christ receive thy Sawle.

From Whinny-moor that thou mayst pass,
Every night and awle,
To Brig o' Dread thou comest at last,
And Christ receive thy Sawle.

From Brig o' Dread that thou mayst pass,
Every night and awle,
To Purgatory fire thou com'st at last,
And Christ receive thy Sawle.

If ever thou gave either Milke or Drinke,
Every night and awle,
The fire shall never make thee shrink,
And Christ receive thy Sawle.

But if milk or drink thou never gave nean,
Every night and awle,
The Fire shall burn thee to the bare beane,
And Christ receive thy Sawle.

15

The Wensleydale Lad

When I were at home wi' mi father an' mother, I nivver had na fun;
They kept me goin' frae morn to neet, so I thowt frae them I'd run.
Leeds Fair were coomin' on, an' I thowt I'd have a spree,
So I put on mi Sunday cooat, an' went right merrily.

First thing I saw were t'factory, I nivver seed one afore;
There were threads an' tapes, an' tapes an' silks, to sell by monny a score.
Owd Ned turn'd iv'ry wheel, an' iv'ry wheel a strap,
'Begor!' says I to t'maister-man, 'Owd Ned's a rare strong chap.'

Next I went to Leeds Owd Church—I were nivver i' one i' mi days,
An' I were maistly ashamed o' misel, for I didn't knaw their ways;
There were thirty or forty folk, i' tubs an' boxes sat,
When up cooms a saucy owd fellow. Says he, 'Noo, lad, tak off thi hat.'

Then in there cooms a great Lord Mayor, an' over his shooders a club,
An' he gat into a white sack-poke, an' gat into t'topmost tub.
An' then there cooms anither chap, I thinks they called him Ned,
An' he gat into t'bottommost tub, an' mocked all t'other chap said.

An' then I heard a shufflin' row, I couldn't mak what aboot,
An' t'chap donn'd up i' t'white sack-poke began a-shootin' oot,
Tellin' o' t'rich folk's road to Heaven, an' t'poor folk's road to Hell.
Thowt I to misel, tha silly owd fooil, tha doesn't knaw t'road thisel.

So they began to preach an' pray, they prayed for George, oor King;
When up jumps t'chap i' t'bottommost tub. Says he, 'Good folks, let's sing.'
I thowt some sang varra weel, while others did grunt an' groan,
Ivvery man sang just what he wad, so I sang 'Darby an' Joan.'

When preachin' an' prayin' were over, an' folks were gangin' away,
I went to t'chap i' t'topmost tub. Says I, 'Lad, what's to pay?'
'Why, nowt,' says he, 'my lad.' Begor! I were right fain.
So I clicked hod o' mi gret club stick, an' went whistlin' oot again.

16

Ballad on the Goodmanham Mule or Mute

Johnny Fowler bowt a mute,
His wife Hannah thowt it wadn't suit;
O but I think it will!
Says Willy-up-o'-th'Hill.
Give her a sly prick!
Says Milner Mick.
Give her a pinchin'!
Says David Quinchin.

Hoo nicely she goes!
Says Hatfield and Rose.
She's as hard as nails!
Says Dicky Dales.
Know weel or ommass!
Says Robert Thomas.
Why—what's her trade!
Says Mistress Wade.
Carryin' a spice stall!
Says Nanny Hall.
Noo what's her rate!
Says Tommy Tate.
Seaven mile i' th'hoor!
Says Billy Moor.
I'll trot her to Driffil!
Says aud Ship Withill.
An' back agean fore dark!
Says aud Dan Clark.
An' I'll trot her to Selby!
Says aud Len Kirby.
O, bud she's a tight un!
Says aud Robert Leighton.
She gangs like a hoss!
Says young Dicky Ross.
Mair like an ass!
Says Ramskill lass.
Thou's a great feeal!
Says Lizzy Beal.
She gangs like a creckit!
Says Mister Beckett.
Just trot her on!
Says fine young John.
It's nowt but malice!
Says Rhoda and Alice.
Tee her up to th' church!
Says silly Willy Perch.
An' I'll let her lowse!
Says aud Nan Towse.
I hope she'll reward 'em!
Says good Mister Guardam.
Are ye sure an' sartain!
Says aud Nanny Garten.

She's varra slo!
        Says Mister Blo.
She isn't yan o' th' best!
        Says aud Mister West.

An' efter all their noise an' bodder,
Th' poor mute was led awa to fodder.

17

Come A Hunting

Come alang, let's awaay, wa mun all on uz gan,
It's t'last daay at wa s'hearken ti t'hoonds;
Ti t'sweetest o' music at ivver fills t'wood,
T'whinney, er spinney, ther's nowt near si good
Ez t'sang yan hears sung, lad, biv t'hoonds.
Ther'll bi all mak's an' manders o' hosses, Ah ween,
An' yauds, an' blood tits, an' fussocks an' all;
Ther'll bi Tommy on Farmer, Ah'll wager a pun',
It 'ud bunch a lahl cockle, it wad Ah'll be bun:
An' yan's sarten ti finnd young Willie fra t'farm
Astride of his mudher's au'd meer,
Weel gingered fer t'daay, like a tweea 'ear au'd coult
Prancin' an' dancin', it' tail like a boult
Thoff ti t'market it's jogged monny a year.
Ther'll be Bobby' bay meer at yance raaced a coo
An' lost by three len'ths an' a field,
Ther'll be Pull Back, an' Fear Nowt, an' Hedge Peepin' Tom,
An' Sucker, an' Slimmer an' Sly
On stringolts, an' rooarers, baith bare-backs an' pads,
An' mebbe ther'll be Mistress Fry,
An' Jack frev his stithy, an' Bob frev his last,
An' Sammy'll lig doon his birch:
T'sand booard mun idle, an' t'horn-beeak this daay
Shutten s'all be whahl t'scholars awaay
Draw t'parson fra prayin' i' t'chetch:
An' Ah wadn't be 'mazed if Mistress Duncombe shewed up,
An' it's wo'th monny a mile fer ti gan
Ti ken hoo sha'll ride wi' t'best on 'em theear,
Ower hedge, dyke, an' stell, theears nowt sha weean't clear,
Sha'll bring sham say ti monny a man.

Ther's nivver neea sayin', like ez nowt it mud be
Mistress Nancy fra Fadmoor mud com'.
If't happen sha diz, Ah'll bi bun fer ti saay
Ther's neean sha'll let beeat her at 's huntin' ti-daay,
Fer sha rides like Au'd Harry, by gum!
Bud ov all at could happen ti mak' uz good spoort
Efther t'brush, heead, an' pad's gi'en ti t'winner,
Is fer t'parson an' t'squire t'ane t'ither ti lip
Sikens mainly good frien's bud oors deean't sip
Fra t'seeam bottle noo efther dinner.

18

A Rustic's Courtship

'Foine neet, monny stars!
Tongs an' poiker just like ahrs.
Ah come i' courtin' did yo knaw?
Ah tell'd thi fatther. Did he tell yo
Ah love tha Betty?'

'Thoo loves ma, Billy!
Ay, bud Ah wonder wheear?'

'I' me heart, Betty.'

'I' thee heart, Billy?
Ah wonder it duzzant appear.'

'Ah'll marry tha, Betty.'

'Thoo'll marry ma, Billy?
Ay, bud Ah wonder when.'

'A Sunday, Betty!'

'A Sunday, Billy?
Ah wish it wor Sunday, then.'

19

On Ilkla Moor Baht 'at

Wheear wor ta bahn when Ah saw thee?
On Ilkla Moor baht 'at.

Tha's been a-courtin', Mary Jane.
On Ilkla Moor baht 'at.

Tha's bahn ta get thi deeath o' cowd.
On Ilkla Moor baht 'at.

Then we sal ha ta bury thee.
On Ilkla Moor baht 'at.

Then t'worms'll come an' eit thee up.
On Ilkla Moor baht 'at.

Then t'ducks 'll come an' eit up t'worms.
On Ilkla Moor baht 'at.

Then we sal come an' eit up t'ducks.
On Ilkla Moor baht 'at.

Then we sal hev etten thee.
On Ilka Moor baht 'at.

RICHARD ABBAY

20

Gan Yam, Gan Yam, Ma Bonnie Lass

Gan yam, gan yam, ma bonnie lass,
    Thoo maunt be oot alaane;
Ther's monny a man'll deea tha wrang,
    They've nowt bud hearts o' staane.

Gan yam, gan yam, ma bonnie lass,
    Ah'll see tha doon to t'dike:
Ther's waastril Tom, Will Louse-i'-t'heft,
    An' hauf a scoor o' sike.

Gan yam, gan yam, ma bonnie lass,
Whahl thoo's an honest naame;
They've bonnie wods an' bonnie deeds,
An' then there's nowt bud shaame.

Gan yam, gan yam, ma bonnie lass,
Thoo maunt come here an' stot;
Thee faather'd lowp fra oot his graave
If owt sud deea tha hot.

Ah will gan yam, at yance, Ah will,
Thoo's better nor a brudder;
There's naan sall saay, Ah yance gat wrang;
Ah'll bide at yam wi' mudder.

WILLIAM BEAUMONT

21

The Proposal

Maggie, tha'rt bonny,
As bonny as onny;
Mi sovereigns are few
An' mi maisters are monny;
Bud whahle Ah can weyve,
An' whahle tha can spin,
We'll keep trouble aht,
An' happiness in.

22

The Weaver to his Son

Be wary, be chary,
Tak' heed who tha courts.
Ther's lasses i' plenty,
I' sahzes an' sorts;
Bud if tha s'be happy,
Tak' on wi' a lass
'At's nimble wi' t'thimble
An' careful wi' t'brass.

GERALDINE BINNALL

23

Oor Awd Spot

We've lived theer thotty year,
Ye mun believe't or not,
'Tis t'bonniest plaace as ivver was,
Is oor awd spot.

She's prood on't t'missis is,
An' doan't I ketch it hot
When I gans traapsin' mud aboot
Iv oor awd spot.

Childer? Aye, we've hed ten;
Still livin'? Aye, all t'lot;
An' t'lahl 'uns, they was t'life an' joy
Ov oor awd spot.

It hots us, though, to think,
Oor eldest, leyke as not,
'Ull tak a weyfe as willna' bide
Iv oor awd spot.

Ye've getten nowt to dae
To-neet? I tell ye wot,
Just come wi' me an' hev a leuk
Roond oor awd spot.

THOMAS BLACKAH

24

Noo Wilta Gan wi' Me

Noo wilta gan wi' me fer rubbin' steeans, Nanny,
They say thar's some good uns o' t'top o' t'Back Moor.
Ah've neeabody wi' me bud curly-hair'd Annie,
An' if ta be thrang, we'll be back in an hoor.
Ah've summat to tell tha, barn, when we git thither,
Ah know it'll pleease tha, lass, excellent weel;
Seea don on thi bonnet, we'll beeath gan togither,
We can put all wer rubbin' steeans into my creel.

Noo seesta yon hillock at Benty Clooase boddum,
Thar's two or three lasses, they're comin' this way;
They're gannin' fer scorrin' steeans too, Ah'll uphod 'em,
By jingo, weea worth 'em! They'll hear what we say.
What thinks ta, lass! Charlie last neet com an' whistled,
An' fair befooare t'winder he brazzandly stood.
Seea Ah slipt on mi clogs, then Ah shoved an' Ah nestled,
An' slyed oot ta meet him as weel as Ah cud.

He seemed to be all in a fearful queer flutter,
Ah cud hear his heart knock, lass, as fair as a die.
He said, 'Wilta wed me, Poll?' all in a splutter,
Ah cuddent say 'Nay', nor Ah diddent say 'Aye'.
Bud barn, Ah hev rued, an' t'next time Ah see him,
Ah sal tell him at yance hoo uneeasy Ah've been;
Fer let me walk oot, or be onywheer wi' him,
Ah's allus as pleeased an' content as a Queen.

25

Pateley Reeaces

Attention all, baith great an' small,
An' dooan't screw up yer feeaces;
While I rehearse, i' simple verse,
A coont o' Pateley Reeaces.

Fra all ower t'moors, they com bi scoores,
Girt skelpin' lads an' lasses;
An' cats an' dogs, an' coos an' hogs,
An' hosses, mules, an' asses.

Oade foaks wer thar, fra near an' far,
At cuddant fairly hopple;
An' laughin' brats, as wild as cats,
Ower heeads an' heels did topple.

The Darley lads, arrived i' squads,
Wi' smiles all ower ther feeaces,
An' Hartwith youths, wi' screw'd-up mooths,
In wonder watch'd the reeaces.

Fra Menwith Hill, and Folly Gill,
 Thorntyat, an' Deacre Paster,
Fra Thruscross Green, an' t'Heets wer seen
 Croods cumin' thick an' faster.

'Tween Bardin Brigg and Threshfield Rig
 Oade Wharfedeeale gat a thinnin';
An' Gerston plods laid heavy odds
 On Creeaven Lass fer winnin'.

Sich lots wer seen o' Hebdin Green,
 Ready seean on i' t'mornin',
While Aptrick chaps, i' carts an' traps,
 Wer off ta Patela' spernin.

All Greenho' Hill, past Coadsteeanes kill,
 Com taltherin' an' singin',
Harcastle coves, like sheep i' droves,
 Oade Palmer Simp wer bringin'.

Baith short an' tall, past Gowthit Hall,
 T'up-deealers kept on steerin',
For ne'er before, roond Middlesmoor,
 Had ther been sich a clearin'.

All kinds and sorts o' games an' sports
 Had t'Patela' chaps pervided,
An' weel did t'few, ther business do,
 At ower 'em persided.

'Twad tak a swell a munth ta tell
 All t'ins an' oots o' t'reeaces,
Hoo far the' ran, which hosses wan,
 An' which wer' back'd for pleeaces.

Oade Billy Broon lost hauf-a-croon
 Wi' Taty-Hawker backin',
For Green Crag flew, ower t'hurdles true,
 An' wan t'match like a stockin'.

An' Creeaven Lass won lots o' brass,
 Besides delightin' t'Brockils,
An' Eva danc'd, an' rear'd an' pranc'd;
 As gif she stood o' cockles.

But t'donkey reeace wer t'star o' t'pleeace,
  For oade an' young observers;
'Twad meeade a nun fra t'convent run
  An' ne'er again bi nervous.

Tom Hemp fra t'Stean cried oot, ' Weel deean,'
  An' t'wife began o' chaffin';
Whal Kirby Jack stack up his back,
  An' nearly brast wi' laughin'.

Sly Wilsill Bin, fra een ta chin,
  Wer plaister'd up wi' toffy,
An' lang-leg'd Jane, he'd browt fra t'Plain
  Full bent on winnin' t'coffee.

Young pronsy flirts, i' drabbl'd skirts,
  Like painted peeacocks stritches;
While girt chignons like milkin'-cans
  On ther top-garrits perches.

Fat Sal fra t'Knott scarce gat ta t'spot,
  Afore sha lost her bustle,
Which sad mishap quite spoil'd her shap,
  An' meeade her itch an' hustle.

Lile pug-nooas'd Nell, fra Kettlewell,
  Com in her Dolly Vardin,
All frill'd an' starch'd sha proodly march'd
  Wi' squintin' Jooa fra Bardin.

Ther cuffs an' falls, tunics an' shawls,
  An' fancy pollaneeses,
All sham displays, ower tatter'd stays,
  An' hard-worn ragg'd chemises.

Ther mushroom fops, fra fields an' shops,
  Fine cigarettes wer sookin',
An' lots o' youths wi' beardless mooths,
  All kinds o' pipes wer smookin'.

An' when at last the sports were past,
  All heeamward turn'd ther feeaces;
Ta ne'er relent at e'er the' spent
  A day wi' Patela' Reeaces.

RICHARD BLAKEBOROUGH

26

Nowt Bud Luv Could Be

T'meean war leeakin' doon on t'yeth
Leyke a silver ball yah neeght,
An' stars war twinklin' ivver seea,
Whahl t'sky war all aleeght
Wi' t'gems ov Heaven up aboon.
Seea gran' tha leeak'd ti t'e'e,
Yan felt fair capp'd ti think doon here
'At owt bud luv could be.
Four beetles hummed ez roond tha swirled,
An' t'crake called for its maate,
An' t'bleat o' monny lambs yan heeard,
An' t'moths cam oot ti late
Ther suppers fra some neeghtly bloom,
An' t'wo'lld war fair ti see,
Whahl somehoo yan felt bet ti knaw
Hoo owt bud luv could be.
A twitterin' noos an' then yan heeard
Fra t'lahl bo'ds i' ther nist,
Ez croodled under t'muther wing
Tha teeak ther neeghtly rist.
T'noisy creeaks 'ed geean ti reeast,
Ther war nowt yan could see
Ti mak it hard upon this yeth
For owt bud luv ti be.
Bud whahl yan tried ti mak it oot,
A flittermoose fligg'd by,
An' t'ullot's shadow darken'd t'grund,
An' t'neeght-jar gav its cry,
An' t'fox yapp'd wiv its neese ti t'grund,
Whahl t'rezzel slank alang,
An' t'rabbit's squeeal tell'd plaan eneeaf
O' parlous deed amang
T'weeak critters, whahl yan's forced ti awn
It's seeam amang wersels—
I' t'heart, wheer nowt bud luv s'ud be,
Unkindness offen dwells.

HENRIETTA BLAKESTON

27

Music on t' Wawds

Yah neet when Ah'd a-finished wark, an' we'd a-getten tea,
Ah gets oot paaper an' mi specs to read a bit, yer see;
An' ther was sike a lot aboot a concert 'at there'd been,
Wheer some grand choir 'ad a-sung afoor oor King an' Queen;
An' when Ah gies up readin', Ah just thinks, 'It's all fer t'swells,
Ah sal nivver hear sike music, as a-what that paaper tells.'
Bud it's nowt te what oor concerts are, 'ere i' t'lanes an' t'fawds,
Wheer all daay lang ther echoes roond oor music 'ere on t'Wawds.

It soonds in t'snarlin' wind fra t'sea, 'at howls awaay ti t'west,
It soonds in t'breeze 'at gently hushes coontry sahd ti rest,
It soonds in t'flutterin' swaal o' t'leaves, in t'rustlin' swish o' t'corn,
It soonds in t'crawin' uv all t'cocks i' t'staggarth ivvery morn;
An' t'bleat o' t'lambs an' t'yowes in t'fields, in t'songs o' t'bo'ds an' t'bairns,
An' t'cattle comin' 'oame at neet, a-lowin' oot in t'lanes.
All mak oop t'sweetest music 'at te me all coontry hods,
Oor choruses o' t'hills an' daales, t'music 'ere on t'Wawds.

Ther's t'creak o' t'carrier waggin ivvery Thosda afthernoon,
All thranged wi' foak wi' parcils comin' yam fra market-toon;
Ther's t'shoot o' Kessmass mornin' uv t'lads a-givin' cheers,
Some say it's nobbut bawlin', bud it's music i' ma ears;
It mahnds me uv awd tahmes when Ah went shootin' village through,
'If yer haven't got a penny, whah! a 'awpenny will do.'
An' some foak can't abahd it, an' gies 'em nowt bud scawds,
It's 'cos ther hearts has nivver larned oor music 'ere on t'Wawds.

Soa thuf Ah reads o' concerts grand, it nivver worrits me,
'At Ah sal nivver gan tiv 'ear 'em singin', dost tha see?
Fer they'd nut fill mi heart wi' peace, nor help me when Ah'm sad,
Like t'soonds Ah've allus loved soa, ivver sen Ah wor a lad.

Ah dean't knaw mich o' what t'songs o' heaven's goin' tae be,
An' mebbe Ah can't sing 'em, bud it allus seeams ta me
'At if Ah reaches yonder, an' t'gaate fer me unfawds,
Ah sal finnd 'at t'music's summat like oor music 'ere on
t'Wawds.

FRED BROWN

28

Old Servants

What ails mi loom?
It's all awry,
Summat snaps
And t'shuttles fly;

T'tuner comes,
'Nah what's amiss?'
Bangs at that,
And screws at this.

We're off agean
And kneyding-in,
'Nowt ner waar
So 'odd thi din'.

Metal stalls
And leather wears,
T'owd loom's run
For fifty years.

Sometahms tuned
Wi' loving care,
Sometahms sluppered
Run somehaah.

A bit o' wire
A bit o' band,
T'owd loom's passed
Through monny a hand.

Lightest weyve
Or heaviest picks,
Who wer't first
To learn its tricks?

Paid bi' tahme
Or paid bi t'tack,
T'loom an' me's
Cloathed monny a back.

Me an' t'owd loom's
Hed wer day,
Let's get downed
And lay away.

THOMAS BROWNE

29

Awd Daisy: An Eclogue

GOORGY. Weel met, good Robert, saw ye my awd meer;
I've lated her an hoor, i' t'loonin' here,
But, howsumiver, spite of all my care,
I cannot spy her, nowther heead nor hair!

ROBERT. Whah, Goorgy, I've te teyl ye dowly news,
Sike as I's varra seer will mak' ye muse;
I just this minute left your poor awd tyke,
Deead as a steean i' Johnny Dobson' dyke.

GOORGY. Whoor! what's that, Robin? tell us owre ageean;
You're joking, or you've mebby been misteean.

ROBERT. Nay, marry, Goorgy, I seer I can't be wrang,
You kno' I've keyn't awd Daisy now se lang;
Her breead-ratch'd feeace, an' twa white hinder-legs
Preeav'd it was her, as seer as eggs is eggs.

GOORGY. Poor thing! what deead then?—had she laid there lang?
Whor abouts is she? Robert, will ye gang?

ROBERT. I care nut, Goorgy, I han't much te deea,
A good hour's labour, or may happen tweea;
Bud as I nivver like te hing behind
When I can deea a kaundness tiv a frind
An' I can help ye wi' my hand or teeam,
I'll help te skin her, or te bring her heeam.

GOORGY. Thank ye, good Robert, I can't think belike
How t'poor awd creature tumbled inte t'dyke.

ROBERT. Ye maund she'd fun hersen just gaun te dee,
An' seea laid down by t'side (as seeams te me)
An' when she felt the pains o' death within,
She fick'd an' struggled, an' seea towpled in.

GOORGY. Meeast lickly; bud—what, was she deead outreet
When ye furst gat up? when ye gat t'furst seet?

ROBERT. You s'hear: as I was gaun down t'looan I spy'd
A scoore or mair o' crows by t'gutter side,
All se thrang, hoppin' un, and hoppin' out,
I wonder'd what i' the warld they were about.
I leuks, an' then I sees an awd yode laid
Gaspin' an' pantin' there, an' ommost deead;
An' as they pick'd it' een, and pick'd ageean,
It just cud lift it' leg, an' give a greean;
But when I fand awd Daisy was their prey,
I wav'd my hat, an' shoo'd 'em all away.
Poor Daise! ye maund, she's now woorn fairly out,
She's lang been quite hard sett te trail about.
But yonder, Goorgy, loo' ye whoor she's laid,
An' tweea'r three Nanpies chatt'rin' owre her heead.

GOORGY. Aye, marry! this I nivver wish'd te see,
She's been se good, se true a frind te me!
An' is thou cum te this, my poor awd meer?
Thou's been a trusty sarvant monny a year,
An' better treeatment thou's desarv'd fra me
Than thus neglected in a dyke te dee!
Monny a daywark we ha' wrought togither,
An' bidden monny a blast o' wind and weather;

Monny a lang dree mahle, owre moss an' moor,
An' monny a hill and deeal we've travell'd owre;
But now, weeas me! thou'll nivver trot ne mair,
Te nowther kirk nor market, spoort nor fair;
An' now, for t'future, thoff I's awd and leeam,
I mun be foorc'd te walk, or stay at heeam.
Ne mair thou'll bring me cooals fra Blakey Brow,
Or sticks fra t'wood, or turves fra Leaf How Cow.
My poor awd Daise! afoor I dig thy greeave,
Thy weel-worn shoon I will for keepseeakes seeave;
Thy hide, poor lass! I'll hev it taun'd wi' care,
'Twill mak' a cover te my awd arm-chair,
An' pairt an appron for my wife te weear
When cardin' woul or weshin' t'parlour fleer.
Deep i' t'cawd yearth I will thy carcase pleeace,
'At thy poor beeans may lig and rest i' peeace;
Deep i' t'cawd yearth, 'at dogs mayn't scrat thee out,
An' rahve thy flesh, an' trail thy beeans about.
Thou's been se faithful for se lang te me,
Thou sannut at thy death neglected be;
Seyldom a Christian 'at yan now can find
Wad be mair trusty or mair true a frind.

30

A Song

Ye loit'rin' minutes faster flee,
Y'are all ower slow by hauf for me,
  That wait impatient for the mornin':
To-morn's the lang, lang-wish'd-for fair,
I'll try to shine the forremost there,
  Mysen in finest claes adornin',
      To grace the day.

I'll put my best white stockin's on,
An' pair o' new cauf-leather shoon,
  My clane wash'd gown o' printed cotton;
Aboot my neck a muslin shawl,
A new silk handkerchee ower all,
  Wi' sike a careless air I'll put on,
      I'll shine this day.

My partner Ned, I know, thinks he,
He'll mak hissen secure o' me,
He's often said he'd treat me rarely;
But I's think o' some other fun,
I'll aim for some rich farmer's son,
An' cheat oor simple Neddy fairly,
Sae sly this day.

Why mud not I succeed as weel,
An' get a man full oot genteel,
As awd John Darby's daughter Nelly?
I think misen as good as she,
She can't mak cheese or spin like me,
That's mair 'an beauty, let me tell ye,
On onny day.

Then hey! for sports and puppy shows,
An' temptin' spice-stalls rang'd i' rows,
An' danglin' dolls by t'necks all hangin':
An' thoosand other pratty seets,
An' lasses traul'd alang the streets,
Wi' lads to t'yal-hoose gangin'
To drink this day.

Let's leuk at t'winder, I can see't,
It seems as tho' 'twas growin' leet,
The cloods wi' early rays adornin
Ye loit'rin' minutes faster flee,
Y'are all ower slow by hauf for me,
'At wait impatient for the mornin
O' sike a day.

31

I Leotly Lov'd a Lass

I leotly lov'd a lass right weel,
Was beautiful and witty;
But all I said (an' 'twas a deal)
Could never raise her pity,
Or mak' her love me.

I tell'd her ower an' ower again
  Did monie reasons render,
She'd never fynd another swain
  Wad be se fond and tender,
      If she'd bud love me.

I'd tent my sheep i' field or faud
  Wi' spirits light and cheery,
Thro' summer's heat and winter's caud,
  If she wad be my deary,
      And say she'd love me.

I's nobbut a poor shepherd lad,
  My hands aleean mainteean me;
Waes me! weel may I be sae sad,
  That maks the lass disdeean me,
      'At winnot love me.

I thought at first, i' my despair,
  I'd gang and get me listed,
And bravely meet my death i' war,
  Because the lass insisted
      She wad not love me.

But noo I've teean another mind,
  I'll try to quite forget her;
Another lass may be mair kind,
  I'se like as weel or better,
      An' she may love me.

H. P. BRUFTON

32

T'Owd Hammer

Nah mi owd hammer, tha's come loise i' t'heead,
If tha doesn't ger a drink, tha'll come off Aw'm feeard,
Aw mun sooak thi' and wedge thi afore Aw do owt,
For a heead wi'aht shaft is noa good for nowt.

Aw've used thi for nigh upo' twenty-foive year,
Aw forget what tha cost, tho' tha worn't varry dear,
But a reight good owd pal tha's e'er been to me,
An' a better owd tooil Aw ne'er wish to see.

That thumb hoil i' t'shaft shows a bit o' good wood,
An' being reight deep shows what wark on't it's stood.
Tha used to be heavy, but tha's leetened a lot,
An' like me tha's mellowed wi' t'age 'at tha's got.

Ne'er heed, mi owd pal, but we nivver shall part,
Ther's nobody on earth knows ha useful tha art,
Soa when Aw can't use thi, Aw'll hing thi on t'wall,
An' theer Aw can see thi, thumb mark an' all.

An' t'times 'at Aw've rubbed thi wi' t'gritstooan i' t'morn,
Aw cannot remember, but Aw see hah tha's worn.
An' t'steel 'at tha's bashed wi' monny a big welt,
Tha's come dahn reight on it, and made thisen felt.

But sooin Aw'm afeeard we'll booath ha to end,
Wheer's nawther hammer, na steel, na bellows to mend,
We've booath had good innings an' done what we could,
Soa we mawn't start repining, but end brave as we should.

JAMES BURNLEY

33

Jim's Letter

What's this? A letter thro' Jim?
  God bless him! What hes he to say?
Here, Lizzie, my een's gettin' dim,
  Just read it, lass, reight straight away.
Tha trem'les, Liz. What is there up?
  Abaat thy awn cousin tha surely can read;
His ways varry oft had made bitter my cup,
  But theer, I forgive him, read on, nivver heed.

That's it—' as it leaves me at present '—
  His father's expression to nowt!
Go on, lass, t'beginning's so pleasant
  It couldn't be mended wi' owt.
What's that? He has sent a surprise?
  What is't, lass? Go on, a new gaan, I'll be bun,
Or happen a nugget o' famous girt size?
  Whativver it is, it's t'best thing under t'sun.

Ay, lad, I dare say, 'life is rough,'
For t'best on 't is nut varry smooth;
I' England it's hilly enough,
Nivver name wi' them diggers uncouth.
But theer, Liz, be sharp, an' let's have his surprise,
I'm capt wheer tha's gotten that stammerin' cough;
Tha reads a deal better nor that when tha tries.
Good gracious! What's t'matter? Shoo's fainted reight off!

Hey! Lizzie, tha flays me; come here,
An' sit wheer tha'll get some fresh air:
Tha'rt lookin' so bad at I fear
Tha's much war nor I were aware.
That's reight, lass, get tul it once more,
Just read reight to t'end on 't, an' then
We'll just tak a walk for a bit aht o' t'door,
Whol tha feels rayther more like thisen.

What! Bless us! Aar Jim gotten wed!
It is a surprise, on my word.
Whi is she? That's all 'at he's said?
I wish then I nivver had heard.
At one time I thowt happen thee he'd admire,
An' that's haa we all sud have liked it to be.
Bud, sithee! What's that, Liz, 'at's burnin' on t'fire?
It's t'ribbin Jim bowt thee! Ay, ay, lass, I see.

TAKKY BURTON

34

Elphi, T'Devil, an' T'Witch

The devil an' t'witch quarted ower ther reets;
Baith claimed ti tak cess fra them at took t'wath.
Fra yon side an' this side they cursed an' they sware,
Weel marrowed they war, an ill-gotten pair.
On owther side t'ane on 'em held t'path,
So tha fowght all throff t'neet
Wi' spells an' wi' charms fra t'yeth an' fra t'air,
Fra watter an' fire, I can't say what mair,

Each other ti best, an' claim ther awn reet,
An' while they were fighting Hob Elphi slipped ower
Shakkin' wi' laughter he beealed out, 'It's too late
I've gotten clean ower without onny gate:
Waal fightin' t'ane t'ither, I've brokken your power,
I've done you, I've done you,' Hob Elphi did roar.
'But lahl did ya hod sike as me ya did watch,
Thoff humped i' my back, an' bandy i' t'leg,
No cess did I pay, no favour did beg:
But i' me ye 'ev both met your match.'
  T'awd witch dag her nails iv her awn rasseled cheeks,
An' Scrat brak off t'tip of his tail,
An' Hell fire spat i' t'awd witches tail,
While she poked iv his face her guts clam o' spleen
Which turned him both kreatchy an' pale.
Both were done an' they knew it,
So both slank away
Cursing their softness like many before;
While haggling for t'happings they lost their whole store,
An' ther reet ti claim cess evermore.

ABEL BYWATER

35

Sheffield Cutler's Song

Coom all you cutlin' heroes, where'ersome 'er you be,
All you what works at flat-backs, coom listen unto me;
        A basketful for a shillin',
        To mak 'em we are willin',
Or swap 'em for red herrin's, aar bellies to be fillin',
Or swap 'em for red herrin's, aar bellies to be fillin'.

A basketful o' flat-backs, I'm sure we'll mak, or more,
To ger reight into t'gallery, wheer we can rant an' roar,
        Throw flat-backs, stones an' sticks,
        Red herrin's, bones an' bricks,
If they don't play 'Nancy's fancy' or onny tune we fix,
We'll do the best at e'er we can to break some o' their necks.

Hey! Jont, lad, is that thee, where art ta waddlin' to?
Does ta work at flat-backs yit, as tha's been used to do?
Ho! coom, an' tha s'go wi' me,
An' a sample I will gie thee,
It's one 'at I've just forged upon Geffrey's bran-new stiddy.
Look at it well, it does excel all t'flat-backs i' aar smithy.

Let's send for a pitcher o' ale, lad, for I'm gerrin' varry droy,
I'm ommost chok'd wi' smithy sleck, the wind it is so hoigh.
Gie Rafe an' Jer a drop,
They sen they cannot stop,
They're i' sich a moighty hurry to get to t'penny hop,
They're i' sich a moighty hurry to get to t'penny hop.

Here's Steem at lives at Heeley, he'll soon be here, I knaw,
He's larnt a new maccaroni step, the best you ivver saw;
He has it so complete,
He troies up ivvery street,
An' ommost breaks all t'pavors, wi' swattin' daan his feet.
An' Anak troies to beat him, whenivver they doon meet.

We'll raise a tail by Sunda, Steem; I knaw who's one to sell,
We'll tee a hammer heead at t'end to mak it balance well.
It's a reight new Lunnon tail,
We'll wear it kale for kale,
Aar Anak browt it wi' him, that neet he coom by t'mail.
We'll drink success unto it—hey! Jont, lad, teem aat t'ale.

J. A. CARLILL

36

Love and Pie

Whin Ah got hoired et Beacon Farm
A year last Martinmas
Ah funnd we'd got a vory bonny
Soort o' kitchen lass,
And so Ah tell'd her plooing maade
Me hoongry, thot was why
Ah allus was a lahtle sthrong
On pudden and on pie.

And efther thot Ah thowt the pie
Was mebbe middling large,
And so Ah aate it fur her saake,
Theer wasn't ony charge,
Oontil it seems th'missus asked
Her raything sharply why
She allus yowsed th'biggest dish
Fur pudden and fur pie :

Ah wasn't much of yowse yer knaw
Et this-heer fancy talking;
She hed noa chance of gooing oot
Fur arming it and walking.
Boot thin Ah knawed Ah got her loove
Whin Ah cud see th'pies,
Ah knawed her thowts o' me wer' big
Bi bigness o' their soize.
The pies and gell Ah thowt thot gead,
Th' hardlins cud be beaten;
She knawed Ah'd allus thowts on her
Bi waay th'pies wer' eaten,
Oontil it seems th' missus asked
Her raything sharply why
She allus yowsed th' biggest dish
Fur pudden and fur pie.

Noo joost thoo wait a bit and see,
Ah'm ooanly thod-lad noo :
Ah moight be wagoner or hoind
Within a year or two,
And thin thoo'll see, or Ah'm a cawf,
Ah'll mak 'em ring choch bell
And carry aff, et Martinmas,
Yon prize pie-makking gell;
And whin thoo's buying cooats and beats
Wi' waages thot yer taake,
It's Ah'll be buying boxes for
Th' lahtle bits o' caake,
And whin Ah've got a missus theer'll
Be noo more asking why
She allus gers oor biggest dish
Fur pudden and fur pie.

F. A. CARTER

37

Downer

Aye dear, I'm fair heart-sluffened;
  I's nivver be nowt noo moor,
For Downer-yar Downer! is bet, mun,
  'At nivver were bet afoor.
I thowt he were fast as ivver,
  'At he were bun' to win;
But Snapdragon bet him bi inches.
  Ah, I were reight ta'en in.

'There's nowt beeats owd'uns but young'uns,'
  That's what they allis say.
Well, Downer an' me's booath owd'uns,
  We'n booath on us had us day.
An' ivver sin he were a whelp, mun,
  Reight thra his varry start,
Downer's been t'leet o' me een, mun;
  Downer's been t'pride o' me heart.

An' talk about t'dog bein' sluffened!
  His feet trailed as heavy as leead.
He looked fit to sink into t'yearth, mun,
  Soo I ran an' patted his heead,
An' I says to him: 'Nivver 'eed, lad,
  Tha couldn't do moor nor thi best.
We'n allis stuck cloise together,
  An' we'll stick together for t'rest.

An' if he should dee afoor me
  He'll wait for me theer grown young,
His little whip tail i-waggin',
  Ready wi' quick red tongue.
An' if he's nooan theer i' Heaven,
  Waitin' me whistle or call,
If it's 'Nooa Dogs Admitted,'
  They mun manage baat me an' all.

Yar owd lass says I'm dooatin';
  Shoo says: 'For shame o' thee sen!'
Ah! shoo knows plenty religion,
  But nowt abaat dogs an' men!
Or shoo'd a' had some soort o' nooation
  What Downer's been to me,
An' thoiled t'bit o' brass for his license
  For theer we could nivver agree.

Yar owd lass gooas to t'Chapil
  Shoo says i' Heaven there'll be
All on us playin' an' singin',
  Wi' seeats an' hymnbooks free,
But that soort o' spot wodn't suit me,
  As far as a sinner can tell,
For I nivver could sing when sowber,
  An' I nivver played nowt but Hell.

Sooa they can keep their music;
  We'll do baat t'trumpets'saand.
Let's have a two-or-thry whippets
  An' a nice little racin'-graand.
Ah, Downer an' me 'ud be suited
  Wi' just that soort 'n a spot,
Wi' eytin' an' suppin' an' racin',
  An' Downer 'ull down all t'lot.

JOHN CASTILLO

38

Awd Isaac

Oft hev Ah lang'd yon hill te clim,
Te hev a bit mare prooase wi' him,
Wheas coonsel like a pleeasin dreeam,
        Is deear te me;
Sin' roond the warld sike men as he
        Seea few ther be.

Corrupted bukes he did detest,
For his wur ov the varry best;
This meead him wiser than the rest
O' t'neeaburs roond,
Tho' poor i' purse, wi' senses blest,
An' judgment soond.

Befoore the silvery neeght ov age,
The precepts ov the sacred page,
His meditation did engage,
That race te run;
Like thooase, who 'spite o' Satan's age,
The praaze hed won.

Bud noo his een's geean dim i' deeath,
Neea mare a-pilgrim here on earth,
His sowl flits fra' her shell beneeath,
Te reealms o' day,
Whoor carpin care, an' pain, an' deeath,
Are deean away.

DOUGLAS CHARLESWORTH

39

T'Poorly Beemaister

Eh lass! my limbs are crammly,
Ah dither through an' through,
My heead feels leet an' wammely,
Ah doant knaw what Ah s'do.
Just pool my bed to t'winder
Wheer t'wind goas softly by,
An' wheer there's nowt to hinder
T'sunbeeams through t'summer sky.

Ah hear i' t'garden singing
My busy bonnie bees,
Up into t'sky they're winging,
Like t'sand o' distant seas.
They sarch all t'world for treasure
By field an' wood an' moor,
An' whoa can tak the measure
Of all their wondrous store?

Lang sin i' t'days o' summer
  Ah've set i' t'front o' t'hive,
An' watched each busy hummer
  On t'leeting-board arrive;
An' dreaming, dreaming, dreaming,
  Emang the scented trees,
Been lulled to slumber seeming
  Wi' t'hum o' t'flying bees.

Noa more i' t'time o' kesting
  Ah'll hoppit t'cluthered swairm,
Or efter t'Queen goa questing
  'Mang t'combs sa soft an' wairm.
Noa more they'll yield their sweetness
  I' rich sweet luscious flow,
Or fill my heairt wi' leetness
  A-murmuring saft an' low.

Hark! there's young Queens a-calling,
  My soul maun tak its fleet,
As quiet as dewdrops falling
  I' t'summer dawn's first leet.
Their wings sal gently bear me
  To t'Happy Dale afar,
On t'Dawn-wind's breeath Ah'll fare me
  Wheer t'joys for ivver are.

An' lass, when life is over,
  An' Ah am hived aloft,
Goa tell each little rover
  Dahn theer i' t'garden-croft.
Just rap on t'hoppet gently,
  Put crepe o' t'top o' t'thack,
An' t'bees a-murmuring faintly
  'Ull send their answer back.

HENRY COOKSON

40

T'Owd Lot to T'Young Lot

You dunnot clack to yer wark i' clogs,
  As t'owd lot used to do;
Bud i' dainty hats, an' sometimes gloves,
  An' blouses pink an' blue.

An' we're glad to see yer donn'd sa smart,
  Though times are dark and dree:
They're a gert deal better i' ivvery way
  Ner t'owd times used to be.

Aw'm fair dahn capt ha yer mothers contrived
  Wi' nobbut a paand a week,
An' sometimes six or seven to feed,
  Whal livin' i' some back street.

They struggled an' tewed i' them grim days,
  An' nivver gat hawf ther due:
Just try ta leeten ther burden nah,
  You'll nivver hev cause ta rue.

An' doan't be ashamed when you kneel ta pray,
  Bud whal you're dahn on yer nogs,
Thank God you're living i' happier days,
  Ner i' days o' porridge an' clogs.

An' when life's warp is finished at last
  An' t'weyver ligs away,
If t'piece be marr'd you've a kindly judge,
  An' he'll tak nowt off yer pay.

W. COWLEY

41

Emigrant

Noo lass, wilt cum wi' ma tineet?
    Wa'll santther doon thruff Ladhill Gill,
    Bi Haazelshaw an' Honey Hill,
An' t'Moor Yat, wheer wa used ti meet.

It's gauvin' tahm, bud t'meean's as breet
    As t'neet Ah traapsed tha doon bi t'Mill
    Fra Coo Wath ower ti Gowerdil,
An' Banniscu' war baathed wi' leet.

Ah'll nut ha'e thee mich langer, lass;
    Thoo knaws Ah's off a week timoorn;
Ah'll nivver see yon moorland grass
    Ageean, ner Ryedil's gowden coorn—
Whya lass, what aails tha? Is thoo bad?
    'Ah's comin' wi' tha lad!'

GEORGE H. COWLING

42

A's Gotten T'Bliss

A's gotten t'bliss o' moonten-tops ti-neet,
    Thof A's i' bondage noo, an' blind, an' deaf.
Brethren, A's stown! An' fand it vary sweet,
    Sea strike my neam off, if't be your beleaf
        A's slidin' back.
Last neet, as A were shoggin' on up t'street,
        A acted t'theaf.

Ye think A's hardened, Ay! A see ye lewk.
    A stell't, it's true; bud, brethren, A'll repay.
A'll pay back ten-foad ivrything A tewk,
    An' fuaks mun say whate'er they like tae say.
        It were a kiss.
An' t'lass hes promist iv oor ingle-newk
        Tae neam t'day.

WILLIAM CUDWORTH

43

A Hearthstone Gem

I pept into a little cot,
    No cosier could it be,
Though humble sewer wor t'earthly lot
    O' t'little family.

Three youngsters clustered rahnd a maid
    Who bade 'em all ' be still '
Whal in reply to me shoo said,
    ' Mi mother goes to t'mill.'

A hearthrug made o' worsed tabs
    Afore the fire wor spread;
A seemin-glass, wi' gilded knobs
    Fair dazzled owerhead.
A crate well filled wi' haver-cake
    Its burden leetly bore,
An' thease i' one brief glance I took
    Whal lewkin' in at t'door.

' Ay, bless tha, lass,' I kindly said,
    ' Tha'rt put on past thi years.
Pray can't thi father finnd yer breead,
    Wi'aht—' shoo brast i' tears,
An' answered me, wi' sobbin' tones,
    ' Mi father's liggin' ill.'
I needed nowt to see at once
    Why t'mother went to t'mill.

An' nearly thirteen week shoo'd wrowt
    To finnd them barns some grub,
For what they hed beside wor nowt,
    Just three-an-six thro' t'club.
An' blessings on her mother Heart,
    They'd ne'er been baht a meal,
Though oft eniff shoo'd done wi'aht,
    Whal lowsin' time at t'mill.

An' all the while this lovin' wife,
    Hard-ooined though shoo be,
Ne'er let her trouble dim the life
    O' t'little family.
An' tho' shoo strave, wi' word an 'smile,
    Her husband's heart to cheer,
God knaws her awn wor sore the while,
    For his end wor varry near.

I'm fain to think when t'Maister comes
To sort his jewels rare,
Ameng the richest, rarest forms
Ther'll be one passin' fair:
A jewel fit for ony crahn,
Believe it, them at will:
An' t'marrow on't I've faintly drawn—
Shoo wave at Drummond Mill.

SOL DARREL

44

Th' Owd Tinker

Owd Tim wor a tinker, an' roamed up an' daan,
Thro village to village, an' taan to taan;
He wor clever at patchin up kettles an' pans,
An stopping up hooils in ladin cans.

He wor knawn to all th'women for miles araand,
For often he'd travelled ower th'self-same graand;
All sooarts ov odd jobs they used to keep,
For they saved 'em for mony an' mony a week.

He carried his kit strung across his rig,
An' for nowt and for nobody cared a fig;
But plodded on th'road, amid sunshine an' shaar,
Thro all sooarts o' places, at ivvry haar.

He gat a neet's lodgin whearivver he cud,
An' wor nooan a praad chap bi th'way ov his food;
It wodn't so oft at he slept in a bed,
An sum varry strange lodgins he oftentimes hed.

He wor fond ov his beer, and he oft used ta say,
At he needed a livener to help him on th'way;
But into th'hedge bottoms it caused him to creep,
For more often ner net it wod put him to sleep.

His face wor th'same colour as th'risin sun,
An his nose wor oft means ov causin sum fun;
For th'women advised him, when he'd hed a sup,
To use it for warmin his irons up.

But ther joakin an jestin ne'er bothered owd Tim,
They cud varry near dew as they liked wi him;
He didn't care, if he cud addle a bob,
They cud say what they liked, if they gav him a job.

A merrier owd fellow yo seldom wod see,
He wor cheerful whativver his luck mud be;
If his pockets wor empty, which often wor th'case,
A misfortun like that he cud easily face.

He cud allus mak sum sooart o' shift for a bed,
An wor willin to tackle a crust o' dry bread;
He knew varry weel at he'd hev it to bide,
So he'd patiently wait until th'turnin o' th'tide.

But his ramblin days ha' nah cum to an end,
He'll ne'er want no more pans an' kettles to mend;
Yet fowk often miss poor owd Tim, and they say,
They'd be pleased to see th'owd chap trudgin up th'way.

JAMES HENRY DIXON

45

The Milkin'-Time

Meet me at the fowd at the milkin'-time,
When the dusky sky is gowd at the milkin'-time;
Whan the fog is slant wi'dew,
An' the clocks go hummin' thro'
The wick-sets an' the branches of the owmerin' yew.

Weel ye knaw the hour of the milkin'-time,
The girt bell sounds frev t'tower at the milkin'-time;
Bud as gowd sooin turns to grey,
An' I cannot hev delay,
Dunnot linger by the way at the milkin'-time.

Ye'll find a lass 'at's true at the milkin'-time,
Shoo thinks of nane bud you at the milkin'-time;
Bud my fadder's gittin' owd,
An' he's gien a bit ta scowd,
Whan Ah's ower lang at the fowd at the milkin'-time.

Happen ye're afeard at the milkin'-time,
Mebbe loike ye've heerd at the milkin'-time
The green fowk shak their feet,
Whan t'moon on Heeside's breet,
An' it chances soa ta-neet, at the milkin'-time.

There's yan, an' he knaws weel whan it's milkin'-time;
He'd feace the varra de'il at the milkin'-time.
He'd nut be yan ta wait,
Tho' a barguest war i' t'gate,
If the word Ah'd nobbut say't, at the milkin'-time.

F. W. DOWSON

46

A Daytal Chap

Ah've addled mi brass bi t'sweeat o' mi broo,
Sen a lahtle bit lad aboot ten.
If Ah live whaal next Mart'mas, then eighty Ah's tonn'd,
An' still yabble ti fick for missen.

Neea skeealin' Ah gat i' theeas new-fangl'd waays
Bud Ah hansell'd mi pleeaf ower seean—
Beeath o' Sundays an' war-days Ah plugg'd in at wark
An' gat falder'd bi t'tahm it was deean.

Mi havver-ceeaks teeaf, Ah cowl'd 'em frae t'ass,
Varry thenk-ful ti greease 'em wi' seeam,
O' this mally-mawk breead at they moother i' t'mill,
For an awmus Ah weean't tell mi neeam!

A poddish-pot meeal it clags ti yer ribs,
Suet dumplins an' broth wi' yan's meeat;
Ti theeas gran-bairns at's dainsh'd wi' their peeasts an' their puffs
Sike a jawther's nit menseful ti eeat!

Mi hodden-grey cooat still haps up mi rig,
What a kenspeck Ah is ti be seear!
Bud a feg for yer dandies an' poother-puff weeans—
Ower gaumless ti maaze oot o' t'deear.

47

T'Pleeaf Stots

Here they cum, tidaay seea grand,
Runnin', lowpin', sooards i' hand:
Rooases, ribbins, cooats seea sthraange,
Hoose ti hoose they're gahin' ti raange.

Last back-end when neets was dark,
All t'lads set theirsens ti wark—
Leearnt their steps, an' showed their airt,
Watchin' t'oad foaks deea their pairt.

Hoo they thried an' thried ageean,
Thowt this nivver wad be deean!
Then they dhrissed i' sike fine cleease,
Fancy suits frae heead ti teeas.

'Blews' an' 'pinks' is allus pets:
Seean theease danced i' tweea fine sets.
Watch 'em plet at last their sooards,
Just when theease seeam flung all rooads!

Here's t'oad woman, an' t'oad man!
Peeak'd aboon 'em sits a cloon.
Sike queer 'stots,' an' actin' teea,
Sum on deearsteean, sum i' t'fleear!

Off they gan awaay ower t'green,
Sike a show, was't ivver seen?
Noo they're i' t'foad-garth ti start,
Ivv'ry yan seea glad at heart.

Watch their antics whaal they're there!
Neean bud what is straight an' fair:
Hoo they dance, an' stand up fine,
Just like soldiers iv a line.

All their wods they just fit reet,
And their pairts all suits their feet;
Fost they dance wi' sooards on end,
Then they clap 'em doon an' bend.

Roond an' roond they dance i' t'ring,
Then they talk an' sumtahmes sing:
Grand oad fiddler! Wheea can beeat
Tunes like thine is despert greeat.

Lahtle cloon, cum sit the doon,
Else they'll likely crack thi croon!
Noo they've deean it straight an' sharp,
For they've cutten off thi scaup!

All i' fun they've deean it yance,
Noo thoo'll mebbe leearn ti dance!
If they thry it on ageean
All thi wark'll then be deean.

Laugh an' dance, an' shoot an' sing!
This is t'daay ti hae yer fling:
Keep t'oad plaay up ivv'ry year,
Nowt else like it, we're all seear.

All you lads at's leeakin' on,
Tak yer tons—git t'jackets on!
Deea like t'oad-uns—keep it up,
When it's ower'd fill yer cup!

C. W. EASTWOOD

48

Aw Dar's'n't

Aw met her fust at t'Statties Fair,
Mi bonnie lass wi' t'deep braan hair,
An' smaailin', axed her wod shoo ride
On t'hobby-hosses, at mi saaide?
Shoo nobbut shakked her heead an' sighed,
'Aw dar's'n't.'

Aw tuke her raand ta see all t'fun,
All t'games they laaked an' t'prizes wun,
Then whispered low, 'twor noa gurt sin,
'Doan't tell thi Muther wheer tha's bin.'
Shoo answered wi' a saucy grin,
'Aw dar's'n't.'

When next we met, 'twor Sunda neet,
Aht i' t'mooinleet, paale an' breet;
Aw heeard t'Chu'ch bells sweeatly ring,
An' begged shoo'd gan wi' mea an' sing;
'What! gan wi' thee? Nay, noa sich thing.
Aw dar's'n't.'

Aw met her yance ageean t'steigh,
An' seed t'love glistenin' in her e'e,
But when Aw aimed to tak a kiss,
Shoo tonned her heead, t'saucy Miss,
An' said afore Aw'd tasted bliss,
'Tha dar's'n't.'

But nah we've cooarted three lang year,
Yet still Aw've gitten daat an' fear,
For when Aw axed her wod shoo wed,
Wi' poutin' lips, baith sweat an' red,
An' lewkin' shy, shoo quaaintly said,
'Aw dar's'n't.'

Yet sin, shoo says, shoo's chaanged her maand,
Laaike t'women do, tha'll oft-tahmes faand,
On t'altar nah mi hoapes are reared,
Shoo'll say, 'Aw will,' Aw'se noan afeeared,
Onless bi chonce, shoo lisps asteead,
'Aw dar's'n't.'

J. H. ECCLES

49

Ode Ta T'Mooin

I like ta see thi quaint owd face
Lewk softly daan on me;
E'en tho I ne'er cud find thi noase
Ner catch thee watchful ee.

Full monny times A've seen thee rise,
When busy day wer done,
When daan behint t'owd maantain tops.
Hed pass'd breet evenin' sun.

I like ta see thee, when sweet Spring
  Cums back ta hill an' vale;
When odours rise thro t'hawthorn bush,
  An' float on t'evenin' gaale.

When lovers walk on t'primrose benks,
  An' whisper soft an' low;
Dreamin' just saame, as me an t'wife,
  Did monny years ago.

I like ta see thee when t'June rose
  Is wet wi' fallin' dew;
When t'nightingale maks t'owd woods ring
  Wi' music fresh an' new.

When fairies dance on t'top a t'flaars,
  An' roam thro t'pleasant dells;
Like monarchs i' ther marble halls,
  I' t'lilies virgin bells.

I like ta see thee when t'ripe corn
  Is wavin' to an' fro;
When t'squirril goes a-seekin' nuts,
  An' jumps thro bough ta bough.

When t'purple heather covers t'hills,
  An' t'hunters tired an' worn
Back throo the fairy-haunted glens,
  Unta ther hoams return.

I like ta see thee when all raand
  Is white wi' t'driven snaw;
When t'streams are stopp'd be owd Jack Frost,
  An' foaks slip as they goa.

I like ta see thee all t'year raand,
  When t'sky is fair an' breet;
An' allus hail wi' fond delight,
  The noble queen at neet.

I used ta think at I cud reach,
  Up ta thee face wi' ease,
If I had but a big long stick,
  Fer tha wor but green cheese.

But nah A've got far different thowts,
An' learnt ta understand,
At tha art one o't' wond'rous works
Form'd be t'Girt Maker's hand.

FRANK ELGEE

50

The Pannierman's Song

Climmin' up t'Causey, climmin' up t'Causey,
Ah gans a swankin' Pannierman
Wiv all t'moors afore me, wiv all t'moors afore me!
Gin it haggle, gin it snaw,
Gin it rain or gin it blaw,
Ah lalls alang t'Causey, Ah lalls alang t'Causey.

Swingin' alang t'Causey, swingin' alang t'Causey,
Ah lalls ti t'pannel hosses' bells
'At mak fine music for me, 'at make fine music for me
Ah loups alang, Ah cracks mah whip,
Ah maks t'hosses fairly skip
As Ah lalls alang t'Causey, as Ah lalls alang t'Causey.

Lallin' alang t'Causey, lallin' alang t'Causey
Ah aims Ah'm t'King o' t'Panniermen
Wi' my bouncin' Sall afore me, wi' my bouncin' Sall afore me!
She lalls aloud like t'tumlin' beck,
She is the finest lass on t'yeth,
So Ah lalls alang t'Causey, Ah lalls alang t'Causey.

BRENDA H. ENGLISH

51

Pienannies

Yah pienannie set on t'wall
At Ibrundale.
An' t'snawflags started for ti fall;
Yah pienannie set on t'wall

An' t'land was happed up iv a pall
As wisht as deid, an' nigh as pale.
Yah pienannie set on t'wall
At Ibrundale.

Tweea pienannies set i' t'sun
At Ibrundale,
Bairns loused frae skeeal, an' down they run!
Tweea pienannies set i' t'sun,
Lairkin', for a bit o' fun.
Sky's blue, an' white clouds sail;
Tweea pienannies set i' t'sun
At Ibrundale.

Three pienannies off on t'wing
At Ibrundale.
A little poke o' rice to fling!
Three pienannies off on t'wing,
Ah's got a little gowden ring,
An' a white weddin' veil ti trail.
Three pienannies off on t'wing
At Ibrundale.

Fower pienannies, in t'back-end,
At Ibrundale.
Now we'll 'e ti mak' a fend!
Fower pienannies, in t'back-end,
Ah's got a little lad ti tend.
Ah'll tell 'im just a little tale
O' fower pienannies in t'back-end
At Ibrundale.

52

When Yaffles Yowl

When yaffles yowl
Then Ah can tell
  It's boun' ti rain.
  An' wisht! How plain
  Ti hear, yon train
An' t'awd Chotch bell,
Aback o' t'dell.

There'll be a spell
O' blash an' dowl,
When yaffles yowl!
  My bonnie Jane,
  For bit o' gain,
  Flees down the lane,
Wi' t'umberell.
An' Ah says, ' Well!
A droppy spell!'
  ' Why, aye!' says Jane,
  ' My weathervane
  Says, " Boun' ti rain!" '
When yaffles yowl.

A. FARNELL

53

Owd Things are Best

  Aw like owd stuff,
Mi ancient coit, an' seasoned pipe,
T'owd walking-stick, 'at t'wife once bowt
  When we were young an' ripe;
But moast of all, aw like t'owd friends,
To me they are t'best of owt Time sends.

  Aw like t'owd songs;
T'owd simple tunes an' hoamly rhymes;
An' t'flaysome tales they used to tell
  Us lads i' t'owden times;
An' awst ne'er forget t'owd fields an' loins,
Whear love's first kiss war ta'en unknowins.

  Aw like t'owd twang;
Brooad Yorksher speyks soa plain an' straight;
T'owd native wit 'at caps 'em all,
  Because it's real an' reight.
Ye can call it blunt or owt ye like,
It runs i' t'blood o' t'keenest Tyke.

Aw like t'owd hearth;
White pottery mould, an' t'fender breet;
Wi' t'cratch at t'side, whear t'wife an' me
Sit talking of a neet.
All these Aw've tried, an' fun 'em true,
Soa give me t'owd, an' ye tak t'new.

ELSIE A. GRASSBY

54

Back End

When t'mist cums creepin' ower t'woaad,
An' t'neets is damp an' t'mornin's coaad,
When t'harvist's deean an' t'fields is bare,
An' t'hosses yoked ti t'pleeaf yance mair;
T'apples laaid oot on t'chaamer fleear,
Wha, yan ma' saay 'at Autumn's 'ere.

When t'wind blaws sharp an' t'threes leeaks bare,
Cos t'leeaves is dhroppin' ivv'rywhere;
When t'stacks is threshed an' t'theeakin' deean,
An' t'taaties piked; when t'dark cums seean,
An' t'neets is lang, wha then fer seear
Yan can't bud saay 'at Winther's near.

When t'rooads gets slaape wi' snaw an' frost,
Wi' greeat dhrifts wheer t'poor sheep gets lost,
When t'coaad maks feet an' finngers numb,
When t'vessil-cups begins ti cum,
We're ommast noo at t'end o' t'year,
Yan knaws fer sartin Winther's 'ere.

JAMES R. GREGSON

55

Postscript

Ah saw a tyrant liggin' deead,
An' t'seet fair made me wonder;
Ah thowt o' t'way he'd earned his breead—
Bi rivin' t'world asunder.

Ah thowt o' t'men he'd made an' marred,
Ah thowt o' t'corpses that he'd scarred;
Ah thowt o' t'earhoils that he'd jarred
  Wi' his little tinpot thunder.

Ah saw a nation led bi t'nooase,
  Ah yerd 'em heil his teychin';
An' here he were, wi' cocked-up tooas,
  An' paid put to his preychin'!
As deead as t'lyin' hopes he'd raised;
As deead as t'damnin' lies he'd praised;
As deead as t'crazy fears that blazed
  At his cruel ovver-reychin'.

Ah saw him stark an' cowd i' deeath,
  An' t'seet fair set me blinkin';
Ah thowt of all his wasted breeath,
  Of all his crack-pot thinkin'.
An' here he were—no moor parades,
An' nooan to care if he upbraids,
Wi' hungry worms for chambermaids
  All thrang wi' meyt an' drinkin'.

An' so Ah say, 'Enjoy yer day,
  'Yo tyrants, big-mahthed, lusty;
'Enjoy yer power, ye'r nobbut clay,
  'Yer glory's nobbut musty!
'There's nowt ye'r buildin' that'll keep;
'Yer earnin' nowt but curses deep;
'An' nawther men nor worms'll weep
'When under t'sod yer crawl to sleep,
  'To moulder fahl an' fusty!'

56

Epitaph on a Politician

His clapper's still, his trap is shut,
    He says nowt, false nor clever;
He's no moor use, nor mischief, but
    His ear's to t'grahnd as ever!

WILFRID J. HALLIDAY

57

Sally

Eh! Sally, is it thee, lass?
    Come and sit tha dahn:
Ah'd reyther see thy face, lass,
    Ner ony lass i' t'tahn.

Tha's allus summat breet, lass,
    Whenivver fowk are glum;
Tha allus cheers me up, tha knaws,
    Eh! lass, Ah'm glad tha's come.

Some fowk are nivver happy,
    Wi'aht they mak yer roar;
They tell yer tales o'misery
    Afore they've shutten t'door.

There's Mrs. Huggins, Jonas wife,
    When sho pops in ta tea,
Sho tells tha all her doleful dumps,
    An' who'll be t'next ta dee.

And 'Bimelech's missus, sho's just same,
    Sho's allus summat wreng.
It's awther t'kinkhoast wi' her barns,
    Or else sho's ower threng.

And Martha Ann were here just nah,
    Sho's full o' trouble, too,
Sho's gotten t'gurds that bad, sho says,
    Sho'll nobbut just pool through.

Tha nivver flays me, Sally,
    Tha's allus full o' fun;
And t'hahse is allus breeter,
    Afore tha's gotten done.

Tha brings a bit o' sunshine,
    Wi' all thi smiles an' jokes.
Ah'm sick o' fiddle faces,
    And fowk wi' nowt but croaks.

Eh! Sally, is it thee, lass?
Come and sit tha dahn;
Ah'd reyther see thy face, lass,
Ner ony lass i' t'tahn.

58

T'Owd Days

Aye, things hev changed sin' I war young,
We used to hev to wark:
You lasses don yersens at neet,
And spend yer time gadding i' t'street,
And doan't come in till dark.

We went to t'miln, and twisted t'webs,
And sang as t'shuttle flew:
There war na lumes 'at went wi' steeam,
We hed to treead o' t'wooden beeam,
And pool all t'bobbins through.

You twine a tap for t'watter nah,
We fotched it fro t'owd pump:
I' rain and hail we'd stand wi' t'jug,
And this straight hoam we hed to hug,
Wi' mony a jolt and bump.

We used to fettle ivery neet
All t'harstone and all t'brass:
And t'copper kettle looked reight fine,
We used to rub and mak' it shine;
There war no laking, lass.

And when mi Father killed a pig
A week 'fore Pudsa Tide,
We had to help and render t'fat,
And salt all t'ham i' t'salting vat,
And some o' t'scraps we fried.

We nivver bowt wer breead at t'shop,
We hedn't brass, ye see.
Through t'brewery we fotched wer barm,
And while it still war nice and warm,

We mixed it up to mak' wer doaf,
It used to mak' a champion loaf,
As leet as leet could be.

You talk abaht yer simple life,
I cannot thoyle sich talk:
You use all maks o' doctored stuff
Wi' frozzen mait, mixed baccas, snuff:
You rush abaht i' trains and trams,
And pay a lass to push yer p'rams,
You've gotten too idle to walk.

Gi' me the good owd cheery days
When wark war man's best friend:
And t'women thowt abaht ther barns,
And didn't traipse to other tahns,
But stayed at hoam to mend.

59

Yorkshire Tyke

It's Ripon for rowels, an' Shevvield for steel,
It's Pudsa for puddins, ya knaw varry weel:
At Whitby there's t'abbey whear Caedmon once sung,
At Halifax t'gibbet, whear t'bad uns were hung:
At Ilkla there's t'moors, there's t'Minster at York,
An' I've heeard of a place whear they fratch when they talk.
But for t'marra to t'fowk, you can choose whear you like,
There's nob'dy so friendly as t'real Yorkshire Tyke.

WALTER HAMPSON

60

Owd England

Tha'rt welcome, thrice welcome, Owd England;
It maks my een sparkle wi' glee,
An' does mi heart gooid to behold thee,
For I know tha's a welcome for me.
Let others recaant all thi failin's,
Let traitors upbraid as they will,
I know 'at thy virtues are many,
An' my heart's beeatin' true to thee still.

There's a gladness i' t'sky 'at bends ower thee,
  There's a sweetness i' t'green o' thy grass,
There's a glory i' t'waves 'at embrace thee,
  An' thy beauty there's noan can surpass.
Thy childer enrich iv'ry valley,
  An' add beauty to iv'ry glen,
For tha's mothered a race o' fair women,
  An' true-hearted, practical men.

There's one little spot up i' Yorkshire,
  It's net mich to crack on at t'best,
But to me it's a kingdom most lovely,
  An' it holds t'warmest place i' my breast.
Compared wi' that kingdom, all others
  Are worthless as bubbles o' fooam,
For one thing my rovin' has towt me,
  An' that is, there's no place like hooam.

I know there'll be one theer to greet me,
  'At's proved faithful through many dark days,
An' little feet runnin' to meet me,
  An' een 'at howd love i' their gaze.
An' there's neighbours both hooamly an' kindly,
  An' mates 'at are worthy to trust,
An' friends my adversity's tested,
  'At proved to be generous an' just.

An' net far away there's green valleys,
  An' greeat craggy, towerin' hills,
An' breezes 'at mingle their sweetness
  Wi' t'music o' sparklin' rills;
An' meadows all decked wi' wild-flaars,
  An' hedges wi' blossom all white,
An' a blue sky wheer t'skylark is singin'
  Just to mak known his joy an' delight.

Aye, England, Owd England! I love thee
  Wi' a love 'at each days grows more strong;
In my heart tha sinks deeper an' deeper,
  As year after year rolls along;
An' spite o' thy faults an' thy follies,
  Whativver thy fortune may be,
I' storm or i' sunshine, i' weal or i' woe,
  Tha'll allus be lovely to me.

May thy sons an' thy dowters live happy,
  An' nivver know t'woes o' distress;
May thy friends be for ivver increasin',
  An' thy enemies each day grow less.
May tha nivver let selfish ambition
  Dishonour or tarnish thy swoord,
But use it alooan agean despots
  Whether reignin' at hooam or abrooad.

GEORGE HARDWICK

61

Tentin' Coos

As Ah tents mi coos i' this country lane,
  Cars passes at lightnin' speed;
They think it a dowly job Ah've got,
  But Ah nivver taks no heed.

You can tak a view ti'd heart's content,
  All free fra worries an' cares;
There's field efter field wheerivver ya look,
  Like cross-wods wi' lattle squares.

Doon i' yon valley there's cottages snug,
  Folks workin', an' bairns at play;
An oad choch clock wi' its musical voice
  Is tellin' ya'd time o' day.

A wagon an' fower comes lumberin' by,
  A farm lad, sittin' astride,
His hosses are groomed an' their shinin' flanks
  Bring credit ti'd countryside.

For'd Sunday School outin' he plaits their manes,
  Decks 'em wi' ribbons and straw,
Then wagon is loaded wi' lattle bairns,
  An' off ti the toon they go.

Tiv his left there's a stretch of lovely moors,
  Wi' heather an' purple ling;
An' it's ' Gee wharve, Dobbin ! ' he says ti'd hoss,
  As happy as ony king.

He shouts Goodbye, an' Ah tons ti mi coos,
  Quietly chewin' their cud,
An' wishes that folks was nobbut like them,
  A-workin' for'd common good.

They patiently stand an' nibble away,
  An' works iv a quiet mood,
While they tons green grass tiv a lily white,
  An' maks it a perfect food.

So ya see it isn't a dowly job,
  Quietly tentin' mi coos,
For there's simple joys iv a country lane,
  So this is the life Ah choose.

JOHN HARLAND

62

Reeth Bartle Fair

This mworning as I went to wark,
  I met Curly just cumman heeam;
He had on a new flannin sark,
  An' he saw 'at I'd just gitten'd t'seeam.
'Whar's te been?' said awd Curly to me;
  'I've been down to Reeth Bartle Fair.'
'Swat te down mun sex needles,' said he
  'An' tell us what seets te saw there.'

Wye t'lads all ther best shun had put on,
  An' t'lasses donn'd all ther best cwoats;
I saw five pund of Scotch wether mutton,
  Sell'd by Ward and Tish Tom for five grwoats.
Bowlaway had fine cottons to sell,
  Butteroy lace an' hankutchers browt;
Young Tom Cwoats had a stall tuv hissel,
  An' had ribbons for varra near nowt.

Thar was Enos had good brandy snaps,
  Bill Brown as good spice as could be;
Potter Robin an' mar sike-like chaps
  Had t'bonniest pots te could see.

John Ridley an' awd Willy Walls,
  An' Naylor, an' tweea or three mar,
Had apples an' pears at ther stalls,
  An' Gardener Joe teea was thar.

Thar was scissors an' knives an' reead purses,
  An' plenty of awd cleeathes o' t'nogs,
An' tweea or three awd spavin'd horses,
  An' plenty of shun an' new clogs:
Thar was plenty of good iron pans,
  An' pigs at wad fill all t'deeales hulls;
Thar was baskets an' skeps an' tin cans,
  An' bowls, an' wood thivles for gulls.

Thar was plenty of all maks o' meeat,
  An' plenty of all sworts o' drink,
An' t'lasses gat monny a treeat,
  For t'gruvers war all full o' chink.
I cowp'd my black hat for a white in;
  Lile Jonas had varra cheeap cleeath;
Jem Peacock and Tom talk'd o' feightin',
  But Gudgeon Jem Puke lick'd 'em beeath.

Thar was dancin' an' feightin' for ever,
  Will Wade said at he was quite grieved;
An' Pedlety tell'd 'em he'd never
  Forgit 'em as lang as he leev'd.
They knock'd yan another about,
  Just warse than a sham to be seen,
Carlie Will leuk'd as white as a clout,
  Kit Puke gat a pair o' black een.

I spied our awd lass in a neuk
  Drinkan shrub wi' grim Freesteeane, fond lad;
I gav her a varra grou leuk;
  O' connies, but I was just mad.
Seea I went to John Whaite's to drink,
  Whar I war'd tweea an' seeumpince i' gin;
I knaw not what follow'd, but think
  I paddled through t'muck thick an' thin.

For today, when I gat out o' bed,
  My cleeathes wer all sullied seea sar,
Our Peggy and all our fwoak said
  To Reeth Fair I sud never gang mar;
But it's rake-time, seea I mun away,
  For my partners are all gyan to wark.
Seea I lowp'd up an' bad him good day,
  An' wrowt at t'awd Gang tell t'was dark.

JOHN HARTLEY

63

Bite Bigger

As aw hurried throo th'taan to mi wark,
  Aw wur lat, for all th'whistles had gooan—
Aw happen'd to hear a remark,
  'At ud fotch tears throo th'heart ov a stooan.

It wur raanin', an' snawin', an' cowd,
  An' th'flagstoans wur covered wi' muck,
An' th'east wind booath whistled an' howl'd,
  It saanded like nowt but ill luck;

When two little lads, donn'd i' rags,
  Baght stockins or shoes o' ther feet,
Coom trapesin' away ower th'flags,
  Booath on 'em sodden'd wi' th'weet.

Th'owdest mud happen to be ten,
  Th'young en be hauf on't, noa moor;
As Aw luk'd on, Aw sed to misen,
  'God help fowk this weather, 'at's poor!'

Th' big en sam'd summat off th'graand,
  An' Aw luk'd just to see what't could be;
'Twur a few wizend flaars he'd faand,
  An' they seem'd to ha fill'd him wi' glee.

An' he said, 'Come on, Billy, may be
  We shall find summat else by an' by,
An' if net, tha mun share thease wi' me
  When we get to some spot where it's dry.'

Leet-hearted they trotted away,
An' Aw follow'd, cos 'twur i' mi rooad;
But Aw thowt Aw'd ne'er seen sich a day,
It worn't fit ta be aght for a tooad.

Sooin th'big en agean slipt away,
An' sam'd summat else aght o' th'muck,
An' he cried aght, 'Luk here, Bill! today
Arn't we blest wi' a seet o' gooid luck?

'Here's a apple, an' th'mooast on it's saand,
What's rotten Aw'll throw into th'street,
Worn't it gooid to lig thear to be faand?
Nah booath on us con have a treat.'

Soa he wiped it, an' rubb'd it, an' then
Said, 'Billy, thee bite off a bit;
If tha hasn't been lucky thisen
Tha sal share wi' me sich as Aw get.'

Soa th'little en bate off a touch,
T'other's face beamed wi' pleasure all throo,
An' he said, 'Nay, tha hasn't taen much,
Bite agean, an' bite bigger; nah do!'

Aw waited to hear nowt noa moor,
Thinks Aw, thear's a lesson for me!
Tha's a heart i' thi breast, if tha'rt poor:
Th'world wur richer wi' moor sich as thee!

Tuppince wur all th'brass Aw had,
An' Aw'd ment it for ale when coom nooin,
But Aw thowt Aw'll goa give it yond lad,
He desarves it for what he's been doin'.

Soa Aw said, 'Lad, here's tuppince for thee,
For thi sen,' an' they stared like two geese;
But he said, woll th'tear stood in his e'e,
'Nah, it'll just be a penny apiece.'

'God bless thi! do just as tha will,
An' may better days speedily come;
Tho' clam'd, an' hauf donn'd, mi lad, still
Tha'rt a deal nearer Heaven nur some.'

64

Nelly O' Bobs

Who is it at lives i' that cot on the lea,
Joy o' my heart an leet o' my ee?
Who is that lass at's so dear unto me?
Nelly o' Bob's o' t'Crowtrees.

Who is it goes trippin' ower dew-spangled grass,
Singin' so sweetly? Shoo smiles as I pass,
Bonniest, rosy-cheek'd, gay-hearted lass!
Nelly o' Bob's o' t'Crowtrees.

Who is it I see i' my dreams of a neet?
Who lovingly whispers words tender an' sweet,
Till I wakken to find shoo's nowheer i' t'seet?
Nelly o' Bob's o' t'Crowtrees.

Who is it at leads me so lively a donce,
Yet to tawk serious ne'er gies me a chonce,
An' niver replied when I begged on her once?
Nelly o' Bob's o' t'Crowtrees.

Who is it at ivery chap's hankerin' to get,
Yet tosses her heead an' flies off in a pet,
As mich as to say, 'You've not getten me yet'?
Nelly o' Bob's o' t'Crowtrees.

Who is it could mak life a long summer's day,
Whose smile would drive sorrow an' trouble away,
An' mak t'hardest wark, if for her, seem like play?
Nelly o' Bob's o' t'Crowtrees.

Who is it I'll have if I've iver a wife,
An' love her, her only, to t'end o' my life,
An' nurse her i' sickness, an' guard her from strife?
Nelly o' Bob's o' t'Crowtrees.

Who is it at's promised, to-neet if it's fine,
To meet me at t'corner, o' t'mistal at nine?
Why, it's her at I've langed for so lang to mak mine—
Nelly o' Bob's o' t'Crowtrees.

65

To a Daisy

(Found blooming March 7th)

Aa, Awm feeared tha's come too sooin,
Little daisy!
Pray, whativer wor ta doin'?
Are ta crazy?
Winter winds are blowin' yet,
Tha'll be starved, mi little pet.

Did a gleam o' sunshine warm thee,
An' deceive thee?
Niver let appearance charm thee,
For believe me,
Smiles tha'll find are oft but snares,
Laid to catch thee unawares.

Still Aw think it looks a shame,
To talk sich stuff;
Aw've lost faith, an' tha'll do th'same,
Aye, sooin enough:
If tha'rt happy as tha art,
Trustin' must be th'wisest part.

Come, Aw'll pile some bits o' stooan,
Raand thi dwellin';
They may screen thee when Aw've gooan,
Ther's no tellin';
An' when gentle spring draws near
Aw'll release thee, niver fear.

An' if thi pratty face,
Greets me smilin';
Aw may come an' sit bi th'place,
Time beguilin';
Glad to think Aw'd paar to be,
Of some use, if but to thee.

66

Wayvin' Music

Ther's music i' th'shuttle, i' th'loom, an' i' th'frame,
  Ther's melody mingled i' th' noise:
For th'active ther's praises, for th'idle ther's blame,
  If they'd hearken to th'saand of its voice.
An' when flaggin' a bit, ha refreshin' to feel
As yo pause an' look raand on the throng,
At the clank o' the tappet, the hum o' the wheel,
Sing this plain unmistakable song:
        Nick-a-ting, nock-a-ting,
        Wages keep pocketing;
    Workin' for little is better ner laiking;
        Twist an' twine, reel an' wind,
        Keep a contented mind,
    Troubles are oft of a body's own making.

To see workin' fowk wi' a smile o' ther face
  As they labour thear day after day,
An' hear th'women's voices float sweetly thro' th'place,
  As they join i' some favourite lay;
It saands amang th'din, as the violet seems
'At peeps aat th'green dockens among,
An' spreading a charm over th'rest by its means,
Thus it blends i' that steady owd song:
        Nick-a-ting, nock-a-ting,
        Wages keep pocketing;
    Workin' for little is better ner laiking;
        Twist an' twine, reel an' wind,
        Keep a contented mind,
    Troubles are oft of a body's own making.

An' then see what lessons are laid aat anent us,
  As pick after pick follows time after time,
An' warns us tho' silent to let nowt prevent us
  From strivin' by little endeavours to climb.
Th'world's made o' trifles, its dust forms a maantain,
Then nivver despair as you're trudgin' along;
If troubles will come an' your spirits dishearten,
You'll find ther's relief i' that steady owd song:

Nick-a-ting, nock-a-ting,
Wages keep pocketing,
Workin' for little is better ner laiking;
Twist an' twine, reel an' wind,
Keep a contented mind,
Troubles are oft of a body's own making.

Life's warp comes throo Heaven, th'weft's fun bi us sen,
To finish a piece we're compell'd to ha booath.
Th'warp's reight, but if th'weft should be faulty, ha then?
Noa wayver i' th'world can produce a gooid clooath.
Then let us endeavour, bi working an' striving,
To finish awr piece so as noa fault can be fun,
An' then in return for awr pains an' contriving,
Th' takker-in'll reward us an whisper 'Well done!'
Clink-a-clank, clink-a-clank,
Workin' wi'aat a thank,
May be awr fortun'—if soa nivver mind it!
Strivin' to do awr best,
We shall be reight at last,
If we lack comfort nah, then shall we find it.

EDMUND HATTON

67

Aar Maggie

Aw believe aar Maggie's courtin',
Fur shoo dresses hersen sa smart,
An' shoo's allus runnin' ta t'winda,
When ther's onny o 't'chaps abaat:
Shoo willent wear her owd shawl,
Bud dons a bonnet i' t'sted,
An' laps her can in her gahn,
As shoo goas ta t'weyvin' shed.

Of a neet, wi' snodden'd hair,
An' cheeks like a summer's cherry,
An' lips fair assin' for kisses,
An' een sa black an' sa merry,

Shoo taks her knittin' ta t'meddas,
  An' sits in a shady newk,
An' knits whal shoo sighs an' watches,
  Wi' a dreamy ling'rin' lewk.

Thus knittin', sighin', an' watchin',
  Shoo cahrs aat on t'soft medda grass,
List'nin' ta t'murmurin' brooklet
  An' waitin' for t'sweetheart ta pass;
Shoo drops her wark in her appron,
  An' glints aat on t'settin' sun,
An' wonders if he goes a-courtin'
  When his long day's wark is done.

Bud shoo hears t'chap's footsteps a-comin',
  Soa shoo rises wi' modest grace;
Ah! Mag! tha sly lovin' lassie!
  For shame o' thi bashful face!
Shoo frames ta be goin' home'ards,
  As he lilts ower t'stile,
Bud when he comes anent her,
  Shoo gies him sich a smile.

Then he places his arms araand her,
  An' shoo creeps t'lois up tuv his side,
An' leyns her heead on his waiscoit,
  An' walks wi' an air o' pride,
Bud oh! yo sud see her glances,
  An' oh! yo sud hear 'em kiss—
When they pairt thro' one another!—
  If shoo isn't courtin', who is?

WILLIAM HEATON

68

Ould Malley's Voluntine

Ould Malley threw her knitting dewn
  An' stood awhile a th' floor,
Starin' at summat t'post hed browt
  Unto hur cottage door.

Ther t'shap o' t'Queen stuck on o' t'neuk,
  An' summat else beside,
'At wakkened up ould Malley's pluck
  To see what wor inside.

Hoo oppend it, bud what hoo saw,
  It made hur varry queer;
Thear lots o' varses up an' dewn
  An' picturs here an' theer,
Hoo couldn't read it, bud hoo said,
  'Aw think Aw s't goa to th'skoil,
An' get th'ould man to read it me,
  At learnin' Aw'm a fooil.'

Soa Malley donn'd hur bonnet on,
  Hur shoin an' Sunday gewn;
An' off hoo set, it wor not long
  Afore hoo clapt it dewn,
Upo' ould Johnny's writin' desk,
  Who said, 'Thew cuts a shine,
Who's sent ta this? Aw'm fain ta see
  Thee get a Voluntine.'

'A Voluntine,' hoo said, 'Who'll send
  A Voluntine to me?
Aw think they're wrang i' ther top lock,
  Today Aw'm fifty-three,
An' neaw to hev a voluntine,
  Aw'd nivver one afore;
An' noabdy's whisper'd love to me,
  Fur twenty year an' more.'

'Well, what o' that,' ould Johnny said,
  'It's nut to lat to mend,
Aw sent tha this to let tha knaw
  I want to be thi friend.
Beside Aw knew thaa'd bring it here
  For me to read to thee,
Soa pray tha doff thi bonnet off,
  An' tak a cup o' tea:

An' we will mak it up today,
  If thee hes bud a mind;
Aw connot live be th'dead, thew knaws,
  Soa dunno be unkind:
Bud tak ma neaw for what Aw'm worth,
  Aw'm nawther rich nor fine;
An' mak ma what Aw want to be—
  Thi love, thi Voluntine.'

Ould Malley shamed an' hung hur heead,
  An' blushing gav consent;
Then went an' doft hur bonnet off,
  An' sat her deawn content.
So they wer wed i' Easter wik,
  The day wer varry fine;
An' oft sin then they've laughed an' talked
  Abewt that Voluntine.

RUTH HEDGER

69

London Piece

Ah nivver thowt it 'ud coome ti pass;
Oor Jackie's wedded a city lass!
Wi' poodther an' paint she clarts 'er phiz,
An' she talks lahke fawks on t'Wiyerless diz:
Fower years 'e wer' coortin' Robi'son' niece,
Bood 'e's been an' getten a Loondon Piece.

She walks oop t'village on 'eels that 'igh
All t'lartle lads mocks 'er, mincin' by;
'Er sket's that stright she could nivver fraame
To clim ovver t'stahle; whyah, yer'd think 'er laame,
Till she clicks oop 'er petticawts, bowld as brass—
Yon shameless Piece of a Loondon lass!

Annie Robi'son's awmly; aya,
Bood 'er ooncle's getten a bit put byah;
She's a 'oose-proud lass, is Robi'son Annie—
She's quiet an' menseful, kahnd an' canny;
An' she'll get 'is brass when 'e dees, will t'niece;
Jack's getten nowt wiv 'is Loondon Piece.

She can't baake breead an' she weean't scroob t'floor,
Nor yet wesh t'step on 'er awn froont door;
'Is Dad wer allus a careful man,
Bood she's maade Jack buy on t'instalment plan;
' E'll rew,' says t'Meeasther, ' bood t'fond yoong ass
Mun fick it oot, wiv 'is Loondon lass.'

W. HIRD

70

Darby an' Joan an' their Daughter Nell

DARBY. Joan ! Ah noo hev thowt seea mich about it,
Ah seearly nivver mair s'all doot it;
At moorn an' neeght, an' neeght an' moorn,
Ah sumtahm wish Ah'd ne'er been born.

JOAN. Whya, Darby, prithee, let ma see,
Ah whoap it's nowt 'at's bad o' me.

DARBY. Thee, Joan ! neea, marry, neea sike thing.
Think bad o' thee ! 'twad be a sin.
Ah think, indeed, Ah war a feeal
Ti send oor Nell ti t'Boordin'-skeeal.
Sike mauky feeals ez them, Ah think,
Hev filled her heead wi' prahd an' stink,
Foor sin' sha went, sha's grown seea fine,
Sha caan't deea nowt wi 'oot her wine,
When t'dinner's owered, an' sha's seea neyce,
Sha weean't eat puddin' meead o' rice,
Thoff when at skeeale an' put ti t'pinch,
Fra sike good stuff sha'd nivver flinch.
An' all her notions are seea raased
It's fit ti to'n her feyther crazed,
Fer leyke a toon wench, Ah declare,
Sha walks abroad wi' breasts all bare;
To show her shoon, an' hosen clocked,
Sha lifts her sket whahl Ah's fair shocked,
Nut 'at Ah care aboot t'fond lass,
Neea mair 'an this—it taks mah brass,
An' wiv her fine lang labberin' tail,
Sha'll git her fahther inti jail.

JOAN. Whya, Darby, bud thoo knaws ther's t'Squire,
An' he, mayhap, will Nell admire,
An' efter all the'r noise an' strife,
Thoo knaws t'young Squire he wants a weyfe.
Then let's be seear ti mak her smairt,
An' teeach her hoo ti plaay her pairt;
Sha seean'll mak him towards her leean,
An' then thoo knaws 'at t'wark is deean.
Ez fer her breasts an' bare at airms,
It's feshion noo ti show yan's chairms.
Men leyke ti knaw, Ah've heeard it said,
What's real an' fause afoor they wed;
Hoose'er, Ah'll try an' deea mah best,
An' leeave ti thee ti mannish t'rest.

DARBY. Bud, then, suppooase oor plot sud fail,
An' me foor debt be sent ti jail,
Poor Nell wad niver be a weyfe,
An' hev ti laabur all her leyfe;
Foor efter sha's seea browten up,
Hoo can sha ivver bahd ti stoop
Ti gan ti sarvice, ur ti spin,
Or ivver ti deea onnything?

JOAN. Whya, Darby, leeave it all ti me,
Ah'll mannish't weel, an' that thoo'll see;
Ah'll be her pilot all mah leyfe,
An' mak her sum rich farmer's weyfe.
Then ez the' gan ti chetch, doon t'toon,
Ah's seear thoo'll say, 'Weel, deean, oor Joan.'

FLORENCE MAY HOPPER

71

Cottage Scene

Neea face ti greet 'im
When a cooms through'd geate,
Neabody ti say 'is tea's riddy,
An' e's leate.

Nea smell a baakin'
Though it's baakin' daya,
Nea fire id greate
An' ivery sowl awaya.

'E leeaks roond t'kitchin,
An' 'e thinks t'oad clock
'Es niver spokken wi' sike
A clooud ' tick-tock.'

'Is lartle 'eart sinks,
An' 'e gets doon on t'mat
An' buries 'is feeace
Id warmth ad oad cat.

Tears isn't far frev 'is ees.
Thas a lump iv 'is throoat,
As 'e pulls off 'is lartle oad cap,
An' chucks doon 'is cooat.

Someweears aboon a creeakin' step
Moves quiet owerd fleear,
A thin wail rises, an' it spreeads
Through'd oppen chamber deear.

A woman's voice is 'eard above
' Is that thoo, Bob?' it ses,
' Come the wayas up, an' seed new bairn
The Mam's getten 'ere a bed.'

ROBERT HORSPOOL

72

A Song of Heeam

Aye, t'sea's reet blae at Reighton, an' t'girt cliffs wheyte an' graay,
An' yalla's t'sand 'at ligs along fra theer ti Fila Bay;
Wheer t'lappin' waaves ton softly ower an' glimmer as they breeak;
Ee, Ah'd fain be heeam i' Reighton when t'daays o' Spring awaake.

Theer's primroses at Reighton doon in a lahtle deale,
An' i' spinney nigh-hand beck, thoo knaws, theer's 'nemones as weel.
Theer, ower anenst t'becksahd cam, Ah'd fain bahd all t'tahm,
An' care nowt for t'morrow, if this yah daay be mahn.

Ah knaws a neuk i' Reighton wheer gaay t'gesses grow,
Wheer buttherflees flig cantily, a-liltin' tiv an' fro;
An' theer Ah'd lig a-skahmin' oop t'wheyte cloods roond an' big
'At flit ower t'gap at Reighton an' on ti Fila' Brig.

Ee, summer morn at Reighton, wi t'wheyte roke rollin' free;
Wi' glowin' sun a-liftin' oop frev oot t'graay North Sea
Whahl't oppens wide t'curtain 'at hides t'coomin' dawn,
An' gliffs across t'deep ti ma, a-waaitin' of t'morn.

Ee, summer eve at Reighton, when soft t'sea winds blow
An' wheyte-sailed cobles slidder by on ebbin' tahd aflow;
Ah sees t'chaangin' colours, t'purple, green an' graay
Creeap ower t'sea at Reighton an' on ti Fila' bay.

But summer neet at Reighton, maist allus is t'best
When t'silver moon hings oop aloft an' glents t'soft sea's breast;
When roond aboot's all peaceful leyke an' yannerly as t'deead,
An' t'lantern leets at heaven's yat are skimmerin' owerheead.

Ah knaws a song o' Reighton 'at's whispered intiv air
An' tuned for ma wheereer Ah gans; an' leyke a muther's praayer
Will coom ageean when Ah's fair stalled, afar i' foreign land;
An' Ah s'll hear it when Ah sleeps an' hearin', unnerstand.

H. M. HUDSON

73

Oh Wheer 'as it Gone, Lad?

Aa lad, Ah mind times as is noan so far back
When Ah wanted for nowt 'at a lassie mun lack;
A man o' mi oan, both luvin' an' kind,
Honest o' heart an' straight in 'is mind;

But it seeams t'mi laately 'at summat be wrong,
The touch o' thi 'and 'at said Ah wor the one,
Oh wheer 'as it gone, lad, an' what 'ave Ah done?

An' Ah mind of a neet when tha cummed 'ome thro' t'pit,
Achin' an' weary, an' reight glad t'sit
Wahm afore t'fire wal Ah set Aht a bit,
Wi' eyes grimed an' bleary tha'd watch mi kind-like,
But it seeams t'mi laately 'at summat be wrong;
Thi prahd look, thi glad look, the luvlight 'at shone,
Oh wheer 'as it gone, lad, an' what 'ave Ah done?

Tha's noan one for talk, but Ah mind 'ow tha'd say
Things breet-like, an' laugh i' thi sho't quiet way,
An' tha'd sing soft sometimes, lad, like one wi'aht care
In a voice 'at wor tuneful an' pleasin' to 'ear,
But it seeams t'mi laately 'at summat be wrong;
The life i' thi speykin', nah deead as a stoan,
Oh wheer 'as it gone, lad, an' what ave Ah done?

Theer all nobbut small things, Ah knaw, lad, Ah knaw,
But they do say as straws 'll tell 'ow the winds blaw,
'Tis the gamesome light 'eart o' thee, lad, 'at Ah miss
I' thi walk an' thi talk, i' thi look an' thi kiss;
An' it seeams t'mi laately 'at summat be wrong.
Doan't think Ah doan't luv thee, doan't think Ah mak moan,
But wheer 'as it gone, lad, an' what 'ave Ah done?

F. AUSTIN HYDE

74

Depper, Awd Meer

Hev I ony awd 'osses, young fellow frev 'Ull?
Thoo's willin' tae buy 'em, gie value i' full?
Why yis, I have yan, i' this paddock doon here,
Cohip, then! Coom on, then! Coom, Depper, awd meer!

No, she dizn't coom gallopin', bud then, you see,
Meer's a bit wankle like, tonned twenty three.
Thoo'll mebbe not be quite sae frisky thisen
When thoo's seen thi greeat-grandsons grow up tae be men!

Weel, what will I tak for her? Why noo, she's fat,
An' they tell me you give a bit extry for that,
Bud Ah might as well tell tha, thoo'll not buy that meer
If thoo stands there an' bids me fra noo tae next year,

She was t'fost fooal I 'ad when I com' upo'd place,
An' fost she's been allus, i' shaft, pole or thrace.
She's ploughed, drilled an' harrowed, rolled, scruffled an' led,
An' mothered Beaut, Boxer, Prince, Cobby an' Ned.

If threshin' machine gat stuck fast on its way,
Young 'osses wad plunge, rahve an' tew hauf o'd day,
Bud afoor it gat shifted it allus was ' Here,
Away thoo gans, Thoddy, an' fetch us t'awd meer ! '

When stacks was afire, afoor motor car days,
She galloped tae Driffield when t'spot was ablaze,
Ower field, ditch and hedgerow for t'gainest way doon,
Saved buildings, an' hoos an' three pikes, I'll be boon !

When t'missus took badly, when t'babby was born,
'Twas a life an' death jonny for t'doctor that morn,
An' though she'd been workin' at t'plough all day lang
T'meer galloped as tho' she knew summat was wrang.

Wi' never a whip, not a jerk on her rein,
She went like a whirlwind an' flew back again,
Wi' t'doctor an' nuss, just i' time tae save life—
Aye, Depper, I owe thoo baith dowter an' wife.

On friends 'at's sae faithful we dooan't turn wer backs,
Nor send 'em for slaughter tae'd foreigner's axe,
Nor let 'em be worked tae their death across t'sea,
Wheer nivver a Yorkshire voice shouts ' Wahve ' nor ' Gee.'

No, noo 'at she's neither young, bonny nor sound,
She awns t'lahtle paddock, it's pensioner's ground,
An' stall i' yon stable, hay, beddin' an' corn,
Ah reckon she's addled a spot of her awn !

An' when the day comes 'at we do hae tae pairt,
She'll gan in a way 'at'll not brek her hairt,
An' t'land 'at she's worked on an' loved twenty year
At last'll lig leet on my faithful awd meer.

A. K.

75

Thoughts for a Sermon

Wi' monny a flout and gibe ther's them at
Aaim t'au'd heeads are bud clatter pans;
Bud let 'em gen, t'wo'lld's nut ez tha wad ha'e't;
Thoff ivvery age wiv its awn mak' o' daftness
Fets them it fits ti gan ram slap at weeastin' tahm,
Ti randiboo wi' drabs, ti mak swill gullets
Fost o' the'rsens, then other swabs; fit deed fer swine;
Fer all ken wits an' deeacent fau'k ti gaum an' wilder at,
Wheea ken an' ho'd at them an' uz sud all be shappin'
Oor sho't an' footed spell o' daays doon here
Wi' seeamly deeds, an' menseful wark weel deean,
An' nivver raffle tahm an' wits awaay i' that
Which ends i' makkin' nowther bou't nor bow,
An' seea at t'finish up its boond ti be
When Fatther Time wi' measured treead his leear swings,
An' tak's a cleean cut swarth wheearon tha stan':
It's neea good then fer onny yan ti aaim
Ther'll be a chance fer them ti loup aside
Ti beg an' pray fer tahm ti side up t'binch
O' life's warkshop; an' finish off a job or tweea,
O' good wark started yance, bud theear hauf deean.
Sike noo mun lig wheear it war thrawn ham sam
Upon life's binch. Sike cannot lig the'r hand upon
Ya sing'l job weel deean, wi' t'maesther's passmark on't:
All yan can finnd is rusty teeals, blunt and brokken,
A square all oot o' trewth,
A plumb board lackin' t'plummet:
A chalk string, mouths a sarmon, all i' knots,
A spletten mallet, a pointless trooel,
O' chisel sprents on t'grund, a parlous heeap,
Tellin' o' labour lost, bud shewin' nowt ov honest wark.
Neea keysteean here, neea arch war ivver maade;
Hoo mud ther' be, wheear neea foondation steean war ivver
  laaid,
Bud deeath sweeps cleean eeach binch, an' tots up wark.
Wi' tahm for weights: life's wark in t'scaale-pan's thrawn:

Some fau'k, Ah ween, i' baith pans aaim ti sit,
Bud t'scaal at weighs yan's yethly deeds tilts strang
Ez eeach yan finnds when his tahm-beeak is for trewth livvered up
It's witless wark fer onny here ti aaim at they
A soarin' kite maay be, an' t'clew-stick ho'd.
Some wear a feeace ti match the duds tha don ;
Some nobbut greease the'r heeads when gahin' ti t'chetch,
Some call ' Noo whisht ! be good, it's Sabbath daay.'
Think on ther's six daays cleear ti scheme an' range eeach plan.
This wo'lld is stock'd wi' men ov endless shaps an' mak's
Ez monny shades an' hues ez glints on t'een. . . .

J. L.

76

Elphi Bandy Legs

Elphi bandy legs
Bent an' wide apart;
Neea yan i' this Deeal
Awnes a kinder heart.
Elphi greeatheead,
Grettest ivver seen;
Neea yan i' this Deeal
Awnes a breeter een.
Elphi little chap
Thoff he war sa small
War big wi' deeds o' kindness;
Drink tiv him yan an' all :
Him at fails ti drain dry
Bettin Agar glass
Binnot wo'th a peascod
Nor a boss for onny lass.

GEORGE LANCASTER

77

A Yorkshire Farmer's Address to a Schoolmaster

Good day to you, Misther Skealmaisther, the evenin' is desperate fine,
I thowt I wad gie ye a call aboot that young sonnie o' mine.
I couldn't persuade him to come, sea I left him behont me at yam,
Bud somehoo it's waintly possess'd me to make a skealmaisther o' Sam.
He's a kind of a slack-back, ye knaw, I niver could get him to work,
He scarcelins wad addle his saut wiv a ploo, or a shovel, or fork.
I've tried him agean an' agean, bud I finnd that he's nea use at yam,
Sea me an' my missus agreed to mak a skealmaisther o' Sam.
If I sends him to wark, why, he'll chunther an' gie me the awfullest leaks,
He'd a deal rayther lig upo'd sofy wi' novels an' them soort o' beaks.
Sea I thowt a skealmaisther wad suit him, a lowse soort o' job, do ye see,
Just to keep a few bairns oot o' mischief, as easy as easy can be.
Of coorse you've to larn 'em to coont, an' to figure a bit, an' to read,
An' to sharpen 'em up if they're numskulls, wiv a lalldabber ower their heead,
Bud it's as easy as easy, ye knaw, an' I think it wad just suit oor Sam,
An' my missus, she's just o' my mind, for she says that he's nea use at yam.
It was nobbut this mornin' I sent him to gan an' to harrow some land,
He was boamin' asleep upo'd fauf, wiv a rubbishly beak iv his hand;
I gave him a bunch wi' my feat, an' rattled him yarmin' off yam.
Sea I think that I'll send him to you, you mun mak a skeal-maisther o' Sam.

He's a stiff an' a runty young fellow, I think that he'll grow up a
whopper,
He'd wallop the best lad you've got, an' I think he wad wallop
him proper;
Bud still he's a slack-back, ye knaw, an' seein' he's nea use at
yam,
I think I shall send him to you, you mun mak a skealmaisther o'
Sam.

LETITIA A. LANGSTAFF

78

Nivver Despair

How is't thet nea matther what happens
We nobbut can luik on t'dark side?
It seims human nater teh dew sea,
Fer all folk ti d'syame styake er tied.
But it's time et we altered er outluik,
An' saw fer ersels fair an' square,
Thet whativver muddle we're left in,
Thar's a way out, sea nivver despair!

We whiles git fair slockened wi' d'weather,
It does nowt bud rain ivv'ry day:
We think ivv'rything 'll be ruined,
Git reet down e' d'dumps, as they say.
We nivver sud harbour sac notions,
Fer doesn't that aud Buik declare
Thar'll alw'z be seed time an' harvist,
Sea cheer up, an' nivver despair.

We're leeven e' queer times, Ah's thinken;
Things happen beyond human ken:
Ah guess it wud mak a strange difference
If we leeved t'yane fer t'other: fer then
That day we all lang te see dawnen
Wiv its prospects si pleizen an' fair,
Wud be nearer—aye! waiten e' d'dowersteid:
Sea hope on, an' nivver despair.

Could nations but trist yan another,
Put fear an' suspicion te d'dower,
Then war an' its terrors wud vanish,
Fer nane wud be seeken fer power.
Sea all on ez, younger an' auder,
Mun warrk hard, all dewen er share,
Te mark d'world a plyace grand te leeve in.
It can be. Let's nivver despair!

FRED LAWTON

79

T'Owd Handloom Weyver

Ah'm nobbut a owd handloom weyver,
An' one day Ah sat at mi loom,
An' pondered on t'past an' on t'futur',
An' mi thowts were all lapped up i' gloom.

Mi owd picking-stick swung anent me,
T'temples wanted shiftin', Ah knew;
Ah'd just been a-alterin' t'creeper,
An' two ends were dahn o' dark blue.

Mi treadle were nearly worn through,
Mi healds, nowt original left,
T'owd handtree were ommost i' two,
An' sooin Ah's be lakin' for weft.

There's t'nippins and t'fruzzins on t'flooar,
Mi beetin' is varry near done;
Band? Well, Ah's sooin want some more,
An' bobbins Ah've hardly a one.

Mi warp's bad wi' t'ends allus dahn,
Soa Ah'm bun to mak' floats, owd lass:
Ah think Ah hear t'tacker-in say
'Well, Ah can't help but bate thee some brass.'

Ah'm finished soa tak mi owd loom,
But when Ah meet t'gert Tacker-in,
He'll happen say, 'Well, nivver heed,
Thi warp worn't soa gooid, come thee in.'

SAMUEL LAYCOCK

80

Factory Days

Thirty years Aw've bin a toiler,
  Th'moast o' th'toime i' th'cotton mill;
Sweat as hard as th'best among you,
  Aye, an' lads, Aw'm workin' still:
Workin', when you're noicely dozin',
  Workin' wi' a weakly frame,
Thinkin', feelin', an' composin',
  Not to get misel a name,
But to try an' raise mi brothers,
  Those 'at labour by mi soide,
Sons o' th'same dear English mothers,
  Britain's glory, strength, an' pride,
Oh, may God i' heaven aboon us
  Help me i' mi humble task;
Gie me th'will an' strength to do it,
  Brothers, this is awl aw ask.

DAVID LEWIS

81

The Sweeper and Thieves

A sweeper's lad was late o' th'neeght,
His slape-shod shun had leeam'd his feet;
He call'd to see a good awd deeame,
'At monny a time had trigg'd his wame,
For he wor then fahve miles fra yam:
He ax'd i' t'lair to let him sleep,
An' he'd next day, ther chimlers sweep.
They supper'd him wi' country fare,
Then show'd him tul his hooal i' t'lair.
He crept intul his streay bed,
His poak o' seeat beneath his heead,
He wor content, nur car'd a pin,
An' his good frind then lock'd him in.
The lair fra t'hoose a distance stood,

Between 'em grew a lahtle wood:
Aboot midneeght, or nearer moorn,
Two thieves brak in to steeal ther coorn;
Heving a leeght i' lantern dark,
They seean to winder fell to wark;
And wishing they'd a lad to fill,
Young Brush (wheea yet had ligg'd quite still)
Thinkin' 'at t'men belang'd to t'hoose
An' that he noo mud be of use;
Jump'd doon directly on to t'fleear,
An' t'thieves then beath ran oot at t'deear.
Nor stopt at owt, nur thin, nur thick,
Fully convinc'd it wor awd Nick.
The sweeper lad then ran reeght seean
Ti t'hoose, an' tell'd 'em what wor deean:
Maister an' men then quickly raise,
An' ran to t'lair wi' hoaf ther clais.
Twea horses, secks, an' leeght they fand,
Which had been left by t'thievish band;
These roond i' t'neybourheead they cry'd,
But nut an awner e'er apply'd,
For neean durst horses awn, or secks,
They wor se freeghten'd o' ther necks,
Yan horse an' seck wor judg'd the sweeper's share,
Because he kept the farmer's coorn an' lair.

E. A. LODGE

82

Then an' Nae

When I were but a striplin'
    An' bare a scoor year owd,
I thowt I'd gotten brains enew
    To fill all t'yeds i' t'fowd.

I used to roor wi' laughin'
    At t'sharpness o' my wit,
An' a joke I made one Kersmiss
    Threw my nuncle in a fit.

I used to think my mother
    Were a hundred year behund;
An' my father—well, my father
    Nobbut fourteen aence to t'pund.

An' I often turned it ovver,
    But I ne'er could fairly see
Yaeiver sich owd cronies
    Could hae bred a chap like me.

An' whene'er they went to t'market,
    I put my fillin's in;
Whol my father used to stop me
    Wi' 'Prithee, hold thy din.

'Does ta think we're nobbut childer,
    Wi' as little sense as thee?
When thy advice is wanted,
    We'st axe thee, does ta see?'

But they gate it, wilta, shalta,
    An' I did my levil best
To change their flee-blown notions,
    Whol their yeds were laid to t'west.

This happened thirty year sin;
    Nae I've childer o' my own,
At's gotten t'cheek to tell me
    At I'm a bit flee-blown.

JOHN MALHAM-DEMBLEBY

83

A Kuss

Ye ma bring me gowd bi t'bowlful,
    Gie me lands bi t'mile,
Fling me dewy roses,
    Stoor set on mi smile;
Ye ma cahr ye dahn afoor me,
    Castles for me build,
Twine me laurel garlands,
    Let sweet song be trill'd;

Ye ma let mi meyt be honey,
    Let mi sup be wine,
Gie ma hahnds an' hosses,
    Gie ma sheep an' kine.
Yit one flayd kuss fro her wod gie
    Sweeter bliss to mei,
Nor owt at ye could finnd to name,
    Lait ye thro sea tul sea.

I've seen her hair gleeam gowden
    In t'kersmas yolla sun,
An' ivvry inch o' grahnd sha treeads,
    Belang her seur it mun.
Her smile is sweet as roses,
    An' sweeter far to me;
An' prahd sha hods her heead up
    As lass o' heigh degree.
Bonnie are greean laurel leaves—
    I'd sooiner mi brah feel
T'laughin' lips o' t'lass I love,
    Thoa bays be varry weel.

I'm varry fond o' singin':
    What bonnier could be
Nor mah fair lass hersen agate
    A-singin' love to me!
It's reight to live on spice an' sich,
    An' sup a warmin' glass;
But sweet-stuff's walsh, an' wine is cowd,
    Aside mi lovely lass.
Tak ye yar hahnds an' hosses,
    Tak ye yar sheep an' kine;
To finnd mi lass ower t'hills I'll ride,
    Sha sal be ivver mine!

WILSON MIDGLEY

84

An Old Man to his Dog

Tha's seen a mort o' trouble, lad,
We've hed a main o' fun.
Both of us is owd an' ooined,
Wer better days are done.

It hurts ta hev thee going deaf,
An' knaw tha'rt nearly blind;
Thi tail that once cocked up sa peart
Hangs dreely down behind.

They say a twelvemonth of thy life
Is just like seven o' mine.
Tha'll noan go pegging on mich more,
Tha mun be ninety nine.

It comforts me to knaw that when
We reach a happier clime,
We can live ony gate we like,
An' tak no heed o' time.

JAMES MILLIGAN

85

Aud Willie's Geease

Ah seear at it's a dowly keease,
Consarnin' niber Willie's geease.
He kept her twenty years an' mair,
An' fed an' shelter'd her wi' care:
An' pate o' t'tahm he kept a steg,
Then they wad eeach stand on yah leg
Sumtahmes be t'beck sahd, poor things,
An' put their nebs onder their wings;
An' then in t'spring tahm o' t'year,
Aud Willie's geease laid eggs, Ah seear.

Ti hetch her eggs sha teeak her tahm,
An' then, when t'weather gat mair warm,
Sum downey geslins sha browt out,
An' proud o' them sha was, neea doubt.
Befoor aud Willie breeath'd his last
He showed his lang freendship a vast
By giving Dicky his aud geease,
But sha went back ti Willie's pleeace.
At last we saw t'aud geease was deead;
Sha mud hev had a wack on t'heead,
Or been pelted wi' hard flint steeans,
An' seea had sum brokken beeans,
Or meby had a twisted neck
Befoore sha was thrawn inti t'beck,
Deead as a steean, there left ti flooat
Down where sha used ti flap an' spoort.
Sha'll nivver cackle efter gam
Ageean, nor waddle on t'way yam.

F. W. MOORMAN

86

A Dalesman's Litany

It's hard when fowks can't find their wark
  Wheer they've bin bred an' born;
When I were young I awlus thowt
  I'd bide 'mong t'roots an' corn.
But I've bin forced to work i' towns,
  So here's my litany:
Frae Hull, an' Halifax, an' Hell,
  Gooid Lord, deliver me!

When I were courtin' Mary Ann,
  T'owd squire he says one day:
'I've got no bield for wedded fowks;
  Choose wilt ta wed or stay?'
I couldn't gie up t'lass I loved,
  To t'town we had to flee:
Frae Hull, an' Halifax, an' Hell,
  Gooid Lord, deliver me!

I've wrowt i' Leeds an' Huthersfel',
An' addled honest brass;
I' Bradforth, Keighley, Rotherham,
I've kept my barns an' lass.
I've travelled all three Ridin's round,
And once I went to sea:
Frae forges, mills, an' coalin' boats,
Gooid Lord, deliver me!

I've walked at neet through Sheffield loans,
'T were same as bein' i' Hell;
Furnaces thrast out tongues o' fire,
An' roared like t'wind on t'fell.
I've sammed up coals i' Barnsley pits,
Wi' muck up to my knee:
Frae Sheffield, Barnsley, Rotherham,
Gooid Lord, deliver me!

I've seen grey fog creep ower Leeds Brig
As thick as bastile soup;
I've lived wheer fowks were stowed away
Like rabbits in a coop.
I've watched snow float down Bradforth Beck
As black as ebiny:
Frae Hunslet, Holbeck, Wibsey Slack,
Gooid Lord, deliver me!

But now, when all wer childer's fligged,
To t'coontry we've coom back.
There's fotty mile o' heathery moor
Twix' us an' t'coal-pit slack.
An' when I sit ower t'fire at neet,
I laugh an' shout wi' glee:
Frae Bradforth, Leeds, an' Huthersfel',
Frae Hull, an' Halifax, an' Hell,
T'gooid Lord's delivered me!

87

A Wharfedale Lullaby

There's a storm brewin' out on Beamsley Beacon,
Thunner an' leetnin' round Simon Seat.
Up amang t'clouds ride prior, priest an' deacon,
T'monks hunt ghosts o'red deer to-neet.
Whist thee, my fairy,
Lullaby, Mary;
Bolton's brown monks wean't harm thee, my sweet.

A blue leet is burnin' i' t'Tower up at Barden,
T'Shepherd-lord's castin' a mawmetry spell.
Yew-slivers an' night-shade he's pullen in his garden,
Goat-sucker's blood he's spilled out on t'fell.
Whist thee, my fairy,
Lullaby, Mary;
Shepherd-lord niver wi' thee sal mell.

A witch is abroad in a mole-skin bonnet,
Buildin' a brig o' cobwebs ower t'Strid.
Woe to the lad that sets foot upon it,
Woe to the lass that by morn is hag-rid.
Whist thee, my fairy,
Lullaby, Mary;
Sleep fold her wings ower each eye-lid.

E. IRENE MYERS

88

A Dales Shepherd to his Aged Dog

Come on, awd lad, we mun ga up ta t'fells;
Thou's ligged ower lang this winter efternune,
For t'wind's south-east, thou knaws what that foretells,
Yon blue-black sky'll fotch snaw fer sewer, gey sune.

Thou needna blink thi een at ma like yon,
An' thump thi tail on t'mat whal t'dust mud flee;
I ken thee weel, aye, mair'n I ken mi son,
He thinks we'se ower awd, booath thee an' me.

Ther's younger dogs, but nane mair wick na thee;
Thou'ld wear thi pads, ta t'booan afore thou'ld quit.
Thou kens mi thowts afore I thinks, an' me,
I cannat whistle, soa I trusts thi wit.

Thou's quick an' quiet ta gather scattered flocks,
Wi' t'yowes thou's soft when lambs is comin' up;
Thou nivver flurries up on t'limestun rocks,
Thou's fleead o' nowt, nut gurtest Swa'dill tup.

When snaw's wa' heigh, thou smells an' finnds the lost;
Aye, lad, when thou gies ower, I'se done fer sewer!
But now, yance mair t'land mun be crossed,
Mi leggin's donned, we mun awa up t'muir.

F. J. NEWBOULT

89

Spring

Owd Winter gat notice to quit,
'Cause he'd made sich a pigsty o' t'place,
An' Summer leuked raand when he'd flit,
An' she says, 'It's a daanreyt disgrace!
Sich-like ways!
I niver did see sich a haase to come intil i' all my born days!'

But Spring says, 'It's my job, is this,
I'll sooin put things streyt, niver fear.
Ye go off to t'Spaws a bit, Miss,
An' leave me to fettle up here!'
An' sitha!
Shoo's donned a owd appron, an' tucked up her sleaves, an' set to, with a witha!

Tha can tell, when t'hail pelts tha like mad,
At them floors bides a bit of a scrub;
Tha knaws t'flegstuns mun ha' been bad,
When she teems aat all t'wotter i' t'tub.
Mind thy eyes!
When shoo gets hod o' t'long brush an' sweeps aat them chamers, I'll tell tha, t'dust flies!

Whol shoo's threng tha'll be best aat o' t'gate:
Shoo'll care nowt for soft tawk an' kisses.
To tell her thy mind, tha mun wait
Whol shoo's getten things ready for t'missis.
When shoo's done,
Shoo'll doff her owd appron, an' slip aat i' t'garden, an' call tha to come.

Aye, Summer is t'roses' awn queen,
An' shoo sits i' her state, grandly dressed;
But Spring's twice as bonny agean,
When shoo's donned hersen up i' her best
Gaan o' green,
An' stands all i' a glow, wi' a smile on her slips an' a leet i' her een.

To t'tips of her fingers shoo's wick.
Tha can see t'pulses beat i' her braa.
Tha can feel her soft breath comin' quick,
An' it thrills tha—tha duzn't knaw haa.
When ye part,
Them daffydaandillies shoo's kissed an' then gi'en tha—they'll bloom i' thy heart!

Q. NICHOLAS

90

Cooartin' Days

What's ageeate wi' t'lad theease days?
Whativver meeade 'im mend 'is ways
An' seeave 'is brass?

Why diz 'e sing an' whissil seea
At wark, neea matter what's ti deea
I' ploo or grass?

Why's e' teean ti weearin' floowers
Iv 'is coat, an' spendin' hoowers
At t'leeakin' glass?

Ah lay there mud be summat wrang—
'Od on! Ah's getten it! 'E's thrang
Cooartin' a lass!

91

Lament

There's summat sad aboot a field 'et's cleear
O' cooarn, wi' t'stubble standin' grey an' bare.
It brings ti mind we're neearin' t'ton o' t'year,
When t'lang, warm days i' t'sun'll be neea mair.

It maks thoo nooatice other signs diz t'seet.
Thoo sees 'oo t'swallows sits i' rows on t'wires;
Thoo starts ti feeal a nip i' t'air at neet,
An' thinks it's time thoo started layin' fires.

Thoo 'arks ti t'oonds oot cubbin' yance ageean,
An' t'robin-ridbreast whistlin' nigh at 'and,
Thoo leeaks at t'berries riddenin' i' t'leeane,
An' greeaves ti think 'oo quickly Summer's ganned.

92

Roll of Honour

When, of a Sunda', Ah sits i' mi pew,
Ah sees a list o' lads that yance Ah knew,
An' then it 'ardlins seeams a day sin last
Ah spooake tiv 'em, though monny yeears 'ez passed.

There's Dick that wor a champion wi' t'ploo,
Ti set a rig an' furrow straight an' true,
An' Ben that snickled monny a fine, fat 'are,
'E'll nivver trouble t'keeapers onny mair!

'Arry that oor Sarah used ti cooart,
An' Bob that wor a dab at ivvry spooart,
When Ah wor young Ah palled on wiv 'em all,
Bud noo they're nobbut neeames upon t'choch wall.

GORDON ALLEN NORTH

93

Little Piecer

T'buzzer's blowin', Willie, lad,
    T'leeghts're shewin' daan below.
Pool thisen together, bairn,
    It's ommost tahme for thee ta go.
Yer thee, Wilson's shut his gate,
    Harry Cartwright's crossin' t'fowd;
Cum on, bairn, tha maunt be late,
    Here's thi shooin—it's varry cowd.
T'kettle's boiled, thi cocoa's brewed,
    Tha'll fahnd a bun on t'cellar yed.
Dayleeght's breakin' ovver t'hill.
    Cum on, lad, it's tahme for t'mill.

A. IRVING PARKE

94

A Lownd Neet

Cum thi waays doon Hunny, doon oot o' t'hoose:
Cum tippy-teeas Hunny, whisht as a moose.
Full meean's i' t'sky, Hunny, all's silver breet,
Ullets flig by, Hunny, hunting bi neet.

Mist rises white, sitha, doon theer i' t'slack;
Shadders o' t'trees, sitha, lig sharp an' black,
Beeafs nivver storr, sitha, all's lownd an' still,
Reek gans stright up, sitha, higher nor t'hill.

Oot here aleean, Hunny, just thoo an' me,
Disn't ta feel, Hunny, sumhoo we're three?
Peeace upon t'yeth, Hunny, glowry i' t'sky,
Ti thoo an' me, Hunny, God's varry nigh.

IRENE PETCH

95

When Timothy Rang Oor Awd Choch Bell

It's a vasst o' years sen t'awd Sexton deed
  An' Frank stepped intiv 'is sheean;
Tim—'e were yan o' them real tall chaps,
  All muscle an' skin an' beean.
'E was a roomm 'un for diggin' an' wark,
  My Wod! What a peeal we 'ad
When Timothy rang oor awd Choch bells
  Wi' Jerry, 'is 'prentice lad.

Bob Rimmer, 'e weeared a white button'ole
  When 'e wed oor Emily Jaane;
'E'd joost gat a grand new set o' teeth
  An' 'e couldn't speak oot plaan;
An' she were all of a dither wi' freet,
  Bood wasn't she capped, by Gad!
When Timothy rang oor awd Choch bells
  Wi' Jerry, 'is 'prentice lad.

Ah mahnds when t'Squire' dowter was wed,
  I' satin or summat o' that;
'Twas a real swell deea amang bettermy folks,
  An' neea room i' t'Choch for a cat!
T'likes of us 'ad ti stop ootsahde—
  By Goom! Warn't all t'village mad!—
Bood Timothy rang oor awd Choch bells
  Wi' Jerry, 'is 'prentice lad.

Bood that 'ud be likely afoor your tahme—
  Mebbe thotty-six year or mair . . .
Squire an' t'Missis, an' Jerry Clegg,
  Bob Rimmer, an' Parson Blair,
Lig sahde be sahde i t'Choch-garth noo:
  Ohr! bitter was t'daay an' sad
When Timothy towlled oor awd Choch bell
  For Jerry, 'is 'prentice lad.

BEN PRESTON

96

Come to thi Gronny, Doy

Come to thi Gronny, doy! come to thi Gronny
Bless tha, to me tha'rt as precious as onny;
Mutherless barn of a dowter unwed,
Little tha knaws, doy, the tears 'at Ah've shed;
Trials Ah've knawn boath fur t'heart an' fur t'heead,
Shortness o' wark, ay, an' shortness o' breead.

Thease Ah could bide, bud tho' tha'rt noan to blame,
Bless tha, tha browt ma boath sorrow an' shame;
Gronny, poor sowl, fur a two-munth or moar
Hardly could feshion to lewk aht o' t'doar;
T'neighbours called aht to ma, 'Dunnot stand that,
Aht wi' that hussy, an' aht wi' hur brat.'

Deary me, deary me, what could Ah say?
T'first thing of all, Ah thowt, 'Let ma goa pray.'
T'next time Ah slept Ah'd a dream de ya see,
Ay, an' Ah knew 'at that dream wur fur me:
Tears o' Christ Jesus, Ah saw 'em that neet,
Fall drop be drop onta one at His feet.

After that, saw Him wi' barns rahnd His knee,
Some on 'em, happen, poor crayturs like thee;
Says Ah at last, though Ah sorely wur tried,
Suarly a sinner, a sinner sud bide;
Neighbours may think or may say what they will,
T'muther an' t'dowter sal stop wi' ma still.

Come on't what will, i' mi cot they sal cahr,
Woe be to them 'at maks bad inta war;
Some fowk may call tha a name 'at Ah hate,
Wishing fro t'heart tha wur weel aht o' t'gate;
Oft this hard world inta t'gutter 'll shove tha,
Poar little lamb, wi' no daddy ta luve tha.

Dunnot thee freeat, doy, whol gronny hods up,
Nivver sal tha want a bite or a sup;
What if Ah wark thease owd fingers ta t'boan,
Happen tha'll luve ma long after Ah'm goan.
T'last bite i' t'cupboard wi' thee Ah could share't
Hay! bud tha's stown a rare slice o' my heart.

Spite o' all t'sorra, all t'shame at Ah've seen,
Sunshine comes back to mi heart throo thi een;
Cuddle thi Gronny, doy,
Bless tha, tha'rt bonny, doy,
Rosy an' sweet, thro thi brah to thi feet,
Kingdoms an' crahns wodn't buy tha ta-neet.

97

I Niver Can Call Her My Wife

Aw'm a weyver, ya knaw, an' awf deead,
  So Aw do all at iver Aw can
Ta put away aat o' my heead
  The thowts an' the aims of a man!
Eight shillin' a wick's whot aw arn,
  When Aw've varry gooid wark an' full time,
An' Aw think it a sorry consarn
  Fur a harty young chap in his prime!

But ar maister says things is as well
  As they hae been, ur iver can be;
An' Aw happen sud think soa mysel
  If he'd nobbud swop places wi' me;
Bud he's welcome to all he can get,
  Aw begrudge him o' noan o' his brass,
An' Aw'm nowt bud a madlin ta fret,
  Or ta dream o' yond beautiful lass.

Aw niver can call hur my wife,
  My love aw sal niver mak knawn,
Yit the sorra that darkens hur life
  Thraws a shadda across o' my awn.
An' Aw'm suar when hur heart is at eease,
  Theer is sunshine an' singin' i' mine,
An' misfortunes may cum as they pleease,
  Bud they niver can mak ma repine.

That Chartist wur nowt bud a sloap
  Aw wur fooild be his speeches an' rhymes,
His promises wattered my hoap,
  An' Aw leng'd fur his sunshiny times;
But Aw feel 'at my dearest desire
  Is withrin' within ma away;
Like an ivy-stem trailin' i' t'mire,
  An' deein' fur t'want of a stay!

When Aw laid i' me bed day an' neet,
  An' wur geen up by t'doctor fur deead,
God bless hur, shoo'd come wi' a leet
  An' a basin o' grewil an' breead.
An' Aw once thowt Aw'd aht wi' it all,
  Bud sa kindly shoo chatted an' smiled,
Aw wur fain to turn ovver to t'wall,
  An' to bluther an' roar like a child.

An' Aw said as Aw thowt of her een,
  Each breeter fur t'tear at wur in't;
It's a sin ta be niver forgeen,
  To yoke hur ta famine an' stint;
So Aw'll e'en travel forrud throo life,
  Like a man throo a desert unknawn;
Aw mun ne'er hev a hoam an' a wife,
  Bud my sorras will all be my awn.

Soa Aw trudge on aloan as Aw owt,
  An' whativer my troubles may be,
They'll be sweetened, my lass, wi' the thowt
  At Aw've niver browt trouble ta thee;
Yit a bird hes its young uns ta guard,
  A wild beast, a mate in his den,
An' Aw cannot bud think at it's hard—
    Nay, deng it, A'm roarin' agen!

98

Owd Moxy

Owd Moxy wrowt hard fur his morsil o' breead,
  An' sweetened his wark wi' a sing,
Tho' Time wi' his scythe hed mawn t'crop on his heead,
  An' then fafft it away wi' his wing.

Reyt slavish his labour, reyt little his wage,
His way tuv his grave wor bud rough,
Fur low livin' an' hardships, a deal moar nur age,
Hed swealed dahn his cannal to t'snuff.

One cowd winter morn as he crept aht o' bed,
T'owd waller felt dizzy an' soar;
'Cum, frame us sum breikfast, owd Duckfooit,' he said,
'An' Aw'll finish yon fence up at t'moor.

'Aw'll tew whal I drop wi' me hammer an' mall,
An' Aw'll bring hoam my honey to t'hive.
An' Aw'll pay t'bit o' rent, an' wur shop score an' all,
An' Aw'll dee aht o' debt if Ah live.'

Soa Peg made his pobs an' then futtard abaht,
An' temm'd sum o' t'tea into t'can,
Then teed up his bacon an' breead in a claat,
Fur dearly shoo liked hur owd man.

Then Moxy set aht on his wearisome way,
Wadin' bravely thro' t'snawbroth i' t'dark.
It's a pity a fella 'at's wakely an' grey
Sud hae three mile ta walk tuv his wark.

Bud summat that mornin' made Moxy turn back,
Thoa he hardly knew what it could meean,
Soa, cudlin' owd Peggy, he gav' hur a smack,
An' then started fur t'common ageean.

All t'day a wild hurricane wuther'd up t'glen
An' then flew like a fiend up to t'heath;
An' as Peggy sat knittin', shoo said tuv hursen,
'Aw dear! he'll be starrav'd to t'deeath.'

Peg felt all that day as shoo'd ne'er felt afoar,
An' shoo dreeaded yit hungar'd fur neet;
When harkenin' an' tremlin' shoo heeard abaht t'doar
A muttrin' an' shufflin' o' feet.

Five minutes at after, owd Peg on hur knees,
Wur kissin' a forheead like stoan;
An' to t'men 'at stood by hur wi' tears i' ther ees,
Shoo said, 'Goa, lads, an' leave ma aloan.'

When they streyten'd his body, all ready fur t'kist,
It wor seen 'at he'd thowt of his plan;
Fur t'shop score an' t'rent wur safe locked in his fist,
Soa he deed aht o' debt like a man.

DOROTHY UNA RATCLIFFE

99

October Moors

They're leadin' brekkons doon fra' moors
For cattle-beddin'
On track 'at goes by t'larch plantation
To our Tom steadin'.

Everywhere t'sun shines sae breetly,
Yaller is trees;
Varra drowsy 'mang dead ling-bobs,
Is bumble-bees.

An' Peace is walkin' hand in hand
Wi' t'suther wind—
A Peace sae rare, nobbut on moors
Thoo'll hope to finnd;

An' way up-dale girt hills noo fold
Theer wings sae blue,
As guardian angels do, when work is done
An' neet is new.

100

Thoo

I may not call thee 'Sweetheart,'
'My ain, my dearest Dear,'
Nor 'Darlin',' nor 'Beloved,'
Lest ither folk might hear,
An' even 'Luve's' forbidden,
Wiv all sweet words 'at woo—
Then may I, when thi folk are nigh,
Call thee 'Thoo'?

Aa! there's a vast of meanin'
In that short simple word,
It's sad as wind in t'rushes,
It's blithe as t'lilt o' bird;
It holds a threat o' kisses
To ony courtin' two—
So, may I, when thi folk are nigh,
Call thee 'Thoo'?

101

Wallflowers

Wallflowers i' my border!
At t'hour when blackies sing
Their sweetest sangs, what is ther
Nor ye mair comfortin'?
Menseful ye are an' restful
Aboon all other flowers:
I knaw I wadn't change ye
Fur furrin lily-bowers.

Wallflowers i' my border!
No matter if t'day's lang
An' full o' carkin' worry
Or I've been varra thrang,
If I can sit at gloamin'
An' do my knittin', wheer
Your bonnie heads can greet me,
Sae velvety an' rare.

Roond my cottage winders
T'grand smell o' ye lingers;
It is soothin' just to touch
Your petals wi' my fingers.
Folk 'at's tired gits churlish
An' starts t'owd world's disorders—
Ther'd be less quarrels if they grew
Wallflowers i' their borders.

102

Wensleydale Lullaby

Settle doon, my Poppet joy,
Noo t'birds an' t'beasts are sleepin',
Settle doon, my bonnie boy,
T'breet stars ther watch are keepin';
When thoo wakes, I'll gie to thee
Mony things for laikin'
'At thoo will rejoice to see
An' can have for takin':
Two black lambkins, muther-lorn,
A white an' ginger kitten,
A puppy 'at is newly born,
A 'broidered chair to sit on,
Thoo shall have a dappled foal
An' a leaf-green cart,
Honey in a sky-blue bowl,
My sweetin', my sweetheart!
Settle doon an' close thine eyes
Noo t'birds an' t'beasts are sleepin',
Settle doon, my viewly doy,
T'Lord ha'e thee in His keepin'.

103

Whisper Dale

Wind is soughin'
Thro' t'sycamore top;
T'beck is greetin'
Wivoot a stop:
But thoo mun whisht
An' close thine eyes;
Thoo's bound for t'moors
Wheer Whisper Dale lies.

Ther's balloons like moons,
Wi' wunnerful toys,
An' rainbow bricks
For a' lile boys

'At toddle to bed
When they is bid
An' seek for t'moors
Wheer Whisper Dale's hid.

At morn we'll sam up
Conkers broon;
Make ships to float
Up-beck an' doon.
But noo, lile lad,
Laik not, nor weep,
Thoo's for Whisper Dale
'Mang t'moors of Sleep.

HARRY SHAW

104

To a Snowdrop

Aye ! bonny flaar, tha'rt t'first Aw've seen,
Who could ha thowt 'at tha'd ha been
Wakken bi nah, an' t'wind soa keen !
Aw felt fair capp'd
As sooin as ivver Aw hed mi een
Upon tha clapp'd.

Ther's noan a bud aht upo' t'tree,
Nor bee nor bird, at Aw can see,
Nor nowt else Spring-like, nobbut thee,
Ma pretty flaar !
But nah Aw knaw 'at t'Winter dree
Has hed his haar.

Aw've felt this Winter varry sad,
Aw nivver knew t'times be soa bad,
An' wark for thaasands can't be had,
Whal thaasands more
Hev near as nowt been driven mad
Through t'wolf at t'door.

But what's use grum'lin'? Here tha art
I' all this cowd, as snod an' smart
As God could mak' tha, peepin' aht
On t'world once more,
An' means to stop here, baht a daht,
Though t'snaw tha smoor.

But though, like thaasands more o' t'race,
Aw've felt misfortune's cowd embrace,
Aw'll try like thee to keep mi place
Though hardly pressed,
Cheer'd by thy smile, tha flaar o' grace,
An' hope for t'best.

MOSES SOWERSBY

105

The Old Farmer at a Wedding

Ah's pleeased ti be amang au'd frinds
At sike a tahm as this,
It hez a breezy soort o' feel
Yan wadn't leyke ti miss.

It stors au'd ricollections up,
An' taks yan back ti t'tahm
When we were young an' fost gat wed,
An' went ti t'Manor Farm.

When all wer prospects seeamed as breet
As t'mornin' sun i' Maay
An' we were beeath as blathe as larks
'At sings all t'summer daay.

When wark, it nobbut seeamed leyke laark
We felt si fresh an' strang,
An' went aboot leyke bummle-bees
As brisk, an' quite as thrang.

We've hed oor ups an' doons sen then,
Leyke monny mair besahd
An' heeaps o' things we didn't leyke
We've had ti gen an' bahd.

Bud throo it all we've stuck leyke wax,
    Hes me an' t'misthress there,
An' sahd bi sahd we've breeasted storms
    An' waited whahl 'twas fair.

An' noo Ah just wad leyke ti wish
    This newly-wedded pair,
All t'happiness this wo'lld can gi'
    Two lovin' hearts ti share.

An' Ah wad ricommend 'em beeath
    Ti allus pull yah waay
An' then they'll nivver hev neea cause
    Ti rieu the'r weddin' daay.

IRENE SUTCLIFFE

106

Jinny

Hast' ivver seed Jinny as feat as a linny
A-nimming doon t'loaning wheer t'lovers all gang?
Ah had set mysel doon where the aums meet aboon,
When Jinny jamp oop, and ganned nimming alang.
O Jinny, Ah'll tell tha, my heart gav' a stang
When fost Ah set e'es on tha nimming alang.

Ah deean't coom on well wi' the lasses, mysel',
Ah wor leeamed i' the war, so Ah's not ower strang;
Ah nobbut can praddle an' crammle an' waddle,
But Jinny's like wicksiller nimming alang.
O wait on me, Jinny, thoo's allus si thrang;
Ah'll niver catch oop wi' tha, nimming alang.

She'll pass t'tahm o' day, then she'll off an' away;
She's leet as a larock, wi' broon wings ootflang;
But oft she'll be flyting an' oft, when Ah's lyting,
Wi' doonkessen e'es she gans nimming alang—
O Jinny, my lassie, what hev Ah deean wrang?
Ah's fain for ti follow tha nimming alang.

107

Yakrons for Pigs

There's tonnips for gimmers, and yakrons for pigs,
And clover for t'coos as they feed on the riggs,
There's corn for my filly, and yal for my men;
But what's for a lassie, diz onny one ken?

Ah bowt her some humbugs at t'statis yah day,
And oop gans her bonny wee neb in the air;
'Thoo thinks Ah's a bairn; ay, tha diz that, Ah lay,
But Ah's fair sick o' goodies,' she telt me, 'so there!'

A load o' good mannishment heartens oop t'land,
Owd theakin' 's nae woss for a bit o' fresh band,
A potful o' pent mak's a yat leuk like new;
But Ah deean't knaw what's best for a lassie, diz thoo?

Ah bowt her some ribbins at t'market yah day,
For lassies like fal-lals, or so Ah've heeard tell;
But she just tonned her heead, and she had nowt ti say,
But, 'What are they for? Thoo'd best wear 'em thysel.'

Ah says 'coop' to my filly, and oop she'll away,
My owd bitch is underfoot maist part o' t'day.
Ah've but ti call 'Dacky,' to fetch oop t'owd sow;
What 'tices a lassie, diz onny one know?

Ah seed her go by wi' the sun on her hair;
Ah tried for ti call, but the wods wadn't come;
She's the bonniest lassie Ah've seed onnywhere,
She mak's me feel all of a dither and dumb.

There's tonnips for gimmers, and yakrons for pigs,
And clover for t'coos as they feed on the riggs,
And corn for my filly, and yal for my men;
What diz for a lassie, deea nane o' ye ken?

JOHN THWAITE

108

To a Dipper

Thi bonny briest's as white as sna',
    It's pure, ay, lily pure;
An' puts i' t'shade them bau's o' foam
    At sails away doon Eure.

Yan wonders whaur thoo's bin te skeul,
    Thoo's gey weel trained, Ah lay,
Fer curtsey efter curtsey
    Thoo's gi'en te me teday.

Thoo cooers doon this way an' that,
    Thoo's weel-behaved, fer seur;
Yan nivver kna's just what's astir,
    It's grand te be at t'deur.

Fer noo thoo sings thi gloamin' song,
    'Mang singers thoo's a swell:
Here, back o' t'wau', Ah hev, thoo kna's
    A concert te misel'.

Thaur, keepen time wi' t'tinklen streeam,
    Thoo's nivver nivver flat;
Thoo's full o' tune wi'oot a doot,
    Ah'll allus stick te that.

Ah'd like te shoot ' gan on mi lass,'
    Thoo weel desarves a clap;
But if Ah did thoo'd pop up t'beck,
    Fair scaured at sike a whap.

Thoo's weathered t'stooren, blisteren blast,
    Ah's seur Ah's varra fain;
Good-day fair Peggy, some day seun
    Ah s'mak this way again.

An' when at heeame teneet Ah lig
    Mi heead doon o' me pilla',
An' odd lang thowt, lass, be o' thee,
    A white throoat on' a willa'.

109

Layky Lambs

A snyzy day, a cowd Eeast wind,
But lambs mun stretch the'r legs, ye'll finnd,
I' April's fickle weather;
It's bin a hardish neet, bi t'hime,
It's cappen hoo they stand this clime,
The're meeastly teuf as leather.

When t'sun gits oot it's time fer t'spoorts,
They cut some capers, teu, aw' soorts,
The're aw' i' tip-top fettle;
Ther's yan fast doonhill, yan's a climmer,
A bonny, booncen, black-feeaced gimmer,
They fairly show the'r mettle.

They nivver wait fer t'crood te come
An' egg 'em on—nut they, by gum;
They reeace fer varra joy:
Neea pistil cracks for them, ye'll finnd,
Roond t'wau's they tak til oot o' wind;
The're off again, by goy.

Ther's yan at's near as black as seut,
Like t'owd lad's sel', he leuks gey cute;
Ther's yan i' ivvery flock!
He started badly, but he's strang,
Yan seun finnds oot at he can gang,
He wins, an' aw', by gock!

T'yowes cheg away, gey thrang, hard by,
T'lambs bump back te the'r mothers, dry;
They want neea milkin' pails.
Weel under t'flanks the'r heids they dook,
Hoo greedily they grep an' sook;
Noo watch them waggen tails!

An' ivvery yowe kna's just what's what,
Sha wants ni other owd deeame's brat;
Nay, nowt but what's her ahn!
At times it meeans a blate, a gliff,
Er mebbe noo an' than a sniff,
T'lile tykes seun git weel knahn.

BEN TURNER

110

My Birthday

Ah took a piece to perch last neet,
Mi sixty-third wor done,
An' nah i th'gentle mornin' leet,
Mi sixty-fourth's begun.

An' this fresh cut Ah start today,
Ah trust Ah weyve it streit;
Ah'm 'fraid th'owd perchers bun to say,
At th'last one worn't reit.

It shewed too many floats an' flaws,
An' t'selvidge went askew;
An' when it's soa a weyver knaws
His loom's noan runnin' true.

It's dun—Ah cannot pool it back,
Ther's chonces 'at Ah've had;
Ther's places in it tight an' slack;
It's brokken picks are bad.

Ah hope Ah may weyve better far
Nor ivver yet Ah've done;
An' noan go weyvin' war' an' war
On t'piece Ah've just begun.

May t'cloth as each day passes by
Show more perfection still;
Ah knaw it can be if Ah try
An' weyve it wi' goodwill.

Ah trust Ah've lots o' cuts to weyve,
An' strength, an' skill, an' pluck;
Wi' honest heart an' handy neive,
An' just a bit o' luck.

This warp o' life is brittle stuff,
Though t'weft's been soundly spun;
Ah'll try an' weyve it good enough
To earn th'owd words, 'Well done!'

WALTER F. TURNER

III

The Good Awd Tahmes

The good awd tahmes? The good awd tahmes?
An' ye think at ye'd like 'em back? Then Ah'll tell ye what, by Gaw!
You just sud ha lived as a lad when Ah did, an' then ye'd knaw
Better 'an ti ax for t'good awd tahmes.

They're better awaay, is t'good awd tahmes,
Wi' their hopper an' gallusies, lays an' flaals. It was hard, dree wark;
Gerrin' up i' t'morn afoor leet, an' laabourin' while lang efter dark.
Deean't tell me aboot t'good awd tahmes.

Me faather he threshed, i' t'good awd tahmes,
At Towthrop, a fower mahle walk, an' mebbe be there afore fahve.
An' yance he gat yam afoor seven at neet—he'd getten a drahve—
A rare thing that, i' t'good awd tahmes.

An' what could he addle, i' t'good awd tahmes?
Ah'll tell ye; he addled eight shillin' a week, an' they gav' him his meeat—
An' wi' six growin' bairns at yam, you may be sear there was monny a treeat
Oot o' that for us, i' t'good awd tahmes!

A laabourer's waage, i' them good awd tahmes,
Wad buy aboot tweea steean o' flooer i' t'week, if he weeared it all,
An' wi' seven tahmes seven odd mooths agaape, sike looance is small.
But we did wer best, i' t'good awd tahmes.

Me muther she slaaved, i' t'good awd tahmes
An' scratted, an' tewed, an' rahved, an' wrowt, wer weeams te trig,
Hoed tonnups, an' wick't, an' gethered, an' gleaned, an' kept a pig—
A recklin' she'd begged—i' t'good awd tahmes.

Ah went wiv her oft, i' them good awd tahmes,
Afoor Ah were ten year awd, a-getherin' flints off t'land;
A shillin' a ton we gat, wiv a sad-keeak, o' t'sahze o' my hand,
Te sarve for wer dinners, i' t'good awd tahmes.

Hungery? Say ye? i' t'good awd tahmes?
Aye, bairn, Ah was hungery, allus, at yam when Ah was a lad;
Bud efter Ah went te farm-pleeacin', ye knaw, things wasn't se bad,
At ten year awd, i' t'good awd tahmes.

That was salvaation, i' t'good awd tahmes.
We reckoned nowt aboot wark, if we nobbut had plenty te eeat;
Suet pudden, an' broth, an' baacon, or butcher meeat;
'Twas grand, was that, i' t'good awd tahmes!

D'ye want 'em back, sike good awd tahmes?
Nay, lad, just be content, an' mahnd o' what Ah saay:
I' t'providence o' God, things breetens ivvery daay.
They're better gone, is t'good awd tahmes.

FLORENCE TWEDDELL

112

Cum, Stop at Yam Teneet, Bob!

'Cum, stop at yam teneet, Bob!
Deean't gan out onnywhere:
Thou gets thesel t'leeast vex'd, lad,
When thou sits i' t'awd ame-chair.

'There's Keeat an' Dick beeath want tha
Te stop an' tell a teeal:
Tak little Keeatie o' the knee,
An' Dick'll sit on t'steeal.

'Let's hev a happy neet, Bob!
Tell all t'teeals thou can tell;
For givin' pleeasure te the bairns
Will deea tha good thesel.

'Ah knaw it's seea wi' me, Bob;
Fer oft when Ah've been sad,
Ah've laik'd an' laugh'd wi' them, mon,
Untel me heart's felt glad.

'An' sing that little sang, Bob,
Thou used te sing te me,
When oft we sat at river sahde,
Under t'awd willow tree.

'What happy tahmes them was, Bob,
Thou nivver left me then
Te gan ti t'yal-house neet be neet
Amang all t'drunken men.

'Ah diz me best for thee, Bob,
An' thou sud deea t'seeam fer me:
Just think what things thou promist ma
Asahde t'awd willow tree!'

'Ah prethee say neea mair, lass,
Ah see Ah ha'en't deean reet;
Ah'll think of all thou's said te me,
An' stop at yam teneet.

'Ah'll try te lead a better life—
Ah will, an' that thou'll see!
Fra this tahme foth Ah'll spend me neets
At yam, wi' t'bairns an' thee.'

113

Deean't Mak Gam O' Me

Ah went last week te Stowslay Fair,
Me sweetheart fer te see;
Sheea promis'd sheea wad meet me there—
Bud deean't mak gam o' me:
Oh deean't mak gam o' me!

Ah rigg'd mesel' all i' me best,
As fine as fine could be;
Ah little thowt how things wad to'n—
Bud deean't mak gam o' me:
Oh deean't mak gam o' me!

Ah walk'd ti t'toon, an' bowt a cane,
Te cut a dash, ye see;
An' how Ah swagger'd up an' down!
Bud deean't mak gam o' me:
Oh deean't mak gam o' me!

Ah thowt, if nobbut Poll wad cum,
How happy we sud be!
Ah'd treeat her in ti t'penny show—
But deean't mak gam o' me:
Oh deean't mak gam o' me!

At last Ah saw her cummin' in;
Bud what else did Ah see?
Jack Hodge was walkin' biv her sahde—
Bud deean't mak gam o' me:
Oh deean't mak gam o' me!

Stright up Ah went, an' 'Poll!' sez Ah,
'Ah's waitin', lass, fer thee!'
'Then thou mun wait!' was all sheea said—
Bud deean't mak gam o' me:
Oh deean't mak gam o' me!

Sheea teeak Jack's ame, an' there Ah stead
Quite flabbergash'd ye see:
Ah thowt Ah sud hev dropt ti t'grund—
Bud deean't mak gam o' me:
Oh deean't mak gam o' me!

Poor Nancy Green com seeaglin' up—
' What's matter, Dick? ' sez she :
' Jack Hodge is off wi' Poll ! ' sez Ah—
Bud deean't mak gam o' me :
Oh deean't mak gam o' me !

' Wha, nivver mahnd her ; let her gan ;
Sheea's better geean ! ' said she :
Bud Ah thowt nut, an' then Ah cried—
Bud deean't mak gam o' me :
Oh deean't mak gam o' me !

TOM TWISLETON

114

The Christmas Party

When cowd December's sturdy breeze
In chimley tops did grumble,
Or, tearing through the leafless trees
On long dark neets did rumble,
A lot o' young folks, smart an' gay
An' owd uns, free an' hearty,
Agreed amang thersels at they
Would have a Christmas party
At hame some neet.

A merrier lot than this I name
N'er met at ony party ;
All girt grand balls they put to shame,
They were sae gay an' hearty.
Here yan had made hersel quite fine,
Wi' lace an' braid's assistance ;
An' there a girt grand crinoline,
To keep t'lads at a distance,
Stood out that neet.

Against the host o' good things there
They wage an awful battle ;
They're crying out, ' A lile bit mair ! '
An' plates an' glasses rattle.

Here, yan's nae time a word to pass,
  Thrang supping an' thrang biting;
There, simpering sits a girt soft lass
  That waits for mich inviting
      An' fuss that neet.

An' when this good substantial fare
  Has gi'en 'em satisfaction,
They side all t'chairs, an' stand i' pairs,
  Wi' heels i' tune for action.
See-sawing, t'fiddler now begins
  The best that he is able;
He rosins t'stick an' screws up t'pins
  An' jumps up on to t'table,
      To play that neet.

An' when they've reel'd an' danced their fling,
  Their chairs all round are ranged;
They tell droll tales, they laugh, they sing,
  An' jokes are interchanged.
A merry tune t'girt kettle sings,
  An' t'fire is blazing breetly;
Wi' cheerful din t'owd farmhouse rings
  An' hours fly ower them sweetly
      An' swift that neet.

A. STANLEY UMPLEBY

115

Goosepool

Young kye i' t'byre,
A clog o' t'fire,
  Nut yan i' t'hoose at's scaumin';
A bairn ti praate
Ti doll an' slaate,
  Yan up it' granny claumin';
All reet at t'bank,
Bills owt bud rank,
  Neea paapers at wants scraumin';
A theeak at's theet
Whativver t'neet
  An' t'weyfe o' t'buffet shaumin'.

116

The Fisherman

He didn't larn his job fre beeaks,
  Ther's neean at teeaches breeadin';
Bud let me watch him whippin' heeaks!

At t'settin'-booard wiv heeaks an' feeaks
  Y'u'll offens see him sneeadin';
He didn't larn his job fre beeaks!

An' hoo at heeam he allus leeaks
  When inti t'sea he's weeadin';
Bud let me watch him whippin' heeaks!

When, wiv a conger, t'au'd clep creeaks,
  Or a greeat brat he's bleeadin',
He didn't larn his job fre beeaks!

His lass'll beeak cau'd watther ceeaks
  Whahl i' t'airm-chair he's reeadin',
Bud let me watch him whippin' heeaks!

When ootsahde t'harbour coulpress breeaks,
  An' his is t'coble leeadin',
He didn't larn his job fre beeaks,
  Bud let me watch him whippin' heeaks.

117

T' Widda Weddin'

I' t'haay wi' Tom felted
T'few goodies is melted
An' Ah's aboot swelted
    Bud what div Ah care:
Wa've putten in t'spurrin's
An' cadged a few corrins;
Ther's ceeake, if ni storrin's
    Fer t'weddin' at t'Fair.

Ah yance fancied owther
Jim Green er Bob Lowther;
Bud noo Ah want nowther,
    Ner onny au'd flare:
Wiv all them Ah've brokken;
Ah s'wed wi' t'floss-docken;
Tom's ax'd, an' Ah've spokken
    Fer t'weddin' at t'Fair.

Wheea thowt he wad bid a
Greeat boxin' young widda
Ti santer roond t'midda
    Then ax her ti share
T'lahl pleeace up t'Green Lonnin'
Wheer torves is a-bonnin',
An' fooak'll seean to'n in
    Fer t'weddin' at t'Fair.

Ther's yowes an' lambs bleeatin',
A brawne i' t'ga'th reeatin',
A wye cawf at's freeatin',
    What mud yan want mair?
Tom sheeap-dog o' t'heearthstan,
T'au'd cock-bo'd o' t'deearstan,
A ham, an' nut t'leeast un
    Fer t'weddin' at t'Fair.

118

Uncle Victor's Evacuees

Yon staggarth yat's cum off it' creeak,
  Seea that's anuther shoo'der-yat!
The've geean an' scaaled all t'bit o' theeak,
  An' slitten that new sheet Ah gat;
  The've weeasted t'tin o' waggin fat,
An' towpled ower tweea skeps o' bees;
  The've gi'en t'flay-creeake mi bran-new hat,
Ah s'think it's them evacuees!

Wheea's pulled t'taal-feathers off t'au'd dreeake?
  Ah see the're laid oot theer o' t'mat;
An' t'au'd cock leeaks a queer au'd leeak,
  Ah laay the've hed ti mell o' that;
  Ther's nowt Ah see bud's hed a bat!
The've rovven bark off meeast o' t'trees;
  The've ta'en t'eggs fre t'au'd 'dotte thoo sat,
Ah s'think it's them evacuees!

The've chasst all t'pullets off the'r peeak,
  Pulled hawf o' t'reeaf off wheer the' scrat;
Meead minchmeeat o' t'kye bit o' ceeake,
  Put t'cat i' trap Ah laid fer t'rat:
  Mi clawver pikes is trodden flat
Just when ther's cum a bit o' breeaze:
  If Ah could nobbut cop 'em at't!
Ah s'think it's them evacuees!

What ha'e the' deean tiv oor poor Natt?
  Leeak here, he's cutten beeath his knees!
He's lost sum teeth! That's bleead he spat!
  Ah s'think it's them evacuees!

119

Wood End

A cottage keekin'
  Fre t'siller birks;
An' t'chimla reekin'
  Ni nyber irks:
A runnel chantin'
Wi' t'bo'ds i' t'plantin';
Ther's nowt awantin'
  I' Naatur's kirks.

Up t'lonnin' winndin'
  Fre t'sand ti t'moor's
A bairnie binndin'
  A bunch o' floowers
Whahl t'granny's tewin'
I' t'fence off-skewin'
A stick fer t'yuen
  Ayont her poowers.

Yon's t'grandad scaalin'
  T'few hens the'r coorn;
Ah doot he's faalin'
An' sadly woorn;
Lang geean his sawin';
He's gain-hand t'mawin';
Ti t'reeaper drawin',
  Wheer he wer' boorn.

ETHEL WALTER

120

Yorkshire Girl's Prayer

Ah noan ask for pleasure,
Ah noan ask for ease,
For brass nor fine vittals
Ah noan ask for these.
Ah nobbut want wark
For to keep me fro' sin,
An' Ah'd like some fine day
Mi awn fireside to win,
An' a husband to come
Fro' his wark tuv his tea.
Two chairs bi th'hearthstone
Mak' Heaven for me.
An' who knaws some day
In our haven o' rest
Ah s'll show him ahr stranger
Asleep at mi breast.

A. C. WATSON

121

Heame, Sweet Heame

When oft at neet I wanders heame
To cosy cot an' busy deame,
My hardest day's wark seems but leet,
When I can get back heame at neet,

My wife an' bairns to sit besaade,
Aroond my awn bit firesaade.
What comfort there's i' steep for me,
A laatle prattler on my knee!
What tales I have to listen tea!
But just at fost there's sike to-dea
As niver was. Each laatle dot
Can fain agree for t'fav'rite spot.
Sike problems they can set for me
'Twad puzzle waaser heeads mebbe.
An' questions hawf a scoor they ask,
To anser 'em wad prove a task;
For laatle thowts stray far away
To things mysterious, oot o' t'way.
An' then sike toffer they torn oot,
An' pratty lips begin to poot,
If iverything's nut stowed away
To cumulate frae day to day.
Sike treasures they could niver spare,
But gether mair an' mair an' mair
In ivery pocket. I've nea doot
They've things they think the wo'ld aboot.
An' when their bed-taames drawin' nigh,
Wi' heavy heead an' sleepy eye,
It's varry laatle din they mak,
But slyly try a nap to tak.
An' when on t'lats they've gone aboon,
I fills my pipe an' sattles doon
To have a comfortable smewk.
An' then at t'news I has a lewk;
Or hods a bit o' talk wi' t'wife,
The praade an' comfort o' my life.
Cawd winds may blaw, an' snaw-flakes flee,
An' neets may be beath lang an' dree,
Or it may rain an' rain agean,
Seea lang as I've my day's wark dean,
I wadn't swap my humble heame
For bigger hoose or finer neame.
If all could as contented be,
There'd be mair joy an' less mis'ry.

T. P. WILLIAMSON

122

Jilted

When Cannelmas cam last aboot,
It wor a weary tahm!
Oor coo gat choakt wi' tonnop-root,
An' fayder brak his arm.

Then mudder teeak an' telt ma theer
Ah mun te sarvice gan;
Fer Ah wor tonn'd o' eeghteen year,
An' sheea'd mak shift wi' Nan.

'Sarvice!' Ah said—'a pratty teeal!
An' what 'll Mattha say
(He luvs ma just that desprit weel)
Gin Ah sud gan away?'

Then up sheea spak, as chirp as chips,
'An' Mattha wants te wed,
He'd better let it pass his lips—
Nut keep it iv his heead.'

'He hes ten yacker, ivvery bit,
Tweea coos, an' pigs as weel,
Sum sheep teea, an' a canny tit,
An' t'cawf at's ommest veeal.

'That lass he hes te mind his yam,
Sheea's neea gert shak's it's clear,
An' getten warse sen fost sheea cam,
Bud gat roond him, Ah hear.

'Seea thoo mun gan te Abram Grant's
O' Pinchinthurp toon-end:
They've happen'd twins; an' t'wife sheea wants
A lass at hes sum fend.'

An' seea that neet, when Mattha cam,
Ah telt him all sheea'd said:
He teeak it quiet as a lamb,
An' hing'd his colly heead.

An' when he rahz't 'Fra Commondil
Te yonder spot,' said he,
'It's kittle rooad, an' monny a hill—
Ten mahl, or else Ah lee!'

'Ah've luv'd tha, lass, uncommon strang,
Bud we mun boo te fate;
Ah'm sarten seear, or it be lang,
Thoo'll finn'd anudder mate.'

An' said, as thruff t'lahle yat he past,
'Ah's seear Ah wish tha weel!'
Ah thowt, fer seear, me heart had brast,
As he tonn'd on his heel.

An' seea Ah's noo at Abram Grant's,
An' t'twins tha be seea cross,
Gin t'Lord mah feeble sarvice wants,
Mah life wor nut mich loss!

Ah thinks o' Mattha day an' neet—
Ah's telt he's teean wi' Nan;
Bud, Oh! Ah thinks it can't be reet
To be seea fause a man!

WILLIAM WRIGHT

123

Owd Betty's Advice

So Mary, lass, tha'rt bahn to wed
I' t'mornin' wi' young blacksmith Ned,
An' though it maks thi mother sad,
It's like to be;
I've nowt ageean yon decent lad,
No more ner thee.

Bud let me tell tha what ta do,
For my advice might help tha through:
Be kind, and to thi husband true,
An' I'll be bun
Tha'll nivver hev a day ta rue
For owt tha's done.

Nay, try ta keep thi former knack,
An' do thi weshin' in a crack,
Bud don't be flaid ta bend thi back,
        Tha'll nobbut sweeat;
So try an' hev a bit o' tack,
        An' do it neeat.

Be sure tha keeps fra bein' a flirt,
An' pride thisen i' bein' alert,
An' mind ta mend thi husband's shirt,
        An' keep it cleean;
It wod thi poor owd mother hurt,
        If tha wor meean.

Don't kal abaht like monny a wun,
Then hev ta broil, an' sweeat, an' run;
Bud allus hev thi dinner done
        Withaht a mooild;
If it's nobbut meil, lass, set it on,
        An' hev it boiled.

Nah, Mary, I've no more ta say,
Tha gets thi choice an' tak thi way;
An' if tha leets ta rue, I pray,
        Don't blame thi mother;
I wish yeh monny a happy day,
        Wi' one another.

AMMON WRIGLEY

124

To A Southern Friend

Yo' tell me deawn i' Hereford on a Springtime morn
If Aw've ne'er sin the orchards Aw know not Aw've bin born:
The lung white miles o' blossom an' th'April scented air,
If Aw know not Hereford, Aw know not England's fair.

Yo' tell me deawn i' Devonshire, life is just a dream
O' song an' bloom an' sunshine an' apple wine an' cream,
But yo' may sing their praises wi' honey i' your meauth,
Aw wouldn't swap eaur Winter for Summer i' the seauth.

Your seauth is like a lady i' silken geawn an' lace,
Wi' dainty airs an' graces an' peawder on her face:
Mi north's a hearty woman, an' merry as a lark,
An' awlus op an' doin', an' never feart o' wark.

Come eaüt amung the heather, an' stretch thi legs wi' me,
Where northern winds are lungin' to blow the dust off thee:
Gie me the gipsy moorland, dark-skinned as ony sloe,
An' tha can keep thi Hereford an' Devonshire an' o'.

125

A Song of Parting

Come shap yersel an' let's go wom,
It's getten time to sever:
Th'owd clock's gone reaund, an' towd us o'
We connot stop for ever.

'Tis said the best o' friends mun part,
So it's no use complainin',
For life is like an April day
There's sunshine an' there's rainin'.

We've had a happy neet, good fowks,
An' shared each other's pleasure,
An' while there's joy i' th'world Aw hope
We'st ne'er go short o' measure.

Then let's away an' get to bed,
Like decent fowk an' warty,
An' pray 'at God will help us o',
An' keep us weel an' hearty.

MAY YORKE

126

T'Moor Edge

Ah's waitin' an' Ah's watchin' on tha, darlin',
By t'intak edge o' bonny purple ling;
Bud Ah sees on'y half a score o' moor birds
Flit passt ma on theer strong brown wing.

Ah's thinkin', oh! sae offens on tha, darlin',
  An' wishin', ivver wishin' for a seet
O' t'face ov thane that cums afore ma twa een,
  Sin' time at wa fusst cam ti meet.

Ah's plagued tha, an' tormented tha, ma power lad,
  Forgive tha lass, sha'll nivver dea it more,
Ma heart is oppen noo, sae cum an' fill it,
  'Stead o' beatin' on a fasst-closed door.

Tha'll happen hod ma close, an' say tha loves ma,
  That's what Ah is fair longin' just ti hear;
Ne'er heed, if shamin', Ah had ton away like,
  Kiss ma, sweetheart, an' hev noa fear.

T'sun's varry nigh ti settin' ower Hea'field,
  It's dree ti walk up Greenhow by ma sen;
Bud theer's a form noo movin' along sky line,
  At last tha cums, ma best o' men.

LOCAL RHYMES

127. *A West Riding Grace before Meat*

God bless us all, an' mak' us able
Ta eit all t'stuff what's on this table.

128. *A West Riding Grace after Meat*

We thank the Lord for what we've getten,
But if more had been cutten
Ther' wod more ha' been etten.

129. *A Yorkshireman's Coat of Arms*

A fly, a flea, a magpie, and a flitch of bacon.

A fly will tipple with anybody, so will a Yorkshireman; a flea will bite anybody, so will a Yorkshireman; a magpie will chatter with anybody, so will a Yorkshireman, and a flitch of bacon is never good for anything till it has been hanged up, no more is a Yorkshireman.

130. *A West Riding Toast*

Here's tiv us, all on us, an' me an' all:
May wa nivver want nowt, noan on us,
Ner me nawther.

Two West Riding Commandments

131. See all, hear all, say nowt;
Eit all, sup all, pay nowt,
And if tha ivver does owt fer nowt
Do it for thissel.

132. Cop hod an' stick.

Sayings against Yorkshiremen

133. A Yorkshire Bite.

134. A Yorkshire Tike.

Sayings about Yorkshire

135. A Yorkshire Way-bit.

136. I'se Yorkshire too.

137. Measter's Yorkshire too.

Two Proverbs against Yorkshiremen

138. Shake a bridle over a Yorkshireman's grave, and he will arise and steal a horse.

139. Give a Yorkshireman an halter, and he'll find a horse.

Three Proverbial Similes

140. To take the Darnton trod.

141. Looks as vild as a pair of Yorkshire sleeves in a goldsmith's shop.

142. I eet like a Yorkshar-mon.

Beggars' Litany

143. From Hell, Hull and Halifax good Lord deliver us.

North Riding Litany

144. From witches and wizards and long-tailed buzzards, and creeping things that run in hedge-bottoms, good Lord deliver us.

Yorkshire Families

145. A Dent for a Galloway, a Hind for an ass.

146. *Teesdale*

An otter in the Wear
You may find once a year;
But an otter in the Tees
You may find at your ease.

147. *Cleveland*

Cleveland in the clay,
Bring in two soles
And carry one away.

148. *Swaledale*

From Hollow Hill Cross
To Stollerston Stile
The extent of Swaledale
Is twenty long mile.

149. *Swaledale Sheep*

Back like a brigg
Tail like a lonk,
Horns like a sickle,
Eyes like a weasel.

150. *Cotterdale*

Three halls, two kirks, and a king,
Same road out as goes in.

151. *Grisedale*

He's sure to come again like Grisedale pies.

152. *Nidderdale*

Up Swincliffe, down Swarcliffe,
An' ower t'New Brig into Hartwith.

153. *Wharfedale and Airedale*

Wharfe is clear, and Aire is lythe,
Where the Aire drowns one, Wharfe drowns five.

154. *Craven*

There's Hunt Pot and Hull Pot,
Jingle Pot and Joggle Pot;
A cave without a bottom,
An' another at's deeper still.

Don Valley

155.

Blood-thirsty Dee each year needs three,
But bonny Don, she needs none.

156

The shelvin', slimy river Don,
Each year a daughter or a son.

157. *Hallamshire*

When all the world shall be aloft
Then Hallamshire shall be God's croft.

(*See also* Nos. 158, 241, 242 and 262)

West Riding Towns

158.

Bradford for cash,
Halifax for dash,
Wakefield for pride and poverty;
Huddersfield for show,
Sheffield what's low,
Leeds for dirt and vulgarity.

159

Birstall for ringers, Heckmondwike for singers,
Dewsbury for pedlars, Cleckheaton for sheddlers.

160. *Some West Riding Villages*

Round Ing, Long Ing, Hade Ing, Greave,
Copthurst, Hades, Ellentree Head;
Arrunden, Cartworth, Damhouse, and Cross,
Ubberton, Longley, Choppards is lost;
Far Cliffe, Nar Cliffe, Cliffe, and Cliffe End,
Paddock, West Nelly, Wooldale and Town End.

161. *Ainderby Steeple*

Ainderby Steeple
Where there are more rogues
Than honest people.

Aislaby (see No. 263)

Aldborough (see No. 171)

162. *Alne*

Alne's Alne, but Tollerton's another toon.

163. *Argam*

If you put in a duck at Argam Well
It will come out at Grindall Kell.

Barnard Castle (see No. 211)

164. *Barningham*

They're all clever fowk as live at Barningham;
Owd skeulmaister Coates is a boy for larning 'em.

165. *Barton St. Mary's*

Barton for sartin;
Twea churches and nivver a parson.

166. *Bawtry*

He will be hanged for leaving his liquor, like the saddler of Bawtry.

167. *Bedale*

Bedale bonnets and Bedale faces,
Find nowt ti' beat 'em
In onny places;
For t'forst are fairings
An' t'last are Graces.

168. *Bellasize*

Bellasis! Bellasis! daft was thy knowle,
When thoo swapt Bellasis for Henknoll.

Beverley

169.

Swa mikel fredom give I ye
Swa hert may think or eghe see.

169 (a)

But if ivver he get out ageean,
An' can but raise a friend,
The divel may tak the Toll-shop
At Beverley town-end.

(See also No. 200)

Birstall (see No. 159)

Boroughbridge

170. Barnaby Bright, longest day and shortest night.

171

Boro'brigg keep out o' t'way,
For Auldboro Town
I will ding doon.

172. *Borrowby* (near Staithes)

Borrowby Hills an' Newton Broos
Them's t'spots for hosses an' coos.

173. *Bowes*

When Julius Caesar was a king
Bowes Castle was a famous thing.

174. *Boynton*

Hops, turkeys, carp and beer,
Came into England all in one year.

Bradford (see No. 158)

175. *Brayton*

If Brayton Bargh, and Hamelton Hough
And Burton Bream
Warr all in thy belly, it wad neer be team.

Bridlington (see No. 200)

Brotherton (see No. 251)

176. *Castleford*

Castleford lasses may weel be fair,
For they wesh i' t'Calder, and sind i' t'Aire.

177. *Cleasby*

Gunpowder Plot
Shall ne'er be forgot
As long as Bella Brown
Sells tom-trot.

Cleckheaton (see No. 159)

178. *Cotherstone*

Cotherstone!
Where they christen calves,
Hopple lops,
And kneeband spiders.

Cowton (see No. 181)

Crayke (see No. 248)

179. *Croft*

'Tute again' made the lad leave Yorkshire,
And when he gat into Bisho'brigg he was nivver dune.

180. *Cropton*

On Cropton Cross there is a cup,
And in that cup there is a sup;
Take that cup and drink that sup
And set that cup on Cropton Cross Top.

181. *Dalton-on-Tees*

Dalton in the dirt,
Cowton in the clay;
If you gan i' two shoes,
You'll only bring one away.

Dewsbury (see No. 159)

Diana's Well (see No. 185)

Doncaster

182. Doncaster daggers.

183.

Doncaster Cuts.

Easingwold (see No. 248)

184. *East Layton*

I hoppled him ahint,
I teed him fast afore;
Dearie me Willie Mallom
What could a man do more?

185. *East Witton*

Whoever eats Hammer nuts
And drinks Diana's Water,
Will never leave Witton town
While he's a rag or tatter.

186. *Eccleshill*

In Eccleshill they're stiff and proud,
And few that dwell therein,
Do shew they've any fear of God
Or hatred unto sin.

Egglescliffe (see Nos. 263 and 265)

Enterpen (see No. 206)

Ferrybridge (see No. 251)

187. *Gayle* (near Hawes)

Hy fer t'Gayle!

188. *Gilling* (near Richmond)

When Gilling brews
Durham rues.

Goole (see No. 239)

189. *Golcar*

Gowcar, wheer t'lilies cums thro!

190. *Gormire*

When Gormire riggs shall be clothed with hay,
White Mare of Wissoncliff 'll bear it away.

191. *Great Ayton*

Yattoners wade ower t'beck ti seeave t'brigg.
(See also No. 249)

Grindall (see No. 163)

Halifax

192. At Halifax the law so sharp doth deal,
That whoso more than thirteen pence doth steal,
They have a gin that wondrous quick and well,
Sends thieves all headless into Heaven or Hell.

193

Halifax is built of wax,
Heptonstall o' stooan:
I' Halifax ther's bonny lasses,
I' Heptonstall ther's nooan.

194

When pancake bell begins to ring,
All Halifax lads begin to sing.

195

Gooid brade, butter and cheese
Is good Halifax and good Friese.

(See also Nos. 143 and 158)

Hambleton (see No. 175)

196. *Harrogate*

When lords an' ladies stinking water soss,
High brigs o' stean the Nidd sal cross,
An' a toon be built on Harrogate moss.

197. *Hartforth*

Have at thee Black Hartforth,
But have a care o' Bonny Gilling.

Hartwith (see No. 152)

198. *Hatfield*

There are no rats at Hatfield, nor sparrows at Lindham.

Hawes (see No. 187)

Heckmondwike (see No. 159)

Heptonstall (see No. 193)

199. *Hinderwell*

Ildrewelle chucks aback of a wall,
A speeanfull o' watter wad droon 'em all.

200. *Hornsea*

Hornsea broach when I built thee,
Thou was ten miles from Beverley,
Ten miles from Bridlington
And ten miles from the sea.

201. *Howden*

Bishop Skirlaw indeed was good to his people,
He built them a school and heightened the steeple.

Huddersfield (see No. 158)

Hull

202

You have eaten some Hull cheese.

203

When Dighton is pull'd down,
Hull shall become a great town.

204

As strong as Hull

(See also Nos. 143 and 269)

205. *Hunmanby*

Gilbert Gant
Left Hundmanby Moor
To Hundmanby poor
That they might never want.

206. *Hutton Rudby*

Hutton Rudby, Entrepen
Far more rogues than honest men.

Ingleborough (see Nos. 223 and 224)

207. *Kelk (Great)*

Great Kelk where God never dwelt
And honest man never rode through it.

208. *Kirkby (Malhamdale)*

Hips and haws an' hollin' stubbs
Are good enough for Kirkby cubs.

209. *Kirkby Malzeard*

Barnaby shut,
Wilfra cut.

210. *Knaresborough*

As freely at St. Robert gave his cow.

Knottingley (see No. 251)

211. *Lartington*

Lartington for frogs
An' Barney Castle for butchers' dogs.

212. *Leeds*

Leeds Loiner.
(See also Nos. 158 and 413)

213. *Market Weighton*

Market Weighton
Robert Leighton;
A brick church
And wooden steeple,
A drunken priest
And a wicked people.

214. *Marrick*

Marrick church is seen the best
Just as the sun withdraws to rest.

215. *Marsden*

Marsden, wheer the' put t'pigs o't'wall ta listen ta t'band.

Meaus Abbey (see No. 219)

216. *Mitton*

Hodder, Calder, Ribble and rain
Mingle together in Mitton domain.

217. *Nafferton*

Nafferton Slack wheer the' shoe ducks bi steeam.

Newton (near Hinderwell)
(See No. 172)

218. *Northallerton*

Hit him! He's a Scot!

219. *Nunkeeling*

If you go to Nun Keling,
you shall find your belly filling
of Whig or of Whay:
but go to Swine,
and come betime,
or else you go empty away:
but the Abbot of Meaus
doth keep a good house
by night and by day.

220. *Ossett*

Ossett, wheer the' black-leead t'tram-lines.

221. *Paull*

High Paull and Low Paull and Paull Holme;
There never was a fair maid married at Paull Town.

222. *Pontefract*

As sure as a louse in Pomfret.

Pendle, Ingleborough and Penigent

223

Pendle, Ingleborough and Penigent
Are the three highest hills between Scotland and Trent.

224

Pendle, Penigent and Ingleborough
Are the three highest hills all England thorough.

225. *Pudsey*

Pudsa wheer they've all bald heeads cos they pull 'em aht o' t'pit wi' suckers.

Raskelf

226. A wooden church, a wooden steeple,
Rascally place, and rascally people.

Another version

227

Rascal Town with roguish people,
A bursten bell and wooden church steeple.

228. *Reeth*

Pack 'em in,
Wedge 'em in,
Wack 'em in,
Edge 'em in,
Jack 'em in
Chuck 'em in
Sledge 'em in
Any way to get 'em in.

229. *Richmond*

Potter, Potter Thompson,
If thou had'st either drawn
The sword, or blown the horn,
Thou'd been the luckiest man
That ever yet was born.

Ripon

230. Pees at Ripon
On ilke side Ye kyrke a mile
For all ill deedes and ylke gyle.

231

Except ye Lord keep ye Cittie ye Wakeman waketh in vain.

232

As true steel as Rippon rowels.

233. *Romaldkirk*

Rum old church, rum old steeple,
Rum old parish, rum old people.

234. *Roseberry Topping*

When Roseberrye Toppinge wears a cappe
Let Cleveland then beware a clappe.

235. *Runswick Bay*

Runs'ick men wiv all the'r toil
Cums ti Steeas ti sell the'r oil.

(See also No. 247)

236. *Saxton*

The Lord of Dacres
Was slayne in the North Acres.

Scarborough

237. A Scarborough Warning
A word and a blow
But the blow first.

238

When Oliver' Mount puts on it' hat,
Scarborough, Falsgrave, and Scalby mun pay for that.

239. *Selby*

Selby was a seaport town
When Goole was but a marsh;
Now Goole it is a seaport town
And Selby fares the worse.

240. *Semerwater*

Semer water rise, Semer water sink,
And swallow all the town
But this lile house
Where they gave me meat and drink.

Sheffield

241. Sheffield made, both haft and blade;
London for your life,
Show me such a knife.

242

When Sheffield Park is plowed and sown,
Then little England hold thine own.
(See also No. 158)

243. *Skipton*

Skipton in Craven
Is never a haven,
But many a day of foul weather.
And he that would say
To a pretty girl nay
I wish for his cravat a tether.

244. *Slaithwaite*

Slowit, wheer the' raked t'muin aht o' t'cut.

Snape (see No. 257)

245. *Sprotborough*

Whoso is hungry and lists well to eat,
let him come to Sprotborough for his meat,
and for a night, and for a day
his horse shall have both corn and hay,
and no man shall ask him, when he goeth away.

Staithes

246

Steeas yackers, flither pickers, herrin' guts fer garters!

247

Steeas men wiv all the'r nuts
Gans ti Runs'ick ti fill the'r guts.

(See also No. 235)

248. *Stillington*

If you do wish to find a fool
And do't without mistake;
Take t'first you meet in Stillington,
In Easingwold or Crayke.

249. *Stokesley*

Stowsla's larnt all it knaws fra t'Yatton feeals.

250. *Strensall*

That's a capper o' Strensall.

251. *Sutton*

Sutton boiled mutton, Brotherton beef,
Ferrybridge bonny lasses and Knottingley thief.

Sutton-on-Forest (see No. 268)

Swainby (see No. 260)

Swarcliffe (see No. 152)

Swincliffe (see No. 152)

Swine (see No. 219)

252. *Tadcaster*

(1) The muse in Tadcaster can find no theme
But a most noble bridge without a stream.

(2) The verse before on Tadcaster was just,
But now great floods we see and dirt for dust.

253. *Thornton Steward*

Thornton Steward for wormwood, lees, and sand!

254. *Tickhill*

Tick-hill, God help me!

Tollerton (see No. 162)

Wakefield

255. Merry Wakefield!

256

As good as George o' Green.
(See also No. 158)

Well

257. Well an' Snaape
Wheer the' gin an' gaape,
An' braay hard watter soft wiv a clooase-prop.

257(a). Well always was a lawless place.

258. *West Witton*

In Penhill crags
He tore his rags;
At Hunters thorn
He blew his horn:
At Capplebank stee
He broke his knee,

At Briskillbeck
He brake his neck;
At Wadham's End
He couldn't fend;
At Briskill End
He made his end.
Shout, lads, shout!

259. *Wetherby*

The woful town o' Wetherby.

Whorlton and Swainby

260. The stream flows ever and silently on
Till it meets in the distance another;
The cottages stand in single array,
With Whorlton on one side and Swainby on t'other.

261

Whorlton snobs are all bobs.

262. *Winkabank*

Winkabank and Temple Brough
Will buy all England through and through.

Yarm

263. When Yarm sinks and Egglescliffe swims
Aislaby will be a market town.

264

The only place that was finished when the world was created.

265

No bells can ring like Egglescliffe . . . Yarm can!

York

266

He is lord for a year and a day,
But she is a lady for ever and aye.

267

Lincoln was, London is, but York shall be
The greatest city of the three.

268

As much as York excels foul Sutton.

269

Oxford for learning, London for wit,
Hull for a woman, and York for a tit.

270

Poor, proud, and pretty.

271

Yorke, Yorke, for my monie:
Of all the citties that ever I see,
For mery pastime and companie,
Except the cittie of London.

ROUND THE YEAR

Days of the Week

272. *Days of Birth*

A Monday's bairn'll grow up fair,
A Tuesday's yan i' grace thruf prayer,
A Wednesday's bairn hes monny a pain,
A Thosday's bairn weean't bahde at heeam.
A Friday's bairn is good an sweet,
A Setterday's warks fra morn ti neet,
Bud a Sunday's bairn thruf leyfe is blist
An' seear i' t'end wi' t'saints ti rist.

Cutting Nails

273. Better t'bairn hed ne'er been born,
'An cut its naals on a Sunday morn.

274

Cut 'em o' Monday, cut 'em for health;
Cut 'em o' Tuesday, cut 'em for wealth;
Cut 'em o' Wednesday, cut 'em for news;
Cut 'em o' Thorsday, ya cut for new shoes;
Cut 'em o' Friday, ya cut 'em for sorrow;
Cut 'em o' Settherday, t'bairn nivver need borrow;
Cut 'em o' Sunday, 't hed better be deead,
For ill-luck an' evil'll lig on it' heead.

275. *Washing Days*

They that wash on Monday
Have a whole week to dry;
They that wash on Tuesday
Are not so much awry:
They that wash on Wednesday
May get their clothes clean;
They that wash on Thursday
Are not so much too mean;
They that wash on Friday
Wash for their need;
They that wash on Saturday
Are clarty-paps indeed.

Fridays

276. Friday flits
Have not long sits.

277

Lang Friday's nivver deean
Seea lig i' bed whahl Setterda' neean.

278

Deean't o' Friday buy yer ring,
O' Friday deean't put t'spurrin's in;
Deean't wed o' Friday. Think on o' this,
Nowther blue ner green mun match her dhriss.

279. *Leap Year*

Happy they'll be that wed and wive
Within Leap Year; they're sure to thrive.

New Year's Day

280

Lucky-bo'd, lucky-bo'd, chuck, chuck, chuck!
Measter an' Missis, it's tahme ti git up:
If ya deean't git up, ya'll ha'e neea luck;
Lucky-bo'd, lucky-bo'd, chuck, chuck, chuck!

281

At New Year's tide
Days lengthen a cock-stride.

282. *St. Agnes' Day*

Fair St. Agnes play thy part,
And send to me my own sweetheart:
Not in his best nor worst array,
But in his apparel for every day,
That I tomorrow may him ken
From among all other men.

February

283. February fill-dyke,
Fill it wi' eyther black or white.
March muck it oot,
Wi' a besom an' a cloot.

284

February fire lang, March tide to bed gang.

285

In Yorkshire ancient people say
If February's second day
Be very fair and clear,
It doth portend a scanty year
For hay and grass, but if it rains
They never then perplex their brains.

Candlemas

286. On Can'lemas, a February day,
Throw can'le an' can'lestick away.

287

A Can'lemas crack
Lays monny a sailor on his back.

288

If Can'lemas be lound an' fair,
Ya hauf o' t'winter's ti cum an' mair:
If Can'lemas day be murk an' foul,
Ya hauf o' t'winter's geean at Yule.

289

If the new moon doth shine t'Setterda' afore Can'lemas day,
Sleet, rain an' blash we shall have, folk say,
It's been a bad back-end, an' rent's hard to pay
If you 'a'en't half your hay on Can'lemas day:
If the throstle sings both loud an' long
It yet must sing a sadder song,
And when green grass is easy found
It better have been under the ground
For grisky grass tells very plain
We must have yet both snow and rain;
But if Can'lemas day be sunny and warm
You must darn your old mittens and full up your hurn:
For when Can'lemas shows both fair an' breet
There's winter still ti mak you greet;
But when it comes with cold and rain
Winter's done and won't come again.
But when Can'lemas day is cloudy and black,
It always hugs winter away on its back,
An' bear in mind on Can'lemas day
A goose 'at's worth owt will have started to lay,
An' a hog 'at's well wintered should do without hay.

290

At Candlemas gooid gees al lay.

Good Friday

291. On Good Friday rist thi pleeaf,
Start nowt, end nowt, that's eneeaf.

292

One a penny,
Two a penny
Hot Cross Buns.

March

293. March grows
Never dows

294

A dry March, an' a windy;
A full barn, an' a findy.

295

For every fog i' March, there'll be a frost i' May.

April

296. April noddy's past and gone
You're a fool and I'm none.

297

Tid, Mid, Miserae
Carling, Palm, and Paste Egg Day.

298. *Palm Sunday*

Palm Sunday, palm away;
Next Sunday's Easter-day.

May

299. O' t'fo'sst o' Maay
A good gull 'll laay.

300

Deean't cast a cloot
Till Maay bi oot.

301

Ya moan't wesh blankets i' May,
Or else ya'll wash yer soul away.

302. *Royal Oak Day*

Roy'l oak day,
T'twenty-ninth o' May:
If ya deean't give us hallida'
Wa'll all run awaa'.

303. *St. Swithin's Day*

St. Swithin's day if thou dost rain,
For forty days it will remain;
St. Swithin's day if thou be fair,
For forty day 'twill rain na maar.

Harvest Home and the Mell Sheaf

304. We hev her, we hev her,
A coo iv a tether;
At oor toon end.
A yowe an' a lamb,
A pot an' a pan.
May wa git seeafe in
Wiv oor harvest-yam,
Wiv a sup o' good yal,
An' sum hawpence ti spend.

305

John Metcalfe has gitten all shorn an' mawn,
All but a few standards an' a bit o' lowse corn.
We hev her, we hev her.
Fast i' a tether,
Cum help us ti hod her.
Hurrah! Hurrah! Hurrah!

306

Blest be t'day that Christ was born,
For we've getten t'mell o' t'farmer's corn.
It's weel bun, but better shorn.
Mell! Shout, lads, Mell!

307

Here we are as tite as nip.
We nivver flang ower bud yance iv a grip,
An' then oor Jack gav her the slip
Hip! hip! hurray!

308

Weel bun' an' better shooarn,
Is Mister Reeadheead's kooarn;
We hev her, we hev her,
As fast as a feather.
Hip, hip, hip!
Hurrah! hurrah! hurrah!

309. *September*

September blow soft
Till the fruit's i' th'loft.

310. *Michaelmas*

If t'geease-breest at Michaelmas be dour and dull
We s'hev a sair winter te t'sure an' te t'full.

311. *November*

Cut corn at Brough Hill Fair, ripe or not.

Guy Fawkes' Day

312. Remember, remember, the fifth of November.

313

A stick and a stake
For King James's sake;
Please give us a coil, a coil.

314

Awd Grimey sits upon yon hill,
As black as onny awd craw.
He's gitten on his lang grey coat
Wi' buttons doon afoor.
He's gitten on his lang grey coat
Wi' buttons doon afoor.

315. *The Waits*

Good morning Mister Capstick,
Good morning Mrs. Capstick,
And all the little Capsticks;
It's five o'clock, an' a frosty mornin'.

Christmas

316. A Merry Christmas, and a Happy New Year when it comes.

317. *Children's Christmas-Boxing Nominy*

Ah wish ya a Merry Chris'mas and a Happy New Year;
A pocket full of munny an' a cellar full o' beer;
Two fat pigs, an' a new-coved coo;
Good Maisther an' Misthress hoo di ya do.
Pleease will ya gi' ma a Chris'mas box?

318. *Cleveland Vessell Cups Song*

God rist you merry, gentlemen,
Let nothin' you dismay
Remember Christ oor Saviour
Was boorn o' Kessamas day,
To seeave oor sowls fra Sattan's poower;
Lang tahme we've geean astray.
This brings tahdin's o' cumfort an' joy.

Noo stright they went te Bethlehem,
Wheer oor sweet Saviour lay;
They fan' him iv a manger,
Wheer oxen fed o' hay:
Te seeave oor sowls fra Sattan's poower;
Lang tahme we've geean astray.
This brings tahdin's o' cumfort an' joy.

God bliss t'maister o' this house,
An' t'mistress also,
An' all yer lahtle childeren
That round yer teeable go;
An' all yer kith an' kindered,
That dwell beeath far an' near;
An' Ah wish ya a Merry Kessamas
An' a Happy New Year.

319. *Saying*

Christmas comes but once a year,
And when it comes, it brings good cheer.

FOLK-LORE RHYMES

Weddings

320. A weddin', a woo, a clog an' a shoe,
A pot full o' porridge an' away they go.

321

Green and white
Forsaken quite.

322

Something old, something new,
Something borrowed, something blue.

323

The woman that changes her name
And not the first letter;
Is all for the worse,
And none for the better.

324

Happy is the bride the sun shines on,
Blessed is the corpse the rain falls on.

325

Marry in Lent
You will live to repent.

326

The bridegroom's health we all will sing,
In spite of Turk or Spanish king;
The bride's good health we will not pass,
But put them both into one glass.
See, see, see that he drink it all,
See, see, see that he let none fall,
For if he do, he shall drink two,
And so shall the rest of the company do.

327. *Wedding-ring Mottoes*

(*a*) God for me appointed thee.
(*b*) In thee my choice I do rejoice.
(*c*) Let me in thee most happy be.
(*d*) God hath sent my heart's content.
(*e*) United hearts death only parts.
(*f*) You and I will lovers die.
(*g*) I have obtained what God ordained.
(*h*) Let reason rule affection.
(*i*) God did decree our unity.
(*j*) Live, love and be happie.
(*k*) Thy consent is my content.
(*l*) Of all the rest I love thee best.
(*m*) In thy breast my heart shall rest.
(*n*) I like my choice too well to change,
My love is fixed, I will not range.
(*o*) Well projected if accepted.
(*p*) A loving wife prolongeth life.
(*q*) Love entire is my desire.
(*r*) Let our contest be who loves best.

BABIES' TEETH

328. *Odd*

If a bairn's teeath's odd,
It'll seean gan ti God.

Early Teeth

329. Soon todd, soon with God.

330

Seean teeath, seean teeas.

331. *Losing Teeth*

Fire, fire, tak a beean,
An' send oor Johnny a gooid tooith ageean.

NURSERY RHYMES

332. *Dressing Baby*

Pranky iddity; pranky aye,
Baby hezn't been pranked ti-day.
But let ti-morn come ivver sa soon
Baby sall be pranked bi noon.

333. *Bonny Lass*

Bonny lass, bonny lass,
Wilt thou be mine?
Thou shalt neither wash dishes
Nor sarrow the swine
But sit on a whishon
And sew up a seam,
And eat nothing but
Strawberries and cream.

334. *The Baker's Man*

Clap-a-cake, clap-a-cake, baker's man,
Knead and bake it as fast as you can,
Stick it and prick it, and mark it with T,
And throw it i' t'oven for Tommy and me.

335. *The Cock-Bird*

Cock-a-doodle-do
My daddy's gaan to ploo,
My mammy's lost her pudding poke
And knaws nut what to do.

336. *Cuckoo, Cherry Tree*

Cuckoo, cuckoo, cherry tree,
Catch a penny and give it to me.

337. *The Daffodil*

Daffy-down-dilly has come up to town,
In a yellow petticoat and a green gown.

338. *Diddle, Diddle, Dumpling*

Diddle, diddle, dumpling; my son John
Went to bed with his breeches on;
One stocking off, and one stocking on,
Diddle, diddle, dumpling, my son John.

339. *Little Miss Muffet*

Little Miss Muffet
Sat on a buffet,
Eating her curds and whey;
There came a little spider,
And sat down beside her,
And frightened Miss Muffet away.

340. *The Moon*

Moon penny, bright as silver,
Come and play with little childer.

341. *The White Paternoster*

Matthew, Mark, Luke, and John,
Bless the bed that I lie on!
Four corners to my bed,
Five angels there lie spread;
Two at my head,
Two at my feet,
One at my heart, my soul to keep.

GIRLS' RHYMES

342. *The Peep Show*

A pin a sight, a sat a sight,
A pin to look in.

343

A pin to look in
A very fine thing.

344

A pinnet a piece to look at a show,
All the fine ladies sat in a row.
Blackbirds with blue feet,
Walkin up a new street;
One behind and one before,
And one beknocking at t'barber's door.

BOYS' RHYMES

345. *Barring-Out*

Bar, master, bar; bar for a pin;
If you won't give us a holiday we won't let you in.

Counting-out

346. Holla, bolla, butterfly;
Lie by, stink, out!

347

Meny, meny, miny mo,
I ax ya wheear mun this man go?
Sum gans eeast, an sum gans west,
An sum gans ower the high crake nest.

348. *Late Scholars*

Diller a dollar,
A ten-o'clock scholar,
What maks ye cum se soon?
You us'd ti cum at ten o'clock,
Bud noo you cum at noon.

349. *Bird-nesting*

Robin takker, robbin takker,
Sin, sin, sin!

350. *Tom Plom*

Tom Plom, penny pie,
Kissed a lass and told a lie.

351. *Whip Behind!*

Here we are at oor toon end,
A bottle o' gin, and a croon to spend,
If ya ha'int a penny, a haw'p'ny 'll do,
If ya ha'int a haw'p'ny God bless you.
Hip! Hip! Hooray.

CHILDREN'S RHYMES

352. *Bell-horses*

Bell-horses, bell-horses, what time o' day?
One o'clock, two o'clock, three and away.

353. *Cockelty Bread*

Mah awd granmother, she is deead,
She lane't ma hoo ti mak cockelty breead;
It's up wi' yer heels, an' doon wi' yer heead,
An' that's oor way ti mak cockelty breead.

354. *Dimples*

A dimple on your cheek
Your living to seek;
A dimple on your chin
You'll have your living brought in.

355. *Gifts*

A gift on the thumb
Is seer ti cum;
Bud yan on the finger
Is seer ti linger.

356. *Handy-pandy*

Handy-pandy
Sugar-candy
Which hand is it in?

357. *Hickup-snickup*

Hickup-snickup
Stand up, stick up.

358. *Ifs and Ands*

If ifs an' an's
Were pots an' pans
Ther'd be na trade fer tinklers.

359. *Pins*

See a pin, and pick it up,
All the day you'll have good luck.
See a pin an' let it stay.
Bad luck'll follow all the day

360. *Rain*

Raan, raan, go away
Cum agaan another day.

361. *Sailors' Children's Rhyme*

Suther wind suther,
An' blaw mi faather
Heeame ti mi muther.

362. *Sticks an' Steeans*

Sticks an' steeans
'll brek mi beeans
Bud callin' weean't ho't me.

363. *Dent Knitters' Song*

Sally an' I, Sally an' I
For a good pudding pye
Taa hoaf wheat an' tudder hoaf rye,
Sally and I, for a good pudding pye.

364. *Sweethearting*

When t'whins is oot o' blossom,
Kissin's oot o' fashion.

365. *Apple Pie*

Apple pie without cheese
Is like a kiss without a squeeze.

SINGING GAMES

366. *Little Allisander*

Little Allisander
Sat upon a cinder,
Weeping an' crying
For a young man.

367. *The Looby-Looby*

Can you dance, looby looby,
(repeat three times)
All on a Friday night.
You put your right foot in,
And then you take it out,
And wag it, and wag it, and wag it,
Then turn and turn about.

368. *The Jolly Miller*

There was a jolly miller and he lived by himself,
As the mill went round he gained his wealth;
One hand in the hopper and the other in the bag,
As the mill went round he made his grab.

WOMEN, GEESE AND HENS

369. *Tweea Mirricles*

A garthful o' geease an' neea to'ds,
A hooseful o' women an' neea wo'ds.

370. *Whistling Women*

A whistlin' woman, an' a crawin' hen
Wad drahve t'deeavil tiv his den.

371. *Fire*

Storr up t'fire, an' mak a low
Or in this house ther'll be a row.

372. *Horses*

Buy
A horse wiv a weeam
An' a meer wi' neean.

373. *Riding T'Stang*

Hey dilly, how dilly, hey dilly, dang!
It's naythe for thy part, nor my part,
That I ride the stang.
But it's for Jack Solomon,
His wife he did bang.
He bang'd her, he bang'd her,
He bang'd her indeed,
He bang'd t'poor woman
Tho' shoo stood him no need.
He nayther took stick, stain, wire, nor stower,
But he up wi' a besom an' knocked her ower.
So all ye good neighbours who live i' this raw,
I pray ye tak warnin', for this is our law.
An' all ye cross husbands
Who do your wives bang
We'll blow for ye t'horn,
An' ride for ye t'stang.
Hip, hip, hip, hurrah!

FISHERMEN'S RHYMES

374. A spraggy cod'll grow ni fatter
Till it gits a sup o' new May watter.

375

Mair heeaks
Mair dogs.

376

Wag ballock wag,
A westerly wind an' a neeap fleead.

377

When t'tahde flows neean
T'neeaps is deean.

378

T'fo'st fresh i' Maay
Brings t'salmon awaay.

379

A nor'west breet as big as a sheet
An' t'sails 'll tak ni harm ti-neet.

380

When t'wind gans opposite t'sun
Trist it not fer back it'll cum.

381

O the boaty row,
O the boaty row,
O the boaty row,
We shot three lines in Skinnigriff Wyke:
Of fishes we got nine,
Three to boil and three to fry
And three to bait our lines.

SHEEP-SCORING NUMERALS

(The Shepherd's ancient method of counting his sheep.)

	382 Swaledale	383 Wensleydale	384 Nidderdale
One	Yahn	Yan	Yain
Two	Tayhn	Tean	Tain
Three	Tether	Tither	Eddero
Four	Mether	Mither	Peddero
Five	Mimph	Pip	Pitts
Six	Hithher	Teaser	Tayter
Seven	Lithher	Leaser	Later
Eight	Anver	Catra	Overro
Nine	Danver	Horna	Coverro
Ten	Dic	Dick	Dix
Eleven	Yahndic	Yan-dick	Yain-dix
Twelve	Tayhndic	Tean-dick	Tain-dix
Thirteen	Tetherdic	Tither-dick	Eddero-dix
Fourteen	Metherdic	Mither-dick	Peddero-dix
Fifteen	Mimphit or Mump	Bumper	Bumfitt
Sixteen	Yahn-a-mimphit	Yan-a-bum	Yain-o-bumfitt
Seventeen	Tayhn-a-mimphit	Tean-a-bum	Tain-o-bumfitt
Eighteen	Tether-a-mimphit	Tither-a-bum	Eddero-o-bumfitt
Nineteen	Mether-a-mimphit	Mither-a-bum	Peddero-o-bumfitt
Twenty	Jigit	Jigger	Jiggit or Giggit

	385 Craven	386 Knaresborough	387 Mashamshire
One	Arn	Yah	Ine (also een)
Two	Tarn	Tiah	Tine (also teen)
Three	Tethera	Tethera	Tethera
Four	Fethera	Methera	Fethera
Five	Pubs	Pip	Fip
Six	Aayther	Seezar	Slar
Seven	Layather	Leezar	Lar
Eight	Quoather	Cattera	Core
Nine	Quaather	Horna	Cone
Ten	Dugs	Dick	Dick
Eleven	Arnadugs	Yah-dick	Inedick (endick)
Twelve	Tarnadugs	Tiah-dick	Tinedick (tendick)
Thirteen	Tetheradugs	Tether-a-dick	Tetherdick
Fourteen	Fetheradugs	Mether-a-dick	Fetherdick
Fifteen	Buon	Bumper	Bum
Sixteen	Arnabuon	Yah-de-bumper	
Seventeen	Tarnabuon	Tiah-de-bumper	
Eighteen	Tetherabuon	Tether-de-bumper	
Nineteen	Fetherabuon	Mether-de-bumper	
Twenty	Gun-a-gun	Jigger	

388. *The Miller*

Miller, miller, mooter poke,
Teeak a laid an' stale a stroke.

389

Down i' yon lum we have a mill,
If they send more grist we'll grind more still,
With her broad arm an' mighty fist
Shoo rams it into t'mooter-chist.

The Thatcher

390. Theaker, theaker, theake a span
Come off yer lather, an' hang yer man.

391

When my maisther hes thatched all his streeah
He will then cum doon an' hing him that says seeah.

392. *The Weaver*

Ther's t'meyt hung dahn afore t'fire ta rooast,
Ther's t'puddin' on t'brandree afore it ta tooast,
Porates top o' t'hob, they'll be done enif sooin,
But Ah think tha can weive a few more bobbins bi nooin.

393. *The Chimney Sweep*

Chimley-sweeper, blackymoor,
Set o' t'top o' t'chapel door.
Tak a stick an' knock him dahn,
That's the way to Chapeltahn.

394. *The Bellman*

Tak'n oop this foornoon, opud th'nooarth sans,
Two keis, which I hev in my hans,
Wo-iver hes lost 'em mun just cum to mea
An' they sal hev 'em agean, an' we can agreea.

395. *The Bird Tenter*

Shoo way, bods! Shoo way, bods!
Tak a bit, an leeave a bit,
An nivver cum ne ma'e bods.

396. *The Witch's Curse*

Fire cum,
Fire gan,
Curlin' smeeak
Keep oot o' t'pan;
Ther's a teead i' t'fire, a frog on t'hob,
Here's t'heart frev a crimson ask,
Here's a teeath fra t'heead
O' yan at's deead,
At nivver gat thruff his task;
Here's prick'd i' blood a maiden's prayer,
At t'e'e o' man maunt see,
It's prick'd upon a yet warm mask,
An' lapt aboot a breet green ask,
An' it's all fer him an' thee;
It boils,
Thoo'll drink,
He'll speeak,
Thoo'll think,
It boils
Thoo'll see,
He'll speeak
Thoo'll dee.

397. *A Charm*

Tak' tweea at's red an' yan at's blake
O' poison berries three,
Three fresh-cull'd blooms o' Devil's glut,
An' a sprig o' rosemary;
Tak' henbane, bullace, bumm'lkite,
An' t'fluff frev a deead bulrush,
Nahn berries shak' fra t'rowan-tree,
An' nahn fra bottery bush.

398. *A Fairy Rhyme*

The moon shines bright,
The stars give light,
And little Nanny Button-cap
Will come tomorrow night.

399

Ah'll tee on me bonnet
An' put on me shoe,
An' if thoo's not off
Ah'll suan catch thoo!

400. *Hob Rhymes*

Hob-hole Hob!
Mah bairn's getten t'kin-cough;
Tak't off-tak't off!

401

'Hob trush Hob! Where is thou?'
'Ah's tying on mah left fuit shoe
An' Ah'll be wi' thee noo.'

402

Gin Hob mun hae nowght
Bud a hardin hamp;
He'll cum nae mair,
Nowther to berry nor stamp.

403. *Churning Rhyme*

Come butter come,
Come butter come,
Peter stands at the gate
Waiting for a butter cake,
Come butter come.

404. *The Sun*

When t'sun sets clear i' t'watter
ov a Tho'sda neet
It'll be a No'th wind
bi Settera' neet.

The Moon

405. A Setterda's meean
Cums yance i' seven year ower seean.

406

Saturday's moon
And Sunday's full
Is always wet
And always wull.

407

Clear moon
Frost soon.

408

I see t'mean an' t'mean sees me
God bless t'sailors oot on t'sea.

409

A far off brough
Is a storm near enough.

Rain

410. Mair raan
Mair rist.

411

Raan afoor seven
Fair bi eleven.

412

If the rain comes before the wind
Lower your topsails and take them in;
If the wind comes before the rain
Lower your topsails and hoist them again.

413. *Snow*

Snaw, snaw, coom faster,
White as allyblaster;
Poor owd women pickin' geese,
Sendin' t'feathers daan to Leeds.

414. *Frost*

White frosts allus shite thersels.

415. *Fog*

A northern harr
Brings fine weather from afar.

Mist

416. A moorn hag-mist
Is worth gold in a kist.

417

When the mist comes from the hill,
Then good weather it doth spill;
When the mist comes from the sea
Then good weather it will be.

418

An awd meean mist
Is wo'th gowd iv a kist.

Clouds and Sky

419. When it gangs up i' sops
It'll fau down i' drops.

420

If woolly fleeces spread the heavenly way
Be sure no rain disturbs the summer's day.

421

A mackerel sky
Is never long dry.

422

Hen scrats an' filly tails
Maks lofty ships carry law sails.

423

A red sky at night is the shepherd's delight:
A red sky in the morning is the shepherd's warning.

Other Weather Rhymes

424. When the days lengthen
The colds strengthen.

425

As monny haws
Seea monny cau'd teeas.

426

Winter's thunder
Summer's wonder.

427. *The Onion*

Onion skin
Very thin
Mild weather coming in:
Onion skin thick and tough
Coming winter cold and rough.

428. *The Seasons*

Spring: Slippy, drippy, nippy!
Summer: Showery, flowery, bowery;
Autumn: Hoppy, croppy, poppy;
Winter: Wheezy, sneezy, breezy.

BIRD RHYMES

429. *The Bat*

Black black-beearaway
Cum doon bi hereaway.

430

There gans a back-beearaway
On his heead away.

The Crow

431. Craw, craw, gehr art o' me seet
Or else al kill thee fatther and mother toneet.

432

One's unlucky
Two's lucky
Three is health
Four is wealth
Five is sickness
Six is death.

The Cuckoo

433. In the month of Averil,
The gowk comes over the hill,
In a shower of rain.

434

The first cock of hay
Frights the cuckoo away.

435

The cuckoo is a merry bird,
She sings as she flies,
She brings us good tidings
And tells us no lies:
She sucks bonny birds' eggs
To keep her voice clear,
And never sings 'cuckoo'
Till summer is near.

436

T'cuckoo sings iv Aapril,
Then sheea sings i' Maay:
Sings anuther tune i' June,
Then sheea flees awaay.

437. *The Lapwing*

Pee-wit, pee-wit,
I coup'd my nest and I rue it.

438. *The Magpie*

One for sorrow
Two for mirth
Three for a wedding
Four for a birth
Five for a parson
Six for a clerk
Seven for a babe
Buried in the dark.

439

One for sorrow, two for luck,
Three for a wedding, four for a death,
Five for silver, six for gold,
Seven for a bonny lass twenty years old.

440

One is a sign of mischief,
Two is a sign of mirth,
Three is a sign of a wedding,
Four is a sign of death,
Five is a sign of rain,
Six is a sign of a bastard bairn.

441

One's a sign of bad luck,
Two's a sign of good;
Three's a sign of a broken leg,
And four's a sign of a wedding.

442

I crossed t'pynot,
And t' pynot crossed me;
T'Devil take t'pynot
And God save me.

443

Tell pie tit,
Laid a' egg an' couldn't sit.

444

Tell-pie-tit,
Thy tongue's slit,
An' ivvery dog i' t'toon'll git a bit.

445. *The Peacock*

When the peacock loudly bawls,
Soon we'll have both rain and squalls.

446. *The Seagull*

Sea-gull! sea-gull! get thee on t'sand,
It'll nivver be fine while thou's o' t'land.

447

O' t'fo'st o' Maay
A good gull 'll laay.

448. *The Cock*

If the cock crows going to bed
He'll certainly rise with a watery head.

449. *The Sparrow*

There's never a sparrow
Without its marrow.

450. *Ladslove*

Lads love is lassies' delight,
And if lads don't love, lassies will flite.

The Docken

451. Docken in drahve t'nettle oot,
Just leyke an au'd dishcloot.

452

In docken, oot nettle,
Deean't let t'warm blood sattle.

453. *Quaking Grass*

A trimmlin' jock i' t'hoose,
An' you weean't hev a moose.

454. *The Ash Tree*

Keep me either wet or dry
The heart of oak I will defy.

455. *Bees*

A swarm in May
Is worth a load of hay;
A swarm in June
Is worth a silver spoon;
A swarm in July
Is not worth a fly.

456. *The Ladybird*

Cowlady, cowlady, hie thy way wum,
Thy haase is afire, thy childer all gone;
All but poor Nanny, set under a pan,
Weyvin' gold lace as fast as shoo can.

457. *The Snail*

Sneel, sneel, put oot your horn,
Your fayther an' muther 'll gie ye some corn.

458. *The Church Bell*

When I doe ring God's prayses syng
When I doe tole, pray heart and soule.

NOTES ON YORKSHIRE DIALECT VERSE

1. *A Yorkshire Dialogue* (1673)

This, according to the late Professor Skeat, was first printed as a broadside at York by Stephen Bulkby in 1673. The original broadside is lost, but it was printed in the *English Dialect Society's Transactions*, vol. 76, 1896, from a manuscript transcript bought at the sale of Sir F. Madden's books and papers. The poem is noteworthy as the first example of modern dialect poetry. Its authorship is unknown.

2. *A Yorkshire Dialogue* (1683)

The selection here given consists of 106 lines from the complete poem of 440 lines. It is a faithful copy of the first edition of 1683, the only alterations being the modernisation of the punctuation, and one or two corrections of a minor character.

As the details of the early editions have never been correctly given, we give them here.

1683. This, as far as is known, is the First Edition. Its title-page is as follows:

A / Yorkshire / Dialogue / In its pure Natural / Dialect. / As it is now commonly Spoken in the / North parts of York-shire. / Being a Miscellaneous discourse, or Hotchpotch of / several Country Affaires, begun by a Daughter and her / Mother, and continued by the Father, Son, Uncle, / Neese and Land-Lord. /
Note that D. stands for Daughter, M. for Mother. / F. for Father, S. for Son, U. for Uncle, N. for / Neese, and L. for Land-Lord. /

Reader, here's folly, come and Laugh thy fill,
He neer did good, that never did noe Ill.

YORK, Printed by John White, and are to be sold by Richard / Lambert, at the Crown at the Minster-gates. 1683.

The Dialogue occupies eighteen pages. There is a copy in the British Museum (Pressmark 164. l. 72), and one in the Bodleian (Ashm. 1066 (2)).

1685. 'A Yorkshire Dialogue' was published along with a poem in standard English, 'The Praise of Yorkshire Ale' and an 'Alphabetical Clavis.'

Pages 1 to 31 were taken up with 'The Praise of Yorkshire Ale,' pages 35 to 78 with 'A Yorkshire Dialogue' (73 to 78 being the newly-added 'Scould between Bess and Nell'), and pages 79 to 113 with an 'Alphabetical Clavis.'

What calls for special note is that in this edition 'A Yorkshire Dialogue' has a separate title-page, dated 1684. This title-page is as follows:

A Yorkshire / Dialogue / In its pure Natural / Dialect. / As it is now commonly spoken in the / North parts of Yorkeshire. / Being a Miscellaneous Discourse or Hotch- / Potch of several Country Affairs, begun by a / Daughter, and her Mother, and continued / by the Father, Son, Uncle, Neese, and / Land-Lord, after which followes a Scould between / Bess and Nell two Yorkeshire Women. /
Note that D. stands for Daughter, M. for Mother, / F. for Father, S. for Son, U. for Uncle, N. for / Neese, and L. for Land-Lord.

Reader here's Folly come and Laugh thy fill,
He neer did good, that never did no ill.

YORK Printed by J. White, for Francis Hildyard / at the Bible in Stonegate. 1684.

It should be noted that the original dialogue of 1683 has been nearly doubled in length: from 440 lines to 774 lines, inclusive of the 'Scould,' which takes up eighty-eight lines.

1697. This edition contains 'The Praise of Yorkshire Ale,' 'A Yorkshire Dialogue,' and the 'Alphabetical Clavis' (all of which are found in the 1685 edition), with the addition of 'Some Observations on the Dialect and Pronunciation of Words in the East Riding of Yorkshire' and 'A Collection of Significant and Useful Proverbs.'

Again, as in the 1685 edition, there is a separate title-page for 'A Yorkshire Dialogue.' This is as follows:

A Yorkshire / Dialogue / In its pure Natural / Dialect / As it is now commonly spoken in the / North parts of Yorkshire. / Being a Miscellanious Discourse, or Hotch / Potch of several Country Affaires, begun by a / Daughter, and her Mother, and continued / by the Father, Son, Uncle, Neese and / Land-Lord, after which follows a Scould between / Bess and Nell two York-shire Women. / Note that D. stands for Daughter, M. for Mother, / F. for Father, S. for Son, U. for Uncle, N. for / Neese, and L. for Land-Lord. /

Reader here's Folly, come and Laugh thy fill,
He neer did good, that never did no ill.

YORK, Printed by John White for Francis Hildyard, / at the Bible in Stone-gate. 1697.

It will be noted that on no title-page of 'A Yorkshire Dialogue' is the name of the author given. Are we justified, as all previous writers have assumed, in ascribing the authorship to 'G. M. Gent'? Or is he the author of 'The Praise of Yorkshire Ale' only? Although his name appears on the full (i.e. the first) title-page of both the 1685 and the 1697 editions, we know that he was not the author of the Clavis (which first appeared in 1685) or of the Observations on the Dialect and the Proverbs (which first appeared in 1697). These were the work of Francis Brokesby (1637–1714), Fellow of Trinity College, Cambridge, and Rector of Rowley in the East Riding from 1670 to 1690. (He was then deprived of his living as a non-juror, refusing to take the oath to William and Mary.) We know of Brokesby's authorship because Ray printed these Observations and the first six of the Proverbs in the 2nd edition of his *A Collection of Local Words*, 1691, and gave Brokesby as the author. The remaining proverbs were taken from Fuller's *Worthies*, and from Ray. If 'G. M. Gent' intended the reader to think that he was the author of these items when in fact he was not, may he not also have wished to take credit for having written 'A Yorkshire Dialogue'? If the poem was his, why does he not acknowledge authorship in the 1683 edition and on the separate title-pages in the 1685 and 1697 editions? It is a problem which will remain unsolved until more evidence comes to light.

But who is 'G. M. Gent'? We do not know. Skeat says (*Nine Specimens of English Dialects*) that in a copy of the 1685 edition in the Bodleian, F. Douce, the Antiquary, has written, 'G. M. is Giles Morrington of Northallerton.' In *The History and Antiquities of Northallerton* (printed by S. Langdale, 1791) the 'Praise of Yorkshire Ale' is called 'the song of an old provincial and ever local Muse, Mr Giles Morrington of this place.' This is also stated by W. C. Newsam in *The Poets of Yorkshire*, 1845, and repeated by Ingledew in his *History of Northallerton*. But all that we know of this man (from Newsam) is 'that he was of Northallerton but whether a native of the town or only a resident there is uncertain.' No dates are given, and the only edition of the poem that Newsam knew is that of 1697.

Others (Gough and Oldys) have identified 'G. M. Gent' with George Meriton, Attorney (1634–1711). Of him we know that he inherited the family estate at Castle Leavington, that he studied law, became an attorney, and practised at Northallerton. He was the author of several law books, and from 1684 to 1711 lived in Ireland. He died in Dublin.

The problem requires fuller investigation than it would be appropriate to attempt here.

3. *The Yorkshire Horse-dealers*

Ingledew, writing in 1860, says:

This song obtained great popularity a few years ago from the admirable singing of Emery, and is still a favourite.

The descendants of Tommy Towers were resident at Clapham till within a very recent period, and used to take great pleasure in relating the adventure of their progenitor.

Ingledew, *Ballads and Songs of Yorkshire*, 1860.

4. *The Dead Pig*

Gordon Home, *The Evolution of an English Town*, p. 208.

5. *A Fragment: On the Witch Molly Cass*

Richard Blakeborough assigns this fragment to 'about the year 1810' and says it was written by one who wrote under the signature 'R. H.' These initials he identifies with William Hird's father (Blakeborough, *Yorkshire Wit, Character, Folk-lore, and Customs*, 1898).

6. *Willie' Waggin*

We have been unable to trace the author of this poem, which comes from the Robin Hood's Bay district.

7. *Johnny Clagclod*

This poem, written in 1800, is from the late Richard Blakeborough's MSS. collection, and is included by courtesy of Mr J. Fairfax Blakeborough. (See note to No. 12 for information in regard to bridal bands.)

8. *A Dree Neet*

From Richard Blakeborough's 'Old Songs of the Dales,' appended to *T'Hunt o' Yatton Brigg*, 2nd edition (1899), p. 37.

The reference to Whinny Moor and the Brigg o' Dread is to the belief that the soul after death must cross these two perilous places before it finds rest. (See note to No. 14 for further details of this belief.)

Gabriel ratchets or raches or hounds. This expression is found as early as 1483 in the *Catholicon Anglicum.*

Their leader Gabriel is condemned to follow his hounds at night, high in the upper air, till Doomsday, for the sin of having hunted on Sunday.

E. M. Wright, *Rustic Speech and Folk-lore*, 1913.

9. *The Gleaner's Lament*

The date of this poem is 1848. It is taken from the late Richard Blakeborough's MSS. collection by courtesy of Mr J. Fairfax Blakeborough.

10. *A Yorkshire Farmer's Lament*

The probable date of this poem is 1860, and it belongs to the Ampleforth area. It was published in Abraham Holroyd's *A Garland of Poetry by Yorkshire Authors*, 1873. Mr. J. Fairfax Blakeborough has another version with many more verses but we have not seen it.

11. *Drink to the Bridal Garter*

The race for the bride's garter was a common custom in former times in North Yorkshire. To gain it was considered a good augury of success in love for the winner.

Mistress Curtis was wed thys daye Juli 10th 1687. Ta her garter bande was founde stitched a golden piece. On her bande was worked in fine silk these words in two lines of smalle letters with other enchauntyng devices.

> Be thou as true ye lass round whose legge thoult bindens y garter, as I schalle always be to hym who bownde yt rouwn my legge. EC 1687.

But Mistress Bella Mathews who was wed 2 week later mayde a righte cunnynge device, for when she came to lift her skirt, the kneeling winner fownde her bande secure beyond removal, yt being helde faste about her legge by a smalle silver locke, an' hangyng therefrom was a smalle note whyche ye Bride groom begged of ye Winner to remove, the whyche he havyng done, and finding that he could not decipher it, he offered to do the same. . . . and these war the wordes he read, and whyche war alle sae cunnyngely worked on ye bande amang leaves and many flowers and pleasyng scrolls.

(The verses, with the title 'Touche not ye knee,' are unfortunately too free to permit inclusion here.)

At thys the winner axed for ye key, but ye bridegroom unlocked yt, lettinge the winner tayke yt off, thereby saveing great offence. Yt was quite emblematical, and a pretty sighte to witness, but yt wd onlie do for a bride to stand sae longe who was exceedingly well favoured in ye shape of her legges: but Mistress Bella knew the like could not be shewn for miles around. I have yt was a sighte to witness.

From the George Calvert–M. Stapylton manuscript book in possession of Mr J. Fairfax Blakeborough, by whose courtesy this is included.

Butler, *Hudibras*, 1700 edition, p. 71 (Canto II), refers to wedding-garters:

'Which all the Saints and some, since Martyrs,
Wore in their Hats like Wedding-Garters.'

12. *Nance and Tom*

From Richard Blakeborough's 'Old Songs of the Dales,' appended to his *T'Hunt o' Yatton Brigg*, 2nd edition, 1899, p. 44.

It was the custom in harvest time for those maidens whose wedded life was to commence at Martinmas (a favourite time for weddings) to weave for themselves, what was then known as a 'cletching band.' As it was considered a disgrace a hundred years ago to be childless, the prospective wife, about full moon, in secret betook herself to some field, and there plaited herself a garter made of oaten and wheaten straw, as many children as she desired, so many straws did she take, the sex being according to the kind of straw used, wheaten straw gave her boys, oaten girls. The band was plaited and bound about the leg on a Friday night. Whilst doing this a certain charm was recited. This is now forgotten. The garter had to be worn until Monday morning. If it remained in situ all well, but if through any accident it broke away, the charm lost its power; like sad results followed if, whilst wearing it, her lover obtained a sight of it. Nance under the circumstances mentioned (in the Poem 'Nance and Tom') in the Song did not mind her 'cletching band' having been exposed, firstly because Tom was not present, secondly, it did not break away, and lastly because none but a pure maiden dare venture to plait and wear such a band. The charm working evil on every child born even in wedlock if the wearer had strayed from the path of virtue. Anyway it was a badge of virginity. The custom has been long discontinued, and is now remembered only by a few of the very old dames. My informant an old lady in her ninetieth year that was in 187– told me the custom was still alive in 1800, but was then decaying. Some of these bands were quite works of art.

From Richard Blakeborough's MSS. by courtesy of Mr J. Fairfax Blakeborough.

13. *T'Au'd Parson*

The date of this poem is 1807. It is contained in the George Calvert–M. Stapylton manuscript book in possession of Mr J. Fairfax Blakeborough, and it is by his courtesy that it is reproduced.

14. *Cleveland Lyke-wake Dirge*

The text of this version follows, with two slight omissions, that of the earliest known one—the one found in John Aubrey's *Remains of Gentilisme and Judaisme*, 1686–7. (Reprinted in *The Publications of the Folk-lore Society*, vol. 4, 1881.)

The two omissions are: (1) the adjectives 'silly, poor' which precede the word 'sawle' in l. 8, and (2) the phrase 'no brader than a thread' which takes the place of the usual second line in stanza 6. We have retained the word 'milke' in stanza 7, though this may be an error for 'meat.' More recent versions are those of Sir Walter Scott in his *Border Minstrelsy*, and Richard Blakeborough in his *Wit, Character, Folk-lore, and Customs of the North Riding*, which is based on the notes of J. C. Atkinson in his *Glossary of the Cleveland Dialect*. For Scott's version and Blakeborough's version, see Appendix 2.

There are three folk-lore or mythological elements in the poem:

(*a*) The singing of the dirge at a wake for the dead.
(*b*) The passage of the thorny land, Whinny-moor, by the giving of alms, when alive.
(*c*) The passage of the Brig o' Dread.

(*a*) With reference to the lyke-wake, Aubrey says:

At the funerals in Yorkshire to this day (1686) they continue the custom of watching and sitting up all night till the body is interred. In the interim some kneel down and pray by the corpse, some play at cards, some drink and take tobacco. They have also mimical plays and sports: for example they chose a simple young fellow to be a judge, then the suppliants, having first blacked their hands by rubbing them under the bottom of the pot, beseech his Lordship and smut all his face.

Richard Blakeborough records an instance of this dirge's being sung over a corpse about the year 1800 (op. cit., p. 123). Mr H. V. Morton describes his experiences at a wake in Ireland in the twenties of this century (*In Search of Ireland*, 1930, p. 214).

(*b*) The myth of the passage of the thorny land is thus expressed by Aubrey:

The belief in Yorkshire was, among the vulgar (perhaps is in part still), that after the person's death, the soul went over Whinny-moor, and till about 1616–1624 at the funeral, a woman came, like a praefica, and sang the following song.

This myth is very ancient, and has Jewish and Mohammedan cognates. Why is it here related of Yorkshire, and where is Whinny-moor? There seem to be no convincing answers to these two questions.

The anonymous author of *Walks through Leeds*, or *The Strangers Companion* (John Heaton, 1835) says that the battle in A.D. 655 in which Penda, King of Mercia, was utterly defeated by Oswiu (in what Professor Stenton describes as one of the decisive battles of Anglo-Saxon history) gave rise to this superstition. This battle, in which there was great slaughter, was fought somewhere in the country round Leeds, by an unknown stream called Winwaed (Stenton, *Anglo-Saxon England*, 1943, p. 84), and its location is identified by this anonymous author with the Whinny-moor of the dirge. He offers no evidence in support of his conjecture, and we give it for what it is worth. William Wheater argues ingeniously for the location of Winmoor (or Whinny-moor), the site of this battle, 'somewhere north of the Leeds and Selby turnpike road, between Whitkirk and Garforth' (*Old Yorkshire*, 1881, p. 71).

The superstition about the giving of alms to ensure a passage over Whinny-moor is still prevalent. Richard Blakeborough writes of it thus:

Old people will tell you that after death the soul passes over Whinny-moor, a place full of whins and brambles; and according as the soul when a tenant of the body administered to the wants of others, so would its passage over the dreaded moor be made easy. It seems, according to the old belief, every one ought to give at least one pair of new shoes to some poor person, and as often as means would allow, feed and clothe the needy. Whether these rules were faithfully carried out or not, the soul on approaching Whinny-moor would be met by an old man carrying a huge bundle of boots; and if among these could be found a pair which the bare-footed soul had given away during life, the old man gave them to the soul to protect its feet whilst crossing the thorny moor.

Yorkshire Wit, Character, Folk-lore, and Customs, 2nd edition, 1911.

(*c*) The Brig o' Dread represents the last and most difficult part of the soul's journey. It is so narrow and treacherous that only the good can cross it in safety. In one mythology it is finer than a hair and sharper than the edge of a sword. In another it is the scene of fighting between the gods and the unclean spirits for possession of each soul as it arrives.

All these elements are of ancient origin, and may be paralleled in the mythologies of other countries. For further details see Aubrey (op. cit.) and J. C. Atkinson (op. cit.).

Fire and Fleet: fire and house-room. The basic meaning of 'fleet' is 'floor,' but it often signifies 'the inner part of a house' or 'house-room.' (See E.D.D. under 'Flet.')

15. *The Wensleydale Lad*

There are several versions of this song and varying titles, including *Old Harry's a Rare Strong Chap, A Country Lad's Visit to Leeds, Fifty Years Ago, Leeds Owd Church*, etc. The date of composition is unknown, but the reference to King George probably places it in the early nineteenth century.

The earliest printed version we know of appeared in the *Cornhill Magazine* (1864).

The last line of this poem is an echo of the last line of David Garrick's Prologue to Dr Browne's Tragedy, *Barbarossa*, Edinburgh, 1774: 'But pack up all, and whistle whoame again.'

Leeds Fairs. There are two fairs held annually at Leeds; one on the 10th and 11th of July, and the other on the 8th and 9th of November. On the last of these days young persons of both sexes attend to hire as servants. There is likewise a fortnight fair for cattle and sheep, held in the Vicar's Croft Market; also, a quarterly fair for leather, held in the South Market, which is expected to become one of the first in the kingdom.

E. Hargrove, *History of Knaresborough*, 1828, p. 173.

16. *Ballad on the Goodmanham Mule*

Taken from *Country Ballads*, Pateley Bridge, 1869.

When John Fowler, huckster, of the village of Goodmanham (near Market Weighton) having bought a mule or mute at Beverley

Fair, brought it home, the inhabitants of the village expressed the following opinions upon its merits and demerits, which were at once done into rhyme by the poet laureate of the same village.

Op. cit.

Unfortunately the name of the 'poet laureate' is not disclosed.

17. *Come a-Hunting*

This extract is from a lively poem in the collection of the late Richard Blakeborough and is included by courtesy of Mr J. Fairfax Blakeborough.

In a note, the poem is attributed either to the Sinnington or the Bilsdale Hunt, two of the oldest packs in England.

George Villiers, Duke of Buckingham, was one of the first patrons of the Bilsdale Hunt, which, according to Mr J. Fairfax Blakeborough, the well-known hunting authority (*Great Ayton, Stokesley and District Past and Present*, with a chapter on Bilsdale and its Hunt, 1901), is the oldest pack in England.

In the Duke of Buckingham's day the Bilsdale Hunt had the country now held by the Sinnington and Farndale Hunts, and the fox and stag were hunted alternately.

The Bilsdale were the first and last trencher-fed pack.

The late Sir Alfred E. Pease, a great lover of and authority upon both hunting and dialect, in his *The Cleveland Hounds as a Trencher-Fed Pack* (Longmans, Green & Co., 1887) writes:

> Where the hounds that formed the Roxby (Staithes) pack came from I have endeavoured but failed to discover, but in all probability they were originally harriers, hunting hare and pursuing a fox when occasion arose, and afterwards crossed and improved by admixture with the fox-hounds that George Villiers, Duke of Buckingham, who died at Kirby Moorside, 1686, brought into banishment with him, and hunted in the neighbourhood of Helmsley. From these hounds the Bilsdale Hounds derive their origin and probably the Farndale.

The Bilsdale is 'the only pack that claims an earlier origin' than the Sinnington (Gordon Home, *The Evolution of an English Town*, p. 228).

18. *A Rustic's Courtship*

This fragment hails from the Knaresborough district, and is taken from *Yorkshire Anthology*, J. Horsfall Turner, 1901.

19. *Ilkla Moor*

There does not appear to be an authentic text of this popular ballad. Its origin is unknown. Its popularity is of recent growth, and the nineteenth-century writers on Ilkley and the nineteenth-century writers of Yorkshire dialect make, as far as we can discover, no reference to it. The tune to which it is usually sung, 'Cranbrook,' was written by Thomas Clark, and published in 1805. We do not know when the ballad and the tune were first associated, but it appears to have been in recent years.

The version here printed is the one best known to Yorkshire-folk. In the *Official Guide to Ilkley and Ben Rhydding* (1947) there is another version, which we give in Appendix I.

20. *Gan Yam, Gan Yam, Ma Bonnie Lass*

From William Andrew's *North Country Poets*, 1889, where it appears under the title 'Advice.'

24. *Noo wilta gan wi' me*

From *Dialect Poems and Prose by Thomas Blackah*, edited with a short biography by H. J. L. Bruff, n.d. (1937).

25. *Pateley Reeaces*

This lively poem was published as 'Anonymous' by Moorman. It is the work of Thomas Blackah. It appeared in *T'Nidderdale Olminac*, which Blackah wrote and published under the pseudonym of 'Natty Nidds.' Compare with part of Mark Lonsdale's *Th' Upshot: Oor mak o' Talk*, Carlisle, 1946. (For Lakeland Dialect Society.)

26. *Nowt bud Luv could be*

Richard Blakeborough is best known as a dialect poet for his two great dramatic poems, *T'Hunt o' Yatton Brigg* and *Auld Nan o' Sexhow*, both of great imaginative power; and as the historian of the North Riding by his *Yorkshire Wit, Character, Folk-lore, and Customs*. He wrote only a few lyrics. The high lyrical quality of this one makes us regret that he did not write more. Mr J. Fairfax Blakeborough included his father's long narrative poems in *The Hand of Glory* (Grant Richards, Ltd., 1924), with the dialect modified.

29. *Awd Daisy*

The Rev. Thomas Browne was one of the pioneers among early Yorkshire dialect poets. His dialect poems, written about 1790–95 (he was only twenty-eight when he died), were very popular, and were many times reprinted in chap-books and cheap popular editions of dialect works in the first half of the nineteenth-century. Often they were published without their author's name. 'Awd Daisy,' for example, appears in Richard Blakeborough's *Yorkshire Wit, Character, Folk-lore, and Customs*, as anonymous.

34. *Elphi, T'Devil, an' T'Witch*

John Blades, ironmonger of Kirby Moorside telles me he well minds hearing of a despert ferce fight which on a time did happen between ye devil and an old witch over their dues over anenst Yaud Wath, and whilst they did so fight, one, by stealth, did slip himself over, and in that wise did for ever break their spell.

He said one Takky Burton wrate the following lines about ye fight.

Takky Burton, such being his name, did live at Lastingham. He was a poet, and wrate some well putten-together lines. When he died I cannot find out, but he was living, but well on in years, about the year 1700. One Betty Ellis owned much matter both in writing, and by remembrance from hearsay of this same man, for truly he was the wonder of his time in those parts where he lived, and among those who knew him he was likewise a wise marvel.

George Calvert–M. Stapylton manuscript book, in the possession of Mr J. Fairfax Blakeborough.

George Calvert refers to Mistress Betty Ellis of Appleton-le-Moors as 'knowing many things concerning the dales wherein she hath lived always,' and states the poem was taken down from her 'saying of it.'

According to Edward Baines' *History, Directory, and Gazetteer of the County of York* (Leeds Mercury Office, 1823) there was at that time a John Blades in business as an ironmonger in the Market Place at Kirby Moorside.

35. *Sheffield Cutler's Song*

The Cutler's Song seems to be a sort of caricature on certain characters, who were manufacturers of flatbacks, and were passionately fond of plays and dancing: hence originated 'penny hops.' A large room was engaged in some public-house, and youths of both sexes admitted to dance for paying perhaps a penny each, or some small trifle.

Preface to Abel Bywater, *The Sheffield Dialect*, 3rd edition, 1877.

38. *Awd Isaac*

This poem, the first part of which was published by J. Metcalfe at Northallerton in May 1832 under the title *Specimens of the Bilsdale Dialect or Two Poems on Isaac Telltruth and Sammy Standfast*, with an introduction by John Nelson, had a remarkable popularity in the North Riding in the second half of the last century. It is a long poem, depicting the zeal of the old evangelical preachers for the conversion of sinners. There are people to-day in the area who know many stanzas by heart. The poem is too long for insertion in full. We select four typical stanzas.

47. *T'Pleeaf Stots*

The 'Plough Stots' (or Bullocks) is the name of a performance, partly song, partly acting, and partly sword-dancing, which has been practised in the Yorkshire dales at certain villages (especially Goathland) for many centuries. The first performance was usually given on Plough Monday, the first Monday after Epiphany. The company gave the first performance in its own village, and then toured the near-by villages.

In the Goathland Plough Stots the characters were the king and queen, who led the company, sets of 'Toms' or collectors, sword-dancers in sets of six, the fiddler and a clown, the Plough bullocks dragging their plough and dressed in smocks, and lastly an Old Man and Old Woman known as Isaac and Betty.

For an interesting description of the costumes and the figures of the sword dances, see F. W. Dowson, 'Folk-lore of the Plough Stots' in *Transactions of the Yorkshire Dialect Society*, vol. 5, pt. 37, 1936.

50. *The Pannierman's Song*

The Pannierman's Causey was an old, roughly-paved roadway across the moors in the direction of Staithes from Castleton, by which goods were formerly conveyed on the backs of horses and mules.

62. *Reeth Bartle Fair*

'Bartle' is a contraction of St Bartholomew. This Fair at Reeth was held on St Bartholomew's day (24 August).

63. *Bite Bigger*

This is perhaps the best known of John Hartley's poems. It was the first poem he wrote:

> Some time in his early twenties John Hartley became a member of the Beacon Club, a kind of literary institute that held its meetings in the 'Corporation Arms,' Halifax. Here, one night, as his contribution to the evening's entertainment, he wrote and recited 'Bite Bigger.' As a first poem it is an amazing achievement. Directly inspired by Edwin Waugh's 'Come Whoam to thi Childer an' me,' it has all the sincere simplicity and the dramatic sense that is found in the best of Waugh. It was enthusiastically received, was published as a broadside, and sold by the hundred at one penny a copy.
>
> W. J. Halliday, 'John Hartley' in *Transactions of the Yorkshire Dialect Society*, vol. 6, pt. 40, 1939.

68. *Ould Malley's Voluntine*

This poem appeared in *The Country Words of the West Riding*, 1870.

70. *Darby an' Joan an' their daughter Nell*

This was written between 1800 and 1815, and published at Bedale.

75. *Thoughts for a Sermon*

This is from Richard Blakeborough's MS. collection. It was composed in 1840. According to a note by Mr J. Fairfax Blakeborough in Sir Alfred Pease's *Dictionary of the Dialect of the North Riding of Yorkshire*, p. 156, A. K. lived at Bedale.

76. *Elphi Bandy Legs*

This poem is taken from the G. Calvert–M. Stapylton manuscript book by courtesy of Mr J. Fairfax Blakeborough.

Bettin Agar: this is the Calvert version. In the versions of the poem printed in Gordon Home's *Evolution of an English Town*, in *The Hand of Glory*, edited by Mr J. Fairfax Blakeborough, and in F. W. Moorman's *Anthology*, this is given as 'Be it mug or glass.' Bettin Agar is a personal name (perhaps the landlady's). Agar is a common North Yorkshire name.

According to Gordon Home (op. cit.) the poem was written in an old cook-book, and signed 'J. L. 1699.' This makes it one of the earliest Yorkshire dialect lyrics which we possess.

78. *Nivver Despair*

We are pleased to include Teesdale dialect verse from the Yorkshire side of the Tees.

81. *The Sweeper and Thieves*

This poem appeared in *The Landscape and Other Poems* by David Lewis, York, 1815. It was written earlier, as it first appeared in a chap-book of 1808 (*Specimens of Yorkshire Dialect*, J. Kendrew, York). It was printed in this chap-book without the author's name. The poetic merits of the piece are not high, but it is interesting as perhaps the earliest specimen of Yorkshire dialect verse written by a peasant.

86. *A Dalesman's Litany*

It is impossible to take note of this poem and the next without gratefully acknowledging the debt that all Yorkshire dialect lovers owe to their author, the late Professor Moorman. Not only was he a leading spirit in the Yorkshire Dialect Society for a dozen years, he led the way also in a revival of dialect composition in verse, drama, and story by his own original work in these three fields. His *Plays of the Ridings*, *Tales of the Ridings*, and *Songs of the Ridings* were a remarkable literary achievement for one who was not a Yorkshireman, and his *Anthology of Yorkshire Dialect Poems*, first published in 1916, passed through three editions in three years, and gained a popularity that has never diminished. His untimely death in 1919 was a grievous loss to Yorkshire dialect studies.

87. *A Wharfedale Lullaby*

The shepherd-lord is Henry Lord Clifford (1455?–1523), who, when his father was attainted and his estates forfeited in 1461, was brought up as a shepherd. He was restored to his estates at Barden and to his titles on the accession of Henry VII.

Whitaker, in *The History and Antiquities of the Deanery of Craven* (3rd edition, p. 324), writes:

Henry Lord Clifford on the accession of Henry VII emerged from the fells of Cumberland where he had been principally concealed for 25 years with the manners and education of a shepherd.

He returned to Barden to live there 'with a small train of servants.' Whilst a shepherd he had studied astronomy and 'other visionary pursuits.' Whitaker hints that, on his return to Barden, he also practised other esoteric arts, and it is on this belief that Moorman appears to base his second stanza.

But Clifford fought bravely at Flodden, and died in 1523, 'aged about 70.' Whitaker tries to 'appropriate to him a tomb, vault, and chantry in the Church of Bolton,' as he would be sorry to believe that he was buried at a distance from the place he loved so well.

Many readers will remember the references to this shepherd-lord in Wordsworth's 'Brougham Castle' and 'The White Doe of Rylstone.' It is in the former that there is the well-known verse (referring to the shepherd-lord).

> Love had he found in huts where poor men lie,
> His daily teachers had been woods and rills,
> The silence that is in the starry sky,
> The sleep that is among the lonely hills.

Wordsworth hints at the shepherd-lord's commerce with alchemy and fairies and magic arts, in both poems.

93. *Little Piecer*

A pathetic and grim reminder of the days of child labour.

97. *I niver can call her my Wife*

Ben Preston, who shares with John Hartley the highest place among West Riding dialect poets for range and poetic power, is represented here by three poems typical of his lyric gifts, his sympathy with the poor, and his hatred of the tyranny of the purse-proud employer of his day who oppressed the workers. These three poems were published in *The Dialect Poems of Benjamin Preston*, Saltaire, 1872. 'I niver can call her my Wife' appeared originally under the title 'T'Poor Weyver.'

123. *Owd Betty's Advice*

William Wright published his dialect writings under the pseudonym of Bill o' th' Hoylus End.

NOTES ON LOCAL RHYMES

127. *A West Riding Grace before Meat*

J. Cuming Walters, *The Spell of Yorkshire.* Methuen, 1931.

128. *A West Riding Grace after Meat*

C. J. F. Atkinson, *Recollections from a Yorkshire Dale.* Heath Cranton Ltd., 1934.

129. *A Yorkshireman's Coat of Arms*

Francis Grose, *A Provincial Glossary with a Collection of Local Proverbs and Popular Superstitions*, 2nd edition 1790.

Another version:

A magpie behold, and a fly and a flea,
And a Yorkshireman's qualifications you'll see;
To backbite and spunge and to chatter amain,
Or anything else, sir, by which he can gain.
The horse shows they buy a few tho' many they steal,
Unhang'd they're worth nought, does the gammon reveal;
But let censure stand by, and not bias the mind,
For others as bad as the Yorkshire you'll find.

A Yorkshire Mans Coat of Arms. London: published by O. Hodgson, Maiden Lane, Cheapside, n.d.

Cockney fling at the natives of the North Countrie, and with Cocknies all Northerns are either Scots or Yorkshiremen. The Cockneydom explanation is . . . (as text). . . .

The Chronicler of this cutting begs leave to say that, although he is not a native of Broad Yorkshire, should the Londoners ever see proper to alter or make any addition to the heraldic bearings of Yorkshire, they must not omit to give a Fighting Cock as the Yorkshireman's Crest. For a Yorkshire Game Cock of the true breed will turn his tail upon none of his species; and as for a Yorkshire Tyke (i.e., a Yorkshire) I feel that he would not only face three Cockneys, but would give them all, one after another what he would in his awn country phraze, call a 'reet good benzilling.' ARCHOEUS.

Specimens of the Yorkshire Dialect, Richmond.

130. *A West Riding Toast*

Richard Blakeborough (*Yorkshire Toasts, Proverbs, Similes, and Sayings*, Dennis, 1907), gives a North Riding version:

Here's tiv us, tiv all on us
Maay wa nivver want nowt
    Neean on uz.

and George Hardwick (*Stories in Dialect*) gives an East Riding version:

Here's tiv us,
All on us,
All on us ivver:
May neean on us want nowt,
Neean on us nivver.

Another toast often heard fifty years ago:

Here's ti ye an' ti me,
An' ti mah wife's husband,
Nut fergittin' missen.

The sentiment is not exclusively Yorkshire. In the Author's Preface to *Don Quixote* one reads 'God give you health, not forgetting me,' and there is, of course, the Scots:

Here's tae us,
Wha's like us?
    Damn few,
An' they're a' deid

131. *Two West Riding Commandments*

Compare:

Hear all, say nowt,
Sup all, pay nowt,
And if ivver thou does owt for nowt,
Do it for thissen.

Arthur Gaunt, *Pennine Ways from Skipton*. The Saint Catherine Press, Ltd.

132. *Cop hod an' stick*

This is similar to Camden's 'Hold fast when you have it' (*Remains*, p. 324).

133. *A Yorkshire Bite*

According to S. Baring Gould (*Yorkshire Oddities*, vol. 1, p. 212), King George III described the famous Jemmy Hirst as 'A Yorkshire Bite.'

For an amusing account of Jemmy's visit to London see *The Life and Adventures of that most eccentric character James Hirst, of Rawcliffe.* Knottingley, n.d.

It is always used to convey a feeling of mistrust or fear of coming in contact with one more adept in cunning than one's self. It is true Yorkshiremen are keen dealers; this, however, is no detraction —on the contrary, it is evidence of industrious habits. The hospitality for which they are famous gave rise to the term 'Yorkshire Bite.' It is said that the fatted calf and flowing bowl greet the stranger at every step, and after the common salutation, the question 'Will you bite?' or 'Will you sup?' is sure to follow, and from this originated a term, used as a sarcasm, but which, in point of fact, derived as it is, ought to be used as a compliment. This is the opinion of the compiler of *The Etymological Compendium* issued more than half a century ago.

William Andrews, *Picturesque Yorkshire.*

Don't thee think to put Yorkshire o' me, I warn't born in a frost.

William Carr, *The Dialect of Craven*, vol. 1, p. 166, 2nd edition, 1828.

And as for the villain thou hast served him right,
Thou hast put upon him a clean Yorkshire bite.

'The Crafty Plough Boy,' *The Ballads and Songs of Yorkshire.* Ingledew, 1860.

. . . and think'nt put Yorkshar o' fok?

Tim Bobbin's Toy-Shop open'd. Manchester, 1763, p. vi.

Yoast naw put Yorkshar o' me.

Ibid., p. 35.

Bite: a sharper, generally applied disparagingly to Yorkshiremen.

Prevost, *Cumberland Glossary.*

134. *A Yorkshire Tike*

Grose, *A Provincial Glossary*, p. 95.

The earliest reference to 'Yorkshire Tike' given in the *N.E.D.* is 1700; it occurs in *B.E. Dict. Cant. Crew*, where 'Yorkshire tike' is explained as 'a Yorkshire manner of man.'

The saying was used in a song by Henry Carey, the author of 'Sally in our Alley' (words and music), in his ballad opera *The Wonder*; or *An Honest Yorkshireman*, which was performed for one night (11 July 1735) at Lincoln Inn Fields, and afterwards for many nights at the Haymarket and Goodman's Fields. The first edition was printed for Edward Cooke, 1736, and the second, under the title *The Honest Yorkshireman*, was printed for L. Gilliver and J. Clarke, 1736. The song was not printed in dialect in any of the editions of the opera.

As far as we know, this dialect version first appeared in Ingledew's *Ballads and Songs*, and the transcription into Yorkshire dialect may indeed be his work.

The Honest Yorkshireman

Ah is i' truth a country youth,
  Neean used teea Lunnon fashions;
Yet vartue guides, an' still presides,
  Ower all mah steps an' passions.
Neea coortly leear, bud all sincere,
  Neea bribe shall ivver blinnd me;
If thoo can like a Yorkshire tike,
  A rooague thoo'll nivver finnd me.

Thof envy's tongue, seea slimly hung,
  Wad lee aboot oor coonty,
Neea men o' t'eearth booast greter worth,
  Or mair extend ther boonty.
Oor northern breeze wi' us agrees,
  An' does for wark weel fit us;
I' public cares, an' luve affairs,
  Wi' honour we acquit us.

Seea gret a maund is ne'er confahnd,
  Tiv onny shire or nation;
They geean meeast praise wheea weel displays
  A leearned iddication.
Whahl rancour rolls i' lahtle souls,
  By shalla' views discarnin',
They're nobbut wise at awls prize
  Good manners, sense, an' leearnin'.

135. *A Yorkshire Way-bit*

That is, an overplus not accounted in the reckoning which sometimes proves as much as all the rest. Ask a countryman how many miles it is to such a town, and he will return commonly so many miles and a way-bit. Which way-bit is enough to make the weary traveller surfeit of the length thereof. But it is not way-bit, though generally so pronounced, but wee-bit, a pure Yorkshirism, which is a small bit in the Northern language.

Ray, *English Proverbs*, 1817 edition, p. 178.

'A Yorkshire Dialogue' (1697) has 'a mile and a wea bit.' Compare the Scottish saying 'a mile and a bittock.'

Bittock: a small bit or piece. When a wayfarer on the road asks of a chance passer-by at what distance is the place to which he is bound, the probable reply is, that it is two, three, or any other number of miles 'and a *bittock*,' signifying that the respondent will not pledge himself to the exactitude of his reply, adding, with the proverbial cautiousness popularly ascribed in England to his countrymen, that there may be a *bittock* added to his computation; though the qualifying *bittock* has often been found to exceed the primary estimate.

Charles Mackay, *A Dictionary of Lowland Scotch.* Whittaker and Co., 1888.

136. *I'se Yorkshire too*

In *Phrase and Fable* Dr Brewer says, in explanation of above, 'I am as deep as you are, and I am not to be bamboozled.'

William Andrews, *Picturesque Yorkshire.*

A song with the title 'I'ze be Yorkshire too,' which was one of several evidently written for stage Yorkshiremen, appeared in *The Northern Minstrel or Tyne Songster*, Gateshead (1806) and has often been reprinted.

I'ze be Yorkshire too

By t'side of a brig, stands over a brook,
  I was sent by times to school;
I went wi' the stream as I studied ma book,[1]
  And was thought to be no small fool.
I never yet bought a pig in a poke;
  For to give Old Nick his due,
Tho' oft I've dealt wi' Yorkshire folk,
  Yet I was Yorkshire too.

I was pratty weel liked by each country maid,
  At races, wake, or fair;
For my father had addled a vast in trade,
  And I were his son to a hair.[2]

[1] 'hook,' Halliwell, *The Yorkshire Anthology*, 1851.
[2] 'And I were his son and heir' (Moorman, *Yorkshire Dialect Poems, 1673–1915*).

And seeing that I didn't want for brass,
Poor girls came first to woo;
But tho' I delight in a Yorkshire lass,
Yet I were Yorkshire too.

To London, by father, I was sent,
Genteeler manners to see;
But fashion's so dear, I came back as I went,
And so they got nothing by me.
My kind relations wou'd soon ha' found out,
What was best wi' my money to do;
Says I, my dear cousins, I thank you for nought,
But I'm not to be cozen'd by you.
For I'm Yorkshire, &c.

Another song of this type often printed is:

When at Hame wi' Dad

When at hame wi' dad,
We niver had nae fun sir,
Which meeade me sae mad,
I swore away I'd run sir;
I packed up cleease sae smart,
Ribbed stocking, weeastcoats pratty,
Wi' money and leet heart,
Tripped off te Lunnun city.
Fal de ral de ra.

When I did git there,
I geeap'd aboot quite silly,
At all the shows te stare,
In a spot called Piccadilly;
Lord sic charming seets,
Bods i' cages thrive sir,
Coaches, fiddles, feights,
An' crocodiles alive sir,
Fal de ral, &c.

Then did I ga te see,
The gentry in Hyde Park sir,
When a lass pushed reeadely by,
Te whoam I did remark sir,
'Tho' your feeace be e'en sae fair,
I've seen a beear mair civil'
Then the lile bit cleease they weear,
God Lunnun is the devil.
Fal de ral, &c.

Te t'play-hoos then I gaas,
Whar I seed merry feeaces,
And in the lower rows,
Were sarvents keeping pleeaces;
T'players I saw seun,
They managed things quite funny,
By gock! they'd t'Hunny-meean,
Afore they'd matrimony.
Fal de ral, &c.

Now having seen all I could,
And passed away my time sir,
If you think fit and good,
I'll een give up my rhyme sir;
And sud my ditty please,
The poppies in this garden,
Ti me 't wad be heart's-ease,
If not I ax yer pardon.

Anon.

These songs may have been sung at Vauxhall, which was in its prime 1750–90. There was a vogue for Yorkshire songs, and many were written by people without any real knowledge of the dialect. Ingledew was criticized for including so many of this character in his *Ballads and Songs of Yorkshire*.

Vauxhall Gardens were laid out in 1661 and closed 1859. They are mentioned in a song 'In Praise of Yarm' in *The Yorkshire Garland*, York, 1788.

Referring to this type of song, Forshaw in *Holroyd's Collection of Yorkshire Ballads*, p. 221, writes, in reference to a ballad 'Jack's Alive; or the Amphibious Yorkshireman':

Songs like the above were very popular during the wars with the French, in the latter part of the last century and the beginning of the present. They appear to have been composed to be sung in the minor or lower-class theatres. There is not much that is elevated in them, but they were no doubt suited to the popular taste of the time. One is surprised to find so many of these ditties relating how Yorkshiremen went up to London; and how they were 'fleeced' or robbed, and endured strange mishaps during their stay in the city; and suggesting the idea that this kind of song was the composition of some Cockney.

137. *Measter's Yorkshire too*

A Yorkshire hostler, who had lived a considerable time at an inn in London, being asked by a guest how it happened, that he, who was so clever a fellow, and a Yorkshireman into the bargain, remained so long without becoming master of that house, he laconically answered, *Measter's Yorkshire too.* A saying used by persons, on discovering the design of any one to impose on them, implying they are a match for them.

Grose, *A Provincial Glossary.*

138. *A Proverb against Yorkshiremen*

Although this proverb does not appear in any edition of Ray we have seen, Bohn includes it amongst Ray's in *A Hand-Book of Proverbs* (1855).

Yorkshire has long been celebrated for its horses. Fitzherbert, who wrote two hundred and fifty years ago, mentions his going to Rippon fair to buy colts.

Marshall, *Rural Economy of Yorkshire*, vol. 2, p. 160.

According to Warton (*History of English Poetry*, p. 187):

The Archdeacon of Richmond, on his visitation comes to Bridlington . . . in 1216 with 97 horses, 21 dogs and 3 hawks.

Yorkshire was pre-eminently the county for horse-races.

J. L. and Barbara Hammond, *The Town Labourer*, 1920, p. 5

Now it is well known that a Yorkshireman, like a dragoon, is nothing without a horse.

R. S. Surtees, *Jorrock's Jaunts and Jollities.*

According to *A New Dictionary of the Terms Ancient and Modern of the Canting Crew*, Yorkshire was known as Whipshire, and a Whipster was 'a sharp or subtil fellow.'

A saying directed against the propensity of the Yorkshire folks for stealing horses. The two Ridings have always been celebrated for horse-breeding and horse-stealing: the horses from the Cleveland country always make a prominent figure at the C'Leger (St. Leger) at Doncaster. A man once related, that he had put a horse into a meadow over night, where the grass was quite short, and in the morning, nothing was to be seen of him but his head. Ah, said some one else, if that had been in Yorkshire, you would have seen nothing at all of him.

W. Carew Hazlitt, *English Proverbs and Proverbial Phrases*, 1869.

139. *Give a Yorkshireman an halter*

W. Carew Hazlitt, *English Proverbs and Proverbial Phrases*, 1869.

140. *To take the Darnton Trod*

Brockett gives this (*A Glossary of North Country Words*, 1846) as a Yorkshire saying of those fleeing into the Bishoprick to escape justice, but *The Bishoprick Garland* has it:

To take the Darnton Trod—which is the road South, is said figuratively of anyone who wishes to elude pursuit.

Darnton: Darlington.

'Bishoprick . . .' of Durham, by which name the county (of Durham) is sometimes now, as formerly, called by way of eminence, though at the present day it is more frequently used in common conversation by those who are resident on the Yorkshire side of the Tees; as 'he lives ow'r i' Bishobrig.'

F. T. Dinsdale, *A Glossary of Provincial Words used in Teesdale*, 1849.

141. *Looks as vild as . . .*

N. and Q., vol. 7, p. 234.

142. *I eet like a Yorkshar-mon*

Tim Bobbin's Toy-Shop open'd, Manchester, 1763, p. 33.

143. *Beggars' Litany*

On the fifth of September (1639) I hired a guide, and rode to Halifax 16 miles, the ways were so rocky, stony, boggy and mountainous, that it was a days journey to ride so short a way. At HALIFAX I saw the fatal ENGINE, wherewith they do behead pilfering thieves, which Sir Francis Wortley told me was set upon this occasion following.

This town of HALIFAX hath (for time out of mind) liv'd and subsisted by the rich and laudable trade of clothing, and often times their clothes were stolen from the tenterhooks (or tenters) whereupon the King (then reigning) upon their humble suit had privilege granted to the town for ever: That if a thief were taken either of these three ways, which is, HAND-NAPPING, BACK-BEARING, or TONGUE-LETTING, that is either ABOUT TO STEAL, or CARRYING IT AWAY, or CONFESSING, that then the party offending (after trial by a jury of townsmen) if the goods, be it cloth, cattle, or whatsoever is valuable, is judg'd to have their heads struck off with the said Engine, without any assize or sessions. Now the Engine is two high pieces of timber, an ell or yard asunder, fixed and closed on the top, with a cross piece like a gallows; in the inner sides of the two standing pieces are two gutters, and on the top (or cross piece) is a pulley through which they do put a small line or rope, and fastening it to another heavier piece of wood of 100 weight (in which they do fix the sharp-edge tool) then they do pull or hoist up the said weight, and the stolen goods is brought to the place of execution with the malefactor; now the one end of the rope is made fast to a pin or stake, which being cut, the Engine falls so ponderously and speedily, that it severs the head from the body in a moment, but there is no man will or must cut the line, but the owner of the stolen goods, which if he do, he hath all again: if he will not cut it, then he must lose all, and it is employed to some charitable uses; by which means the thief escapes; and this is HALIFAX law.

JOHN TAYLOR, THE WATER POET PART OF THIS SUMMERS TRAVELS Or News From Hell, Hull, and Halifax, from York, Linne, Leicester, Chester, Coventry, Lichfield, Nottingham, and the Divells Ars a Peake.

Imprinted by J. O., n.d.

From WORKS OF JOHN TAYLOR, THE WATER POET, EDITED by Charles Hindley, Esq. London: Reeves and Turner, 196, Strand, W.C. 1876.

Ray gives 'From Hell, Hull, and Halifax . . . deliver us,' and adds, quoting Fuller:

This is a part of the beggers and vagrants litany. Of these three frightful things unto them, it is to be feared, that they least fear the first, conceiting it the farthest from them. Hull is terrible to them as a town of good government, where beggers meet with punitive charity, and it is to be feared are oftener corrected than amended. Halifax is formidable for the law thereof, whereby thieves taken . . . in the very act of stealing cloth, are instantly beheaded with an engine, without any further legal proceedings.

The English Dialect Dictionary, vol. 3, p. 272, gives:

'From Hull, Hell and Halifax, good Lord deliver us,' with the note: 'At Hull vagrants found begging in the streets were whipped and set in the stocks; and at Halifax persons taken in the act of stealing cloth were instantly, and without any process, beheaded with an engine called a maiden.

John Evelyn (*The Diary and Correspondence of John Evelyn*, Routledge & Sons, Ltd, n.d.), writing at Rome, 6 May 1645, says:

At executions I saw one, a gentleman, hanged in his cloak and hat for murder. They struck the malefactor with a club that first stunned him, and then cut his throat. At Naples they use a frame, like ours at Halifax (p. 123).

It may interest you to know that the weird skirling of bagpipes used regularly to be heard at the execution of criminals at Halifax.

J. Sutcliffe Smith, *The Music of the Yorkshire Dales*, Leeds, 1930, p. 51.

Compare:

From Lying at the Mercy of Fire, Water, and a wicked Woman, Good Lord deliver us (Greek).

L'Estrange, *Life of Æsop*, p. 7.

And

From the cold comfort of a fine coach with springs, and a dull husband with none, Good Lord deliver me.

Colley Cibber, *Love Makes a Man*, Act iii. London, 1776.

From the sea, the Spaniard, and the Devil, the Lord deliver me (Dutch).

Howell, *Familiar Letters*, 7th edition, 1705, p. 8.

And

From filthy sluts and from all joayles good Lord deliver us all.

The Roxburghe Ballads, An excellent new Medley. Reeves and Turner, 1873, vol. 1, p. 81.

144. *A Litany from the North Riding*

This was heard at Catterick and reported in *Notes and Queries*, May 4th, 1850.

From *Choice Notes from 'Notes and Queries': Folk-lore.* London, 1859, p. 130. Compare:

From all ghoulies and ghosteses,
From all long-leggedy beasteses,
From things that go wump in the night,
Good Lord, deliver us. (Norfolk.)

A. R. Wright, *English Folk-lore*, p. 59.

145. *Yorkshire Families*

N. and Q., vol. 7, p. 234.

146. *Teesdale Rhyme*

Henry Heavisides, *The Annals of Stockton-on-Tees.* Stockton, 1865.

147. *Cleveland Rhyme*

This saying is included in Gibson's additions to Camden's 'Britannia' (1695) as a 'proverb' (Morris, North Riding). *A Yorkshire Dialogue* (1697) gives:

Cleaveland in the clay,
Bring tway shun,
Carry yane away.

Ray (p. 179) writes:

'Cleveland is that part of Yorkshire which borders upon the bishoprick of Durham, where the ways in winter time are very foul and deep,' and Grose adds, 'but nothing to what those of Kent and Sussex were formerly, for if one had brought forty soles thither, he would not have carried half a one away.'

A Provincial Glossary.

148, 149. *Swaledale Rhymes*

Ella Pontefract and Marie Hartley, *Yorkshire Tour.* J. M. Dent & Sons, Ltd.

150, 151. *Cotterdale and Grisedale Rhymes*

Ella Pontefract and Marie Hartley, *Wensleydale.* J. M. Dent & Sons, Ltd.

John Routh (*Guide to Wensleydale*, 2nd edition, p. 75) writes:

It is a hackneyed phrase in Wensleydale, when any person puts in a frequent appearance, to say he's like Grisedale pies, sure to come again. Grisedale is a small valley at the head of Wensleydale (in the W.R. Wapentake of Ewcross 6 miles E. of Sedbergh) and the saying is based upon a legend to the following effect: a potato pie was once made in Grisedale, and, being forgotten, was not brought out for half a year, when the potatoes are said to have taken root, and grown out at the top of the crust. The pie was frequently afterwards placed upon the table, but nobody seemed fond of it, hence the origin of the saying 'Sure to come again like Grisedale pies.'

A. W. M. Close (in a cuttings book in Darlington Public Library) has a different version:

Said of people who are always turning up to ask some favour. Garsdale housewives had the reputation of making their pastry of such rich ingredients that visitors to the Dale who were accustomed to plainer fare at home, were apt upon partaking too heartily of it to suffer from after effects commonly known as 'a rising of the lights.'

Free livers are astounded by the rising of the lights . . .

Thomas Hood, 'Bartholomew Fair,' *The New Comic Annual* p. 282.

Compare 'They'll come again, as Goodyear's pig,' (i.e. never) (Ray, 125).

It is amusing, in this connection, to recall that Grisedale means 'pigs' valley.'

Jervaux Abbey may be said to mark the place where Yoredale ends and Wensleydale begins.

Tom Bradley, *The Ure*. The Yorkshire Post, 1891.

Wensleydale is generally considered to end a little below Jervaux, at a place called Kilgram Bridge, where the valley has by degrees opened out into a wide open tract of country.

Guide to Wensleydale, its Picturesque Scenery, and its Objects of Antiquity, by a Native Admirer. John Routh, 2nd edition, Hawes, 1879.

About a myle benethe Gervalx Abbey is a great old Bridge of stone on Ure, caullyd Kilgram Bridge.

John Leland, quoted John Fisher, *History of Masham*, p. 21.

152. *Nidderdale*

William Grainge, *Nidderdale*. Pateley Bridge, 1863.

The saying was frequently used about Hampsthwaite and Birstwith fifty years ago.

153. *Wharfedale and Airedale*

Old Yorkshire, edited William Smith, 1881.

154. *Craven*

W. S. Banks, *Walks in Yorkshire*.

155. *Don Valley*

E. &. M. A. Radford, *Encyclopaedia of Superstitions*. Rider, 1947.

156. *Don Valley*

'Dun,' the name of the principal river of Hallamshire, never Don, though in modern times universally so written. Dun has, however, kept its place in the common talk, rhyming with son, as indeed it does in an old saw 'The shelving, etc.' This is, however, a rhyme better known lower on the stream than while it is pursuing its course through the regions to which this book relates; nor is, I think, the river here infamous for accidents of the kind alluded to.

Hunter MS., quoted by S. O. Addy in *A Glossary of Words used in the neighbourhood of Sheffield* (E.D.S.), p. 67.

157. *Hallamshire*

S. O. Addy, *Sheffield Glossary*, p. 92. Bohn, p. 558. Ray, p. 179.

'God's Croft,' the name of a farmhouse lying half-way between Frodsham and Helsby, and supposed to be the place indicated by the prophet Nixon when he was asked where a man should find safety on the Judgment Day.

Holland's Cheshire Glossary, quoted by Addy, p. 92.

Compare:

When all England is aloft
Well are they that are in Christ's Croft;
And where should Christ's Croft be,
But between Ribble and Mersey?

Mr Higson's MSS. Coll. for Droylsden etc., quoted by W. Carew Hazlitt, *English Proverbs and Proverbial Phrases*, 1869.

Between Calder and Aire
Shall be great warfare,
When all the world is aloft
It shall be called Christ's Croft.

(Mother Shipton.)

158. *A Rhyme on the West Riding Towns*

A. R. Wright, *English Folklore*. Benn's Sixpenny Library, No. 33, p. 78.

Bradford a little but a strong town.

Margaret Newcastle, *Life of the Duke*. Everyman edition, p. 44.

Mr Brown and Mr Fisher, with whom I had a good deal of conversation concerning the state of Leeds and its neighbourhood, informed me that the sufferings of the poor in Leeds itself were much less than in the surrounding district, yet they spoke of Leeds itself as exhibiting a face of great wretchedness.

W. Wilberforce, 17 March, 1801, *English Letters of the Nineteenth Century*, edited James Aitken. Pelican Books.

I reckon nowt to Scarborough. T'air tastes o' nowt, an' smells o' nowt: gie me Leeds!

A Leeds woman reported by the Mayor of Scarborough in *Northern Echo*, 1 April, 1948.

159. *Birstall for Ringers, etc.*

Folk-lore Record, 1878, vol. 1, p. 174.

161. *Ainderby Steeple*

A. W. M. Close, *Old Time Quips and Quirks*, MS. book. Darlington Public Library.

163. *Argam*

Folk-lore Society Publication, XLV, 1899.

Charles Cotton, *The Wonders of the Peake*, 3rd ed., records a similar belief in Derbyshire.

164. *Barningham*

A. W. M. Close, 'Let us now praise Famous Men.' Thomas Grainger Coates, schoolmaster, 1827–54. At Barningham the sexton was formerly paid a yearly sum for whipping cats out of the churchyard. (For a reference to dog-whipping see Canon Atkinson's *Cleveland Glossary*, p. 145.)

165. *Barton St. Mary's*

C. P. Nicholson, *In and Around Darlington*. Barton formerly had two churches.

166. *Bawtry*

He was a saddler at Bawtry (Yorkshire) and occasioned this saying, often applied among the lower people to a man who quits his friends too early, and will not stay to finish his bottle. The case was this: There was formerly and indeed it has not long been suppressed, an ale-house, to this day called The Gallows House, situate between the city of York and their Tyburne, at which house the cart used always to stop, and there the convict and the other parties were refreshed with liquors; but the rash and precipitate saddler, under sentence, and on his road to the fatal tree, refused this little regale, and hasten'd on to the place of execution where, very soon after he was turn'd off, a reprieve arrived, insomuch that had he stopped, as was usual, at the Gallows House, the time consumed there would have been the means of saving his life.

Pegges Curialia, 1818, 340–1.

Ray has a corrupt version of this, which quite loses sight of the original story. 'He was hanged that left his drink behind him,' and he appends a note, which shows that he had not met with the story.

W. Carew Hazlitt, *English Proverbs and Proverbial Phrases*, 1869.

The Man was hang'd that left his Liquor behind him.

Swift, *Dialogue II Works.* 4th edition, 1751. Vol. 9, p. 230.

167. *Bedale*

Edmund Bogg, *Richmondshire*, p. 483, and Close, *Old Time Quips and Quirks.*

168. *Bellasize*

A popular saying relative to a foolish exchange of estates in the 15th century.

Holderness Glossary, p. 84.

Bellasize: E.R. a township in the parish of Howden, wapentake of Howdenshire, 1½ miles E. from Howden; inhabitants, 49.

Stephen Reynolds Clarke, *The New Yorkshire Gazetteer.* 1828.

Anthony Belasyse, the original grantee of the site and (Newburgh) priory lands at the Dissolution was the son of Thomas Belasyse of Henknoll county Durham. This family was seated at Bellasis, in the same county, soon after the Conquest, and, at an early period John de Bellasis exchanged that estate with the prior of Durham for Henknoll, a bargain which he afterwards repented if we may believe the following couplet:

Bellysis, Bellysis, daft was thy sowell
When exchanged Bellysis for Henknowell.

Bulmers *History and Directory of North Yorkshire.*

We are not clear which Bellasis was exchanged, the Yorkshire or the Durham one.

'We can only account,' says Mr Halliwell (*Popular Rhymes of England*, 1849, pp. 200–1), 'for the proverb by supposing that, at a former period, Bellasyse had been exchanged for lands, but not the manor of Henknoll.' See his remarks and account of the tradition on which the saying is alleged to be founded (W. Carew Hazlitt, *English Proverbs and Proverbial Phrases*, 1869), in which the following version is given:

Johnny tuth' Bellas daft was thy poll,
When thou changed Bellas for Henknoll.

169. *Beverley*

J. G. Miall, *Yorkshire Illustrations of English History*, London, 1865 and J. R. Witty, 'The Rhyming Charter of Beverley.' *Transactions of the Yorkshire Dialect Society*, pt. XXII, vol. iv.

The *Holderness Glossary* (p. 92) gives 'Als fre mak I thee, As hert may think or egh may see' as being the 'Commencement of Athelstan's charter to the town of Beverley: an early translation from the original.' The lines given are nos. 74 and 75 of the Charter as given by Witty.

169(a). *Beverley*

Quoted in *The Slang Dictionary*, Hotten. London, 3rd edition, 1864, p. 258. From a song popular at Fairs in the East Riding. The song appears in full in *A Glossary of Words used in Holderness* (E.D.S., 1877, p. 19).

170. *Boroughbridge*

Ray, p. 29. The saying was common at Boroughbridge fifty years ago, when Barnaby Fair still retained some of its old glory (Barnaby Fair: 17 June and the following days).

'Barnaby-day, Barnaby bright or long Barnaby, St. Barnabas' Day, the 11th June, in Old Style, reckoned the longest day' (N.E.D.).

> This day the sunne is in his chiefest hight,
> With Barnaby the bright.
>
> Spenser, *Epithalamion*, l. 265.

171. *Boroughbridge*

J. G. Miall, *Yorkshire Illustrations of English History*. The lines have reference to the Devil's Arrows.

173. *Bowes*

Ella Pontefract and Marie Hartley (*Swaledale*. J. M. Dent & Sons, Ltd) have another version:

> When Julius Caesar was a king
> Bowes Castle and Hurst and Arkendale mines was a famous thing.

174. *Boynton*

Turkeys were first brought to England by William Strickland of Boynton on ye Wolds, as it was anciently called, on his return from America, where he had gone with Jean Cabot.

Strickland, *Queens of England*, vol. II, pp. 513–14, 1854 ed., quoted by Frances Elizabeth Cottrill Dormer, *Flamborough Village and Headland*. Hull, 1894.

Compare

Hops, Reformation, Turkeys, carps and Beer,
Came all into England in one year.

Ja. Chetham, *The Angler's Vade Mecum*, p. 127. 3rd edition. London, 1700.

And the Suffolk proverb:

Hops, reformation, baize, and beer,
Came into England all in a year?

Supplement to Vocabulary of East Anglia, E.D.S. 1879.

175. *Brayton*

A Yorkshire Dialogue (1697).

Ray included with 'Hambleton' spelling and note:

It is spoken of a covetous and insatiable person, whom nothing will content. Brayton and Hambleton and Burton are places between Cawood and Pontefract. Brayton bargh is a small hill in a plain country covered with wood. Bargh in the Northern dialect, is properly a horse-way up a steep hill, though here it may be taken for the hill itself.

176. *Castleford*

Old Yorkshire, edited by William Smith, 1881.

177. *Cleasby*

Publications of the Folk-lore Society, XLV, 1899.

Tom-trot: a sticky sweetmeat of half-baked treacle, called tom-trot was a local speciality, and was more particularly prepared by Jenny Dunn and Nancy Walker. The children on the anniversary of Gunpowder Plot invested immensely in that article and sang in the streets:

Gunpowder Plot will never be forgot,
So long as Jenny Dunn sells good Tom Trott,

an admonition which would doubtless secure the attention of the makers.

'Northallerton Fifty Years Ago,' Smithson's *Northallerton Almanack*, 1889.

Stallions proud with ribbands prancing
Joyous fiddling and dancing.
Isaac Horsfield who was there,
He made sport for all the fair.
A handsome show of china ware
Of much variety was there.
Cheese-cakes plenty might be got,
Ginger-bread and good tom-trot.

1847, Askrigg Moor Fair Rhyme, quoted by Ella Pontefract and Marie Hartley in *Wensleydale*. J. M. Dent & Sons, Ltd.

'Tom-trot' is given by Brockett, so it was clearly common to a wide area. There was evidently no bad tom-trot. It is curious that both the Northallerton and Askrigg rhymes should refer to 'good' tom-trot.

178. *Cotherstone*

Morris in *North Riding*, Constance Cotterell in *Holidays in North East England*, and Close each give this. The latter states:

The hopple was a short chain with a strap at each end to fasten round the forelegs of a horse or donkey to prevent him wandering off when turned out to graze.

See also East Layton rhyme, No. 184.

Compare:

To clap on shoes on grasshoppers.

Rabelais, *Works*. London: Gibbings & Company, 1903. Vol. 1, p. 192.

Hazlitt gives another saying: 'Cotherston cheese will cover a multitude of sins.'

179. *Croft*

W. H. D. Longstaffe, *The History and Antiquities of the Parish of Darlington in the Bishoprick*. Darlington & Stockton Times, 1854, p. 21.

There is also a saying in County Durham 'Out o' Bisho'brig into Yorkshire'—i.e., out of the frying-pan into the fire, or, as they say in Upper Wensleydale, 'Oot o' bed inta t'beck.'

Croft Bridge dates from the Edward III period. It collapsed in a flood in 1356, and was probably restored or rebuilt about 1400 (H. D. Pritchell, *The Bridges of the County of Durham*).

Blackwell Bridge was commenced in 1832. There was a ford previously at Stapleton, as there is still at Cleasby and at Neasham, from where Wordsworth got his cousin, Mary Hutchinson, whom he later married at Brompton near Scarborough (by licence, 4 October 1802). De Quincey (*Recollections of the Lakes and the Lake Poets*. Edinburgh: Adam and Charles Black, 1862, p. 187) is rather vague about this.

It was at Alfoxton that Miss Mary Hutchinson visited her cousins the Wordsworths; and there, or previously, in the north of England, at Stockton-upon-Tees and Darlington, that the attachment began between Miss Mary Hutchinson and Wordsworth, which terminated in their marriage about the beginning of the present century. The marriage took place in the north; somewhere, I believe, in Yorkshire; and, immediately after the ceremony, Wordsworth brought his bride to Grasmere.

Lewis Carroll spent much of his boyhood at Croft, where his father was vicar. Amongst Carroll's earliest poetical work was an amusing mock fifteenth-century ballad in the old Northumbrian dialect, 'Ye Fatalle Cheyse.' (*The Lewis Carroll Picture Book*. London, 1899).

Byron spent part of his honeymoon at Hulnaby in the Parish of Croft.

180. *Cropton*

According to Morris (*The North Riding*):

This curious bit of folk-lore occurs with variations in places as widely severed as Lanarkshire (Tinto Hill) and Surrey (Highdown Ball).

181. *Dalton-on-Tees*

This has been attributed to Dalton near Thirsk, but it seems more likely to refer to Dalton-on-Tees which is nearer Cowton, and nearer Cleveland from whose rhyme this has evidently been taken.

182. *Doncaster*

Daggers

Dunmow bacon and Doncaster daggers,
Monmouth caps and Lemster* wooll.

J. Ray, *A Collection of English Proverbs*, 1670, p. 258.

* i.e., Leominster.

183. *Cuts*

Doncaster Cuts, i.e., horses. They were held in small estimation.

In fayth, I set not by the worlds two Dauncester cuttys.

Skelton, *Magnyfycence*, circa 1520; W. Carew Hazlitt, *English Proverbs and Proverbial Phrases*, 1869.

SIR TOBY. An thou hast her not i'the end, call me cut.

Twelfth Night, II, iii.

184. *East Layton*

During the early part of the last century an East Layton labourer whose donkey had been confined in the village pinfold (it had been found straying), defended himself before the village constable in this fashion.

A. W. M. Close, *Richmond Almanack*, 1890; Longstaffe, *Richmondshire, its Ancient Lords and Edifices*.

185. *East Witton*

Speight, *Romantic Richmondshire*, p. 322; Morris, *North Riding*, states:

There are two famous wells in the vicinity—Diana's and Cast-a-Way Wells.

Ella Pontefract (*Wensleydale*, p. 231) writes:

Slaverin' Sal, the local name for the Cast-a-Way or Diana's Well, is on the higher slopes of Witton Fell . . . pins and other articles used to be thrown into the well for luck . . . Hammer Wood, near by, is famous for its nuts.

Walter White (*Month in Yorkshire*, 3rd edition, 1859, p. 201) refers to Witton Fell, 'and its spring, still known as Diana's Bath.'

On the summit is a grotto, and a spring named 'Cast-a-Well,' much frequented by pleasure-seekers.

Edmund Bogg, *From Eden Vale to the Plains of York*, p. 266.

There is a grotto near the well which was built by the Marquis of Aylesbury in 1821. Diana's Well at one time supplied drinking water through a pipe in the mouth of a carved stone head nicknamed 'Slavering Sal.'

Ripon Gazette and Observer, 29 January 1948.

186. *Eccleshill*

Bradford in the Time of John Wesley (W. Scruton, in *Old Yorkshire*, 2nd Series, 1885, p. 285).

187. *Gayle (near Hawes)*

The cry 'Hy fer t'Gayle an' b . . . t'Haas!' was heard nightly forty years ago from the Gayle lads leaving the clubs. In earlier days the reply of the Hawes lads was 'Ya can shout, but ya can't buy nowt i' Gayle!'

188. *Gilling (near Richmond)*

Longstaffe, *Richmondshire, its Ancient Lords and Edifices,* and Spencer's *Richmond Almanack,* 1890.

190. *Gormire*

Smithson's *Northallerton Almanack,* 1886, gives another version:

> When Gormire Riggs shall be covered with hay,
> The White Mare of Whitestone Cliff shall bear it away.

191. *Great Ayton*

Publications of the Folk-lore Society, XLV, 1899.

Joseph Reed (b. Stockton, 1722–87) made the name of Canny Yatton familiar to thousands by his inclusion of the dialect-speaking character Margery Moorpoot, in his play *The Register Office,* which was performed at the Theatre Royal, Drury Lane, in 1761.

A scene from this play, 'Margery and Gulwell,' was printed in the many *Specimens of Yorkshire Dialect* published in the early years of the nineteenth century.

Captain James Cook (1728–80), although born at Marton in Cleveland, spent much of his boyhood with his parents at Great Ayton, in a cottage which was removed to Fitzroy Gardens, Melbourne, Australia some years ago. He later served as an apprentice at Staithes, and went to sea from Whitby.

> When a boy he was sometimes taken from school, to labour in the fields under his father, at Airyholme; and even then he would hold the multiplication table in one hand, and work with the other.

Correctness of computation, mathematical precision, and persevering undaunted resolution, prevailed through life.

Croft Spaw, Yorkshire: A Brief address with digressions, 3rd edition, North Shields. Printed by Mr Appleby, 1882.

See also Walter Besant, *Captain Cook*. Macmillan and Co., 1890.

192. *Halifax*

Taylor, the Water Poet (1630). (See 143 note).

193. *Halifax*

F. H. Marsden, 'The Folk-Lore of Calderdale,' *Transactions of the Yorkshire Dialect Society*, vol. 4, pt. 22.

Ella Pontefract and Marie Hartley, *Yorkshire Tour*. J. M. Dent & Sons, Ltd.

The first two lines refer to the introduction in the eighteenth century of brick for building instead of the local stone. The second two lines were added by a Halifax wit in retaliation. (Marsden)

Halifax is a mongrel, begot by a Leeds merchant and a Lancashire woman, nurs'd by a Dutch frow.

Tim Bobbin: vide *Craven Glossary*, vol. 1, p. 167.

194. *Halifax*

R. V. Taylor, *Yorkshire Anecdotes*, 1883, p. 229.

Sterne's Halifax connection is often overlooked. In *Memoirs of the Life and Family of the Late Rev. Laurence Sterne*, written by Himself, we read:

In this year (one thousand seven hundred and twenty one) I learnt to write, etc. . . . The autumn of that year, or the spring afterwards (I forget which) my father got leave of his colonel to fix me at school—which he did near Halifax, with an able master; with whom I stayed some time, till, by God's care of me, my cousin Sterne, of Elvington, became a father to me, and sent me to the University, etc., etc.

The Complete Works of Laurence Sterne, Nimmo, 1897, p. 4.

A branch of Sterne's family lived near Halifax, at Wood Hall, and a mill on the Calder is still called Sterne's Mill.

J. A. Erskine Stuart, *The Literary Shrines of Yorkshire*, 1892, p. 42.

195. *Halifax*

Mr. Higson's MSS. Coll. for Droylsden, etc. W. Carew Hazlitt, *English Proverbs and Proverbial Phrases*, 1869.

196. *Harrogate*

A Mother Shipton prophecy from *Yorkshire Dialect Poems (1673–1915)*, F. W. Moorman, 1919.

The Oxford Dictionary of English Proverbs gives another Harrogate rhyme:

Said the Devil when flying o'er Harrogate Wells,
I think I am getting near home by the smells.

197. *Hartforth*

It is said the devil was once much vexed with the Hartforth people, who were perhaps too good for him; finding a stone of enormous bulk and weight, to the South of Gilling, his majesty in his rage, raised the ponderous mass in one hand and uttered the extraordinary couplet.

Longstaffe, *Richmondshire, its Ancient Lords and Edifices.*

198. *Hatfield*

N. and Q., vol. 7, p. 234.

Hatfield W.R. a parish and township in the wapentake of Strafforth and Tickhill, 7 miles NE from Doncaster. . . . In this place William of Hatfield, second son of Edward III, was born. The extensive level of Hatfield Chase contains 180,000 acres, half of which were formerly covered with water; it was sold by Charles I. to Cornelius Vermuiden, a naturalized Dutchman, to drain and cultivate, which, to the general surprise, he at length effected, at an expense of £400,000, but the project involved him in tedious and ruinous law suits. In the centre of the Chase stands a farm-house, called Lindholm, surrounded by an almost impassable morass; on the site was anciently a hermitage, inhabited by William of Lindholme, a personage partaking of the contradictory natures of a hermit and a giant, and concerning whom strange traditionary stories are yet extant in the neighbourhood: his remains were discovered in 1747. Edwin, the first christian king of Northumberland, was slain here in a great battle, by Penda, the turbulent king of Mercia.

Stephen Reynolds Clarke, *The New Yorkshire Gazetteer or Topographical Dictionary*, 1828.

199. *Hinderwell*

This is the scathing comment of the inhabitants of a fishing village (Staithes) upon those of an agricultural one. The two villages are in the same parish and there was formerly much rivalry between them.

200. *Hornsea*

Hornsea is now a fashionable watering-place, but in the steeple of the old church which was blown down in 1714 were these lines. *The Court Guide and County Blue Book of the North and East Ridings of Yorkshire*. Charles William Deacon & Co., 1901.

201. *Howden*

Publications of the Folk-lore Society, XLV, 1899.

Bishop Skirlaw was Bishop of Durham (1388–1406).

202. *Hull*

I.e., you are drunk. Hull is famous for strong ale.

Ray.

There at mine Inne, each night I took mine ease,
And there I got a cantle of Hull cheese.

Taylor, *The Water Poet*, 1662.

Dodsley, *A Collection of Poems in Six Volumes by Several Hands*, 1758, vol. 5, p. 293, includes a poem under the title 'Hull Ale' by Mr W. Taylor, the first six lines of which read:

Long time did a silly old proverb prevail,
That meat, drink, and cloth were all found in good ale;
'Till a lover of truth went on purpose to Hull,
And to try an experiment drank his skin full.
He began to see visions, his head it turn'd round,
'Till off from his keffal he fell on the ground.

Similar metaphorical expressions are:

Newcastle cloak—an empty barrel put over a drunkard's shoulders. (Brockett, vol. 2, p. 53.)
White Chappel portion—two torn Smocks and what Nature gave.
Cambridge-Fortune—a woman without any substance.
Dover-Court—all speakers and no hearers.

A New Dictionary of the Terms Ancient and Modern of the Canting Crew in its Several Tribes of Gypsies, Beggers, Thieves, Cheats, etc. (1700).

203. *Hull*

This is rather a prophecy than a proverb. Dighton is a small town not a mile distant from Hull, and was in the time of the late wars for the most part pull'd down. Let Hull make the best they can of it.

Ray, p. 178.

204. *Hull*

The allusion is to the fortifications of that town which were formerly much renowned in these parts.

English Dialect Dictionary.

Let it suffice that it is absolutely accounted the strongest and most defensible town in the kingdom of England, and for good government inferior to none. I might speak somewhat of their good fellowship; but my book would swell big with it.

John Taylor, The Water Poet, *Part of this Summer's Travels.*

205. *Hunmanby*

The Gaunts or Gants sometimes Earls of Lincoln, held Hundmanby in Yorkshire and their name is still kept up among the populace.

Longstaffe, *History and Antiquities of the Parish of Darlington*, p. 60.

206. *Hutton Rudby*

Ord, *History of Cleveland.* Vide Folk-lore Society, pub. XLV, 1899.

207. *Kelk*

Marie Hartley and Joan Ingilby, *Yorkshire Illustrated*, May 1948.

This couplet about a small village near Driffield merely states a fact in that it has no church and has only one side to the village street.

208. *Kirkby*

Marie Hartley and Joan Ingilby, *Yorkshire Illustrated*, May 1948.

209. *Kirkby Malzeard*

This means that the corn shoots into ear at Barnaby Fair time (21 June) and is cut at the Feast of St Wilfrid, in the early days of August. This saying was heard at Ripon, spoken by a young Kirkby Malzeard man. It is current locally.

210. *Knaresborough*

This Robert was a Knaresborough saint, and the old women there can still tell you the legend of the cow.

Ray, p. 151.

Unfortunately we have not been able to find out what the legend was.

Robert Flower, the hermit of Knaresborough, usually called St Robert (though he has not been canonized), was the son of Took Flower, who was twice Mayor of York. He was born towards the close of the twelfth century, and became a monk of the Cistercian Order at York. After some years he removed to Knaresborough, where he resided at a hermitage among the rocks. From hence he removed to Spofforth, but returned to Knaresborough, where he led a hermit's life and ended his days. His reputed sanctity led many persons to visit him, among whom was King John. The cell in which he passed his days still remains, and is known as St. Robert's Cave. It is romantically situated among the rocks overhanging the Nidd, and will be familiar to the readers of Bulwer's romance called 'Eugene Aram' . . . .

History and Topography of the City of York and the North Riding of Yorkshire. Beverley, 1857.

A metrical life of St Robert of Knaresborough from an early MS. was printed for the Roxburghe Club, 1824.

W. Carew Hazlitt, *English Proverbs and Proverbial Phrases*, 1869.

This seat of piety (Saint Robert's Cave) was, in the year 1745, profaned by the murder of Daniel Clark, of Knaresborough who, with Eugene Aram and John Houseman, had confederated to defraud several of their neighbours of plate and goods to a considerable amount.

History of Knaresborough, 1828.

Mother Shipton, Ursula Sonthiel (this being Mother Shipton's maiden name) was born in July, 1488, in the reign of Henry VII, near the Dropping Well, at Knaresborough, in the county of York, and was baptized by the Abbot of Beverley.

E. Hargrove, *History of Knaresborough*, 1828.

For list of early books on Mother Shipton, see *N. and Q.* vol. 5, p. 419 (May 1852 issue).

211. *Lartington*

A. W. M. Close.

Lartington produces no other Dickens' relic, save the clock of Master Humphreys of Barnard Castle, set-up in the little waiting-room of its railway-station.

Charles Eyre Pascoe, *Dickens in Yorkshire.* Sir Isaac Pitman Sons, Ltd, p. 75.

212. *Leeds*

Sol. Darrel, *The Chimney Nook original Almanac*, 1915.

213. *Market Weighton*

Old Yorkshire, edited by William Smith, 1881.

214. *Marrick*

Speight, *Romantic Richmondshire*, p. 208.

216. *Mitton*

Marie Hartley and Joan Ingilby, *Yorkshire Illustrated*, May 1948.

Hazlitt, *English Proverbs and Proverbial Phrases*, 1869, has it Milton and quotes from *MSS. Coll. for Droylsden, etc.*, by Mr Higson.

217. *Nafferton*

A very common saying in the East Riding forty years ago.

218. *Northallerton*

The boys who attended the National School were dubbed 'Charity Bull Dogs' whilst those who hailed from the British were called 'Tithe Barners,' and often in winter disciples in each met in snowball battles with varying success. At that time a favourite term of encouragement was 'Hit him! He's a Scot!' no doubt handed down from the days when Scot and Yorkshireman often met in more deadly conflict in the neighbourhood.

'Northallerton Fifty Years Ago,' *Smithson's Northallerton Almanack*, 1889.

The battle of the Standard which was fought in 1138 under the direction of the Archbishop of York, took place at Northallerton, a place, though locally situated in Yorkshire, was actually a parcel of the county of Durham; but no one questioned its relation to Durham after the battle.

Gaillard Thomas Lapley, *The County Palatine of Durham; A Study in Constitutional History.* Longmans, Green & Co., 1900.

Fra York thai passyt rycht in gud aray.
Northwest thai past in battail buskyt boun,
Thar lugeyng tuk besyd Northallyrtoun,
And cryit his pess, thar market for till stand,
Thai fourty dayis, for pepill off Ingland,
Quha that likyt ony wyttaill till sell.

Henry the Minstrel, *Wallace*, 1869. Buke Aucht, ll. 568–573.

Thai rassyt fyr, brynt wp Northallyrtoun,
Agayn throucht Yorkschyr bauldly maid thaim boun;
Dystroyed the land, als fer as euir thai rid;
Sewyn myle about thai brynt on athir sid.

ibid., ll. 727–730.

The holye prieste doth weepe as he syngs
Hys masses o'er and o'er;
And alle for the soules of them that were slayne,
At the battle of Cuton Moore.

On Monday, 22nd August, 1138, the standard was raised on Cowton Moor, three miles north of Northallerton, and after a severe contest the Scots were defeated and ten thousand of their number slain; the rest, with king David and prince Henry his son, retreated with difficulty to Carlisle.

Ingledew, *The Ballads and Songs of Yorkshire.*

219. *Nunkeeling*

Hunter's Hallamshire Glossary, 1829, quoted by W. Carew Hazlitt, *English Proverbs and Proverbial Phrases*, 1869.

221. *Paull*

Old Yorkshire, edited by William Smith. 1881.

222. *Pontefract*

Ray, p. 154.

I cannot learn the reason of this saying.

Grose.

223, 224. *Pendle, Ingleborough, and Penigent*

Ray states No. 224 is more common in the mouths of the vulgar.

Cross Fell, Mickle Fell, and Whernside are all higher than Ingleborough, the highest of the three mentioned in the two rhymes, and, of course, with respect to No. 224, Ingleborough is exceeded in height by many of the Lakeland hills.

226. *Raskelf*

Baring-Gould, *Yorkshire Oddities*, vol. I, p. 190.

According to Morris, *North Riding*, p. 296, 'The only example of a wooden tower in the Riding.'

227. *Raskelf*

Longstaffe, *History and Antiquities of the Parish of Darlington*, and Frank J. Nash, *The Road to the North*, 2nd edition, give this version.

Marie Hartley and Joan Ingilby, *Yorkshire Illustrated*, May 1948, have another:

Raskelf Town, Roguish people, Stone church, Drunken parson, Wood steeple.

Compare Ainderby (No. 161) and Romaldkirk (No. 233), 'steeple' rhymes, also:

Proud Preston, poor people,
High Church and low steeple.

N. and Q., vol. 6, p. 496.

And

Ugly church, ugly steeple,
Ugly parson, ugly people.

N. and Q., vol. 5, p. 375.

Besides of our own special favour we have granted and given license for ourselves and our heirs, as much as we can, to the aforesaid Ralph (Ralph de Neville, first Earl of Westmoreland) to enclose his wood of Raskelf, called Raskelfe Wode, near our Forest of Galtres, in the county aforesaid, and thereof to make a park, and three places to keep deer in, adjacent to the same park, the length of each of those places to keep deer in to be an hundred feet. *King Richard II*, 1388.

Spencer, *Richmond Almanack*, 1890.

The Forest of Galtres extended from York north to Alne and

Stillington. The first three scenes of the fourth act of *Shakespeare's Henry IV., Pt. II* are laid in the Forest of Galtres.

If any offers are made about the inclosure at Rascal, they must be inclosed to me.

Letters of the late Laurence Sterne, 1794, p. 72.

228. *Reeth*

This refers to the Richmond-Reeth brake in the days before motor cars (*Richmond Almanack*, 1903).

229. *Richmond*

Once upon a time a man with the prosaic name of Potter Thompson was led by a supernatural guide, whom no one has seen before or since, into the depths of this fabulous cell. The sword and the horn were placed, by the guide, in his hands, and he was told to draw the one, and sound the other. He proceeded to withdraw Excalibur from the sheath; but, as he did so, the dead began to rustle their armour, and to move, half awakened from their long sleep. This so terrified the man, that he allowed the sword to slip back into its place. Immediately a strong wind rushed through the vault, and swept him out of the place; but, as he was being driven before it, a bitter cry resounded in his ears:

'If thou hadst either drawn,' etc.

Rev. Thomas Parkinson, *Yorkshire Legends and Traditions*, Stock, 1889, vol. 2, p. 170.

F. W. Moorman, in his dialect play 'Potter Thompson' (*Plays of the Ridings*, Elkin Mathews, 1919), dramatises a somewhat different version of the legend. Potter Thompson finds King Arthur and his sleeping knights in a cavern beneath Richmond Castle, and receives from Arthur his horn, a pledge that peace will at last prevail. 'Daft Potter Thompson' is scorned by the townsfolk when he gives his message, but though we are led to believe that he suffers martyrdom, the play ends in triumph with the promise of universal peace.

230. *Ripon*

Miall's *Yorkshire Illustrations of English History*, p. 101, and Thomas and Katharine Macquoid's *About Yorkshire*, Chatto and Windus (1883), p. 219.

Dugdale, in his Monasticon, has transcribed from an ancient chartulary in the possession of one Lyndal, a charter, by which King Athelstan grants to the monastery of Ripon the privilege of sanctuary, which was to extend a mile on each side of the church. As it was considered the highest crime to take a person from sanctuary, it provides that those who infringe the boundaries shall be punished with loss of life. He also declares that

Na nan that langes me to
In yair Herp-sac sal have to do
And for ik will at yai be sade
I will at yai alkin fredome have:
And in all thinges be als free
As hert may thynke or eygn may see.

The boundaries of the sanctuary were marked by three crosses called Sharow Cross, Archangel Cross, and Athelstan Cross. Sharow Cross still remains, in the shape of a short pillar standing on a base, formed by several large stones. The stump of Archangel Cross stands in a lane leading to Littlethorpe, from the York road; and the Cross of Athelstan was probably situated in a field near Hutton Conyers which still bears the name of 'Athelstane Close.'

The Tourist's Guide being a Concise History and Description of Ripon, Ripon, 1838.

During the autumn of 1947 a notice which reads as under, was erected at Sharow Cross:

Sharow Cross

This cross which belongs to the National Trust, was set up in the Middle Ages to mark the limit of 'Sanctuary,' a privilege which fugitives enjoyed who came within a mile of St Wilfrid's Monastery.

In the thirteenth century there were eight of these crosses around Ripon, but only this one now remains.

The Public are asked to protect so interesting a Relic from damage or injury.

It may be noted that Sharow means 'boundary hill.'

There were also sanctuary rights at Beverley (see note 169) and at Sprotburgh. In regard to the latter the Rev. Scott F. Surtees, *Waifs and Strays of North-Humber History*, 1864, writes:

Beneath this canopy there was, until recently, the remains of stone ornamental work, as if for the support of a raised seat, and near by is a remarkable chair of stone in one piece, similar in height and shape to the 'Frith-stols' of Beverley and Hexham. It has sculptured on it what are evidently heathen idols, Thor, a massive animal denoting strength, with his belt, and Saturn, with his beard. If this was Paulinus' church at Campodono, restored by Wilfrid when he searched out the old places, and re-edified Hexham and Ripon this Minister, in like manner with that of Beverley, as well as others of the same date and age, would have with them the privilege of sanctuary, and as there you find the old Frithstols remaining through successive generations, so here would be the 'Frith-stow' *par eminence* where lay buried their great ancestor, the first settlement and home of those Ethelings from whom their successive kings and princes gloried to derive their race.

231. *Ripon*

The motto of the City of Ripon inscribed outside the Town Hall.

In the year 886, this town was incorporated as a royal borough, by Alfred the Great; and its chief magistrate was styled Vigilarius or Wakeman. He caused a horn to be blown every night, at nine o'clock, after which if any house or shop was robbed before sunrise, the sufferer received compensation for his loss from an annual tax of 4d levied on every inhabitant whose dwelling had but one, and of 8d where it had two outer doors, from which latter circumstance, a double degree of danger might be apprehended. The tax has long since fallen into disuse, but the custom of blowing the horn, continues to this day.

E. Hargrove, *History of Knaresborough*, 1828, p. 183.

The horn is still blown nightly at nine o'clock, once at each of the four corners of the market cross, and three times at the door of the mayor's residence.

It may be of interest to add a note here about the Bainbridge Forest Horn, which, according to the *Richmond Almanack* of 1899, was

blown every night at ten o'clock from Holy rood to Shrovetide. A bell also was rung at Chantry, and a gun fired at Camhouse.

A later note (*Richmond Almanack*, 1907) states:

The old Bainbridge Horn is now at Bolton Castle. The new one is 2½ feet long and bears the inscription 'Presented to the village of Bainbridge by Mr R. H. Harburn of Bishop Auckland, who brought it from South Africa January 11th 1864'.

At the time of writing difficulty is being experienced in finding a horn-blower at Bainbridge.

The horn-blower at Ripon still wears a three-cornered hat and eighteenth century uniform.

Compare:

If God ne kepe not the citee, in ydel wakith he that kepith hit.

Chaucer, *The Tale of Melibeus.*

And

Except the Lord build the house, they labour in vain that build it: except the Lord keep the city, the watchman waketh but in vain.

Psalm 127. 1.

232. *Ripon*

As true steel as Ripon spurs (Fuller's Proverbs).

This was a celebrated make of cock-spurs.

Harrison Weir, *Our Poultry*, vol. 2, p. 802.

It is said of trusty persons, men of metal, faithful in their employments. Rippon is a town famous for the best spurs in England, whose rowels may be enforced to strike through a shilling, and will break sooner than bow.

Ray, 1817 edition, p. 178.

Rippon is famous for its spurs, both those used for horsemanship, and those with which gamecocks are armed. The temper of the first is so good, that it is said they will strike through a shilling without breaking. This proverb is used to signify persons of inflexible honor and integrity.

Grose, *A Provincial Glossary*, p. 94.

Ben Jonson's play 'The Staple of News' (acted 1625, printed 1631) has a character a spurrier, and there is a reference to Ripon spurs in Act I, Sc. 3, l. 52.

Ben Jonson, *Works*, edited Herford and Simpson, vol. 6, 1938.

Spurrier — To my box, sir.
Penny-Boy Jr. — Your box? why, there's an angel; if my spurs
Be not right Rippon—
Spurrier — Give me never a penny
If I strike not thorow your bounty with the rowels.

and Davenant in his play 'Wits' says:

Whip me with wire beaded with rowels of
Sharp Rippon spurs.

Quoted *Guide to Ripon* Ward Lock & Co.

The Witts: A Comedie, presented at the Private House in Blacke Fryers. Richard Meighen, 1636 (1st edition), Sir William Davenant. Pickering & Chatto, Ltd., Cat. 338.

233. *Romaldkirk*

A. W. M. Close. There is no note of the saying in *A Guide to Cotherstone and Neighbourhood*, 1911.

234. *Roseberry Topping*

The History and Antiquities of Cleveland, the Rev. John Graves. Carlisle, 1808, p. 216.

Roseberry Topping, 1057 ft. Phillips, *The Rivers, Mountains, and Sea Coast of Yorkshire*, uses the spelling 'Rosebury.'

Another version of the rhyme is:

> When Roseberry Topping wears a cap,
> Cleveland may beware a clap.
>
> Andrews, *Picturesque History of Yorkshire*, p. 83.

These 'hat' and 'cap' rhymes are found all over England from the Cheviots to Devonshire, and there is at least another in Yorkshire, viz.:

> When Rawdon Billing puts on his cap,
> Calverley Mill will get a slap.
>
> Johnnie Gray, *Through Airedale from Goole to Malham*, 1891.

235. *Runswick Bay*

The fish caught by the Runswick men is sold by auction at Staithes. With their beautiful and sheltered bay, the Runswick fishermen can often get to sea when the Staithes men cannot.

236. *Saxton*

S. R. Clarke, *The New Yorkshire Gazetteer*, 1828; J. G. Miall, *Yorkshire Illustrations of English History*, 1865.

The Lord Dacre was slain in North Acre.

North Acre is, or was, the name of the spot where Lord Dacre perished at the battle of Towton in 1461. He is said to have been shot by a boy out of an elder tree.

Halliwell, quoted W. Carew Hazlitt, *English Proverbs and Proverbial Phrases*, 1869.

237. *A Scarborough Warning*

This terme Scarborow Warnynge grew some say
By hasty hangyng for rank robbery theare.
Who that was met, but suspect in that way,
Streight was thrust up, whatever he weare;
Whereupon theeves thynkynge good to forbeare
Scarborow robbyng they let alone
And take Scarborow warnynge everychone.

A Briefe Balet touching the traytorous Takyng of Scarborow Castle.

Imprinted at London in Fleete Street by Tho. Powell.

Sixteenth-century broadsheet, *Yorkshire Notes and Queries*, vol. 1.

Brewer, *Phrase and Fable* attributes this to John Heywood, 1497?–1580?

Skarborow warning, for a sodaine commandement, allowing no respect or delay to bethinke a man of his business.

George Puttenham, *The Arte of English Poesie*, 1589; Edward Arber, *English Reprints*, 1869, p. 199.

Scarborough Warning is mentioned in Scott's *Redgauntlet*.

A Scarborough Warning, that is none (at) all but a sudden surprise, when mischief is felt before it is suspected. This proverb is but an hundred and four years standing, taking its original from Thomas Stafford, who in the reign of Queen Mary, Anno 1557, with a small company seized on Scarborough Castle, (utterly destitute of provision for resistance) before the townsmen had the least notice of his approach. However, within six days, by industry of the earl of Westmorland, he was taken, brought to London, and beheaded.

Ray, edition of 1817, p. 178.

This statement is disproved by the occurrence of the saying in John Heywood's 'Proverbs' (1546). Heywood's words are:

A day ere I was wed, I bade you, (quoth I).
Scarborough warning I had, (quoth he) whereby
I kept me thence, to serve thee accordingly.

The Dialogue of the Effectual Proverbs in the English Language concerning Marriage, 1546.

Heywood repeats the saying in 'Epigrams upon Proverbs' (1562).

> I gave him Scarborough warning. Scarborough?
> That warning came short to bring good harborough.

An expression which, from the contiguity of Scarborough and Whitby, has, in the latter town, become localised. 'If you do that much longer, I will give you a Scarborough warning' that is, none at all, but a sudden surprise.'

F. K. Robinson, *Whitby Glossary*, 1855, p. 147.

Compare:

> First hang and draw
> Then hear the cause by Lydford Law.

Ray, p. 161.

> Jethart Justice, first hang a man and syne judge him.

Popular Rhymes of Scotland.

Scarcely relevant, perhaps, but we cannot resist:

> Lancashire law, no stakes, no draw.

A saying whereby a person who loses a wager endeavours to evade payment when the wager was merely verbal, and no stake deposited. William Carr, *The Dialect of Craven*, vol. 1, p. 274. (*The Oxford Dictionary of English Proverbs* has this 'Stopford law': Stockport, half in Lancashire and half in Cheshire).

238. *Scarborough*

William Andrews, *Picturesque Yorkshire*, p. 65.

239. *Selby*

Old Yorkshire, edited by William Smith, 1881.

240. *Semerwater*

This refers to the legend which tells how in Apostolic days a poor man was refused alms at every house in Raydale, where there was then a large city, except one small cottage, where he was given bread and milk and cheese and a pallet to lie on. When he departed, the old man spoke the lines above. Immediately an earthquake followed, and the waters of the present lake engulfed all the town except the cottage of the charitable people.

There are many poetical versions of the legend, including one by Sir William Watson, and one by John Routh, the author of the first guides to Wensleydale and Swaledale who was a Hawes man.

See Parkinson's *Legends and Traditions*, Second Series, Stock, 1889; Bogg's *Eden Vale to the Plains of York* and J. Horsfall Turner's *Yorkshire Anthology*, Bingley, 1901.

241. *Sheffield*

Ella Pontefract and Marie Hartley, *Yorkshire Tour*. J. M. Dent & Sons.
Compare 'Oxford knives, London wives.' Ray, edition of 1670, p. 257.

According to some, this saying conveyed a reflection on both, insinuating that their appearance exceeded their real worth; that the Oxford knives were better to look at than to cut with, and that the London wives had more beauty and good breeding than housewifely qualities.

Grose, *A Provincial Glossary*, 1811, p. 87.

Who goes to Westminster for a wife, Pauls for a man and to Smithfield for a horse, may meet with a whore, a knave, and a jade.

Ray, op. cit.

242. *Sheffield*

It hath been plow'd and sown these six or seven years.

Ray, 1817 edition, p. 179.

243. *Skipton*

Marie Hartley and Joan Ingilby, *Yorkshire Illustrated*, May 1948; *Old Yorkshire*, edited by William Smith, 1881, gives first three lines only.

245. *Sprotborough*

Sprotborough, three and a half miles S.W. of Doncaster. *Higson's MSS. Coll.*, No. 22; W. Carew Hazlitt, *English Proverbs and Proverbial Phrases*, 1869.

246, 247. *Staithes*

A. Stanley Umpleby, 'The Dialect of Staithes,' *Y.D.S. Transactions*, Part xxxvi, 1935.

248. *Stillington*

Publications of the Folk-lore Society, XLV, 1899.

Laurence Sterne was vicar of Stillington from 1742–3 to 1768, holding it during the whole of that period in conjunction with Sutton on the Forest, and for the last eight years with Coxwold (Morris, *North Riding*, p. 364).

Writing to his friend John Hall Stevenson of Skelton Castle on 13 November 1764, Sterne says:

'Tis a church militant week with me, full of marches and counter-marches and treaties about Stillington common, which we are going to inclose.

Letters, p. 121.

At this time Mr Sterne was possessed of some good livings, having enjoyed so early as the year 1745, the vicarage of Sutton in the Forest of Galtrees, where he usually performed divine service on Sunday mornings; and in the afternoon he preached at the rectory of Stillington, which he held as one of the Prebends of York, in which capacity he also assisted regularly, in his turn, at the cathedral. Thus he decently lived a becoming ornament of the Church, till his Rabelaisian spirit, which issued from the press, immersed him into the gaieties and frivolities of the world.

Eugenius (John Hall Stevenson), Preface to Yorick's *Sentimental Journey continued*, London, 1769.

In his autobiographical sketch Sterne wrote:

By my wife's means, I got the living of Stillington: a friend of hers in the south had promised her that, if she married a clergyman in Yorkshire, when the living became vacant, he would make her a compliment of it. I remained near twenty years at Sutton doing duty at both places. I had then very good health. Books, painting, fiddling, and shooting were my amusements. As to the Squire of the parish, I cannot say we were upon a very friendly footing, but at Stillington the family of C—— showed us every kindness.

Works of Sterne, Nimmo, 1897, p. 5.

Crayke until 1844 was a part of the County of Durham. Dean Inge was born there.

249. *Stokesley*

Publications of the Folk-lore Society, XLV, 1899.

250. *Strensall*

C. Clough Robinson, *Mid-Yorkshire Glossary*, E.D.S., 1876, p. 138.

251. *Sutton nr. Pontefract*

Clock Almanack, 1944, p. 34. There are many Suttons, and at least four, in different counties, have ' mutton ' rhymes.

252. *Tadcaster*

Dr Eaves, Dean of Winchester (Bulmer's *History and Directory of North Yorkshire*, 1890).

Compare :

Thence to Tadcaster, where stood reared a fair bridge ; no flood appeared.

Richard Braithwaite, *Drunken Barnaby's Four Journeys*.

253. *Thornton Steward*

Publications of the Folk-lore Society, XLV, 1899.

254. *Tickhill*

Can any one tell why a Tickhill man, when asked where he comes from, says, ' Tickhill, God help me '? Is it because the people at Tickhill are famed for misery, as the neighbouring town of Blythe seems to have been so called from its jolly citizens.

Notes and Queries, 12 February 1850.

Compare :

Many of the mendicants who ramble the county of Suffolk in search of relief, when asked where they come from, reply in pitiful tone ' Saffron Walden, God help me.'

Oxford Dictionary oj Engish Proverbs.

255. *Wakefield*

What peculiar cause of mirth this town hath above others, Fuller acknowledges he cannot tell unless that it may be entitled to that epithet from its cheapness, and the plenty of good cheer. Might it not be mirrie, that is faithful to Wakefield? and allude to some event in the disputes between the houses of York and Lancaster; mirrie-men a term that frequently occurs in old ballads, signifying true or faithful men.

Francis Grose, *A Provincial Glossary with a Collection of Local Proverbs*. London, 1811.

There are six references to 'mery Carleile' in the ballads 'Adam Bell,' 'Clym of the Clough,' and 'William of Cloudesly,' *Reliques of Ancient English Poetry*, Thomas Percy, 1765, and Leigh Hunt, *The Town*, has a note on 'Merrie London.'

256. *Wakefield*

This George of Green was that famous *Pindar of Wakefield*, who fought with Robin Hood and little John both together, and got the better of them, as the old ballad tells us.

Ray, p. 151.

But the ballad tells us that Scarlet was there too, and that it was three to one.

See *Robin Hood: Ballads and Songs Relating to that celebrated outlaw*. Bell and Daldy, 1865.

Witts Recreations, 1640, reprinted 1817, p. 378.

This George of Green was the famous Pindar of Wakefield, who fought with Robin Hood and little John both together, and got the better of them, as the old ballad tells us (Ray). But the old ballad does not tell us what is quite true, as George was a much later hero than Robin Hood, and his companions. A prose history of the celebrated Pinner was in print before 1600, but no edition anterior to 1632 is at present known. A drama, founded on his real or supposed achievements, was published in 1590; it is attributed to the pen of Robert Greene.

(W. Carew Hazlitt, *English Proverbs and Proverbial Phrases*, 1869,)

See, however, *The Cambridge History of English Literature*, vol. 5, p. 34, where it is suggested (after Chambers) that Robin, the type-name of the shepherd lover, taken from the early May-game, became confused with the Robin Hood of the ballads.

And were y'as good as George a Green,
I shall make bold to turn agen.

Butler, *Hudibras*. The Second Part, Canto II, 1700 edition, p. 253.

257. *Well and Snape*

This was given by a Well lady as 'Snape wheer the' gin an' gape.' Seeking confirmation we heard a Ripon tradesman add 'an' bray hard watter soft wiv a clooas-prop,' and a Ripon varnish-worker say, 'Naay, it's Well an' Snaape.' This illustrates the difficulty experienced in getting complete and authentic versions of these village sayings.

Compare:

Wae worth the man
  Wha first did shape
That vile wanchancie
  Thing—a rape!
It maks guid fellows
  Girn an' gape. . . .

Robert Burns, *Poor Mailie's Elegy*.

257 (a). *Well*

Thomas Horsfall, *The Manor of Well and Snape*, 1912, p. 174.

258. *West Witton*

Edmund Bogg, *From Eden Vale to the Plains of York*.

This rhyme refers to the effigy-burning ceremony of the 'Burning of Bartle' on St. Bartholomew's Day.

It is doubtful if the old time annual Wensleydale ceremony . . . would have continued so long and so regularly had it not been for the enthusiasm of Mr George Stockdale of West Witton who passed away on Friday and whose funeral took place at West Witton on Tuesday.

Mr Stockdale, who was 56 years of age, was formerly employed as a porter at Leyburn railway station for some years. He was one of those responsible for the retaining of the old custom. For many years he made the effigy of Bartle and carried the huge figure at the head of a long procession which marched down the village in the eerie night hours of the celebrations.

No one knows the origin of the old custom, but it is said that some ruffian haunted the Wensleydale Forest on Penhill, just above the long village of West Witton, and carried out despicable acts that, in due time, dalesfolk rounded on 'Bartle' and, according to the legend, he was eventually burnt in Grassgill Lane, not before he had been pretty well 'done in' by his hunters.

Whether the time honoured tradition will continue after the passing of such a local enthusiast as Mr Stockdale remains to be seen. After the effigy had been consumed in flames he was, invariably, requested to bring out his concertina on which he played old time tunes to the delight of a throng of dalesfolk. George . . . will be most missed.

Ripon Gazette and Observer, 22 January 1948.

. . . he had been flea'd alive, and bedevil'd and used worse than St. Bartholomew, at every stage he had come at. . . .

Sterne, *Sentimental Journey*, 1769, p. 34.

259. *Wetherby*

N. and Q., vol. 7, p. 233.

260 and 261. *Whorlton and Swainby*

A. W. M. Close.

263. *Yarm*

Publications of the Folk-lore Society, XLV, 1899. (A Mother Shipton prophecy.)

264. *Yarm*

A. W. M. Close.

265. *Yarm*

A boys' saying: 'Whilst Egglescliffe has a full peal of bells, Yarm has but two.'

266. *York*

The Lord Mayors of London and York and the Lord Provost of Edinburgh have the style by ancient prescriptive usage, the Lord Mayor of Dublin by the Act 3 and 4 Vic. Cap. 108. Section 12. The Lord Provost of Glasgow and the Lord Mayor of Belfast were granted the style by His Majesty in 1912 and 1923 respectively.

In precedence, on state and public occasions, the Lord Mayor of London comes first, then the Lord Mayor of York, and other Lord Mayors in order, according to priority of date of their specific grants.

The only Lord Mayors in England and Wales who may be addressed as the Right Honourable are the Lord Mayors of London and York. All other Lord Mayors should be addressed as the Lord Mayor.

If the Lord Mayor was married, his wife, who fulfilled many felicitous duties, enjoyed by prescription the analogous and respectful title Lady Mayoress, and in former days her ladyship, by the courtesy of an old York custom, retained her title though her husband relinquished his when his term of office expired. . . .

In an oft-repeated rhyme her life-long tenure of the honour is recognized:

> My Lord is a Lord for a year and a day,
> But she is a Lady for ever and aye.

T. P. Cooper, *York, the Titles 'Lord Mayor' and 'Right Honourable.'*

267. *York*

Compare:

Rising was, Lynn is, and Downham shall be,
The greatest seaport of the three.
N. and Q., vol. 3, p. 206

Woking was, Guildford is, Godalming shall be,
N. and Q., vol. 8, p. 616.

Limerick was, Dublin is, and Cork shall be,
The finest city of the three.
N. and Q., vol. 8, p. 102.

York was, London is, but Lincoln shall be
The greatest city of all the three.
N. and Q., vol. 6, p. 146.

London streets shall run with blood
and at last shall sink;
So that it shall be fulfilled,
That Lincoln was, London is, and York shall be
The finest city of the three.

Prophecies of Nixon the Cheshire Merlin who lived nobody knows when, *N. and Q.*, vol. 8, p. 257.
This version was quoted by Taylor 1622.

268. *York*

Although this is not included in Ray's 1817 edition, Bohn includes it amongst Ray's. Henry G. Bohn, *A Hand-book of Proverbs*, 1855, p. 191.

For some time he (Sterne) lived in a retired manner at Sutton in the forest of Galtrees, a small vicarage in Yorkshire, and probably would have remained in the same obscurity, if his lively genius had not displayed itself upon an occasion which secured him a friend, and paved the way for his promotion. A person who filled a lucrative benefice, was not satisfied with enjoying it during his own lifetime, but exerted all his interest to have it entailed upon his wife and son after his decease. The gentleman that expected the reversion of this post was Mr Sterne's friend, who had not, however, sufficient influence to prevent the success of his adversary. At this critical time Sterne's satyrical pen operated so strongly, that the intended monopolizer informed him, if he would suppress the publication of his sarcasm, he would resign his pretensions to the next candidate. The title of this piece, it appears, was to have been 'The history of a good warm watch-coat, with which the present possessor is not content to cover his own shoulders, unless he can cut out of it a petticoat for his wife, and a pair of breeches for his son.' The pamphlet was suppressed, the reversion took place, and Mr Sterne was requited, by the interest of his Patron, with the Prebendaryship of York.

Eugenius, *Preface to Yorick's Sentimental Journey Continued.* London, 1769.

I then came to York, and my uncle got me the living of Sutton.

Sterne, *Memoir*, Nimmo, p. 5. (This was his first appointment.)

See also note 248 for reference to Sterne's connection with Sutton.

269. *York*

Smithson, *Northallerton Almanack*, 1886.

270 *York*

Three P's of York: Pretty, Poor, Proud.

Higson's MSS. Coll., 208, quoted by W. Carew Hazlitt, *English Proverbs and Proverbial Phrases*, 1869.

271. *York*

Yorke, Yorke, for my monie. (1584.)

From Ritson's *Northern Garland*.

The lines are the chorus of a ballad containing 22 verses. The ballad was written by William Elderton, of the 'ale-crammed nose,' the famous ballad writer. He died *c.* 1592.

John Taylor (1580–1653), known as the 'Water Poet,' gave the sub-title 'York for my Money' to his poem *A Very Merry Wherry-Ferry Voyage* (1622).

NOTES ON ROUND THE YEAR

272. *Days of Birth*

Richard Blakeborough, *Yorkshire Wit, Character, Folk-lore, and Customs*, 1898, p. 106.

Other versions appear in A. R. Wright's *English Folk-lore*; Grace Rhys' *Cradle Songs and Nursery Rhymes*; 'Canterbury Poets,' *The Northallerton Almanack*, 1913; and *Notes and Queries*, vol. 2, p. 515 (1850).

273, 274. *Cutting Nails*

Richard Blakeborough, *Yorkshire Wit, Character, Folk-lore, and Customs*, 1898, p. 113.

NAMES OF FINGERS

In Sheffield these are: Little man (little finger), Ling man (leech man), long man (long finger), lick pot (index finger), thomb-a-thomb (thumb). . . . It is said that there is a direct communication between the ring-finger (leech man) and the heart. In this connection *thumb* is sometimes called *thumper*.

S. O. Addy, *Sheffield Glossary*, 1888, p. 74.

NAMES OF TOES

The following names of the toes are taught to children in the neighbourhood of Sheffield:

Great toe: Tom Thumbkin. First toe: Billy Bumkin.
Second toe: Long Daniel. Third toe: Hickspickit.
Little toe: Little Dick.

S. O. Addy, *Supplement to Sheffield Glossary*, 1891, p. 59.

275. *Washing Days*

Smithson, *Northallerton Almanack*, 1913 (a Devonshire version appeared in *N. and Q.*, vol. 2, p. 515).

Monday was washing day, Tuesday ironing, Wednesday and Saturday baking, Thursday 'turning out' upstairs and churning, Friday 'turning out' downstairs.

Herbert Read, *Annals of Innocence and Experience*, p. 21, Faber and Faber (1946 ed.).

276. *Fridays*

S. O. Addy, *Sheffield Glossary*, p. 77.

It is said that 'three flittings are as bad as a fire.'

277. *Lang Friday*

Richard Blakeborough, *Yorkshire Wit, Character, Folk-lore, and Customs*, 1898, p. 75.

278. *Engagements and Marriages*

Richard Blakeborough, *Yorkshire Wit, Character, Folk-Lore, and Customs*, 1898, p. 95.

279. *Leap Year*

Publications of the Folk-lore Society, XLV, 1899.

280. *New Year*

Yorkshire Dialect Poems (1673–1915), edited by F. W. Moorman.

281. *New Year*

S. O. Addy, *Sheffield Glossary*, p. 48.

Addy gives the meaning of 'cock-stride' as being 'a considerable length.' It is, of course, the opposite.

Noo gan on' wi' tha, an' deean't be si lang: it's nobbut a cock-stride!

Harrison Weir, that great artist and authority on the game-fowl, in the glossary to his monumental work *Our Poultry* (Hutchinson & Co.), says, quoting *Gentleman's Mag.*, 1759, p. 16.

A cock's stride: The countryman has a method of making a guess at the lengthening or shortening of the day, concerning which he has a saying that, I believe, is very general all over England:

At New Year's-tide
They are lengthened by a cock's stride.

Everybody knows the meaning of this saying, to wit, that it intends to express the lengthening of the days in a small but perceptible degree; but very few are aware of the ground or occasion of it, which is less to be wondered at since there is something uncommon.

Our Poultry, vol. 2, p. 810.

282. *St Agnes' Day*

I am also told by the elder dames that it was a common custom in days past for those maids who were in troth such of them to repair unto St. Cedd's well at Lastingham on the Eve of St. Agnes, and there perform the office of washing of their garters. The doing of the like was held of all to be most binding vow to so remain true maids. A bit of sock, a pair of garters was by times unravelled and knittened or worked into something for the chap they loved to wear, and it would never fail for to hold true love to a true maid. . . ."

Eve of St. Agnes note in George Calvert–M. Stapylton manuscript book in the possession of Mr J. Fairfax Blakeborough.

283. *February Fill-Dyke*

Yorkshire Dialect Poems (1673–1915), edited F. W. Moorman, and Frederick Ross, *Holderness Glossary*, E.D.S., 1877.
Compare:

February Fill-Dyke
When it's white
It's better to like.

S. O. Addy, *Sheffield Glossary*, p. 73.

284. *February fire lang*

William Carr, *The Dialect of Craven*, vol. I, p. 144, 'A Craven proverb, which seems to have eluded the researches of Ray.'

285. *February*

Horace Annesley Vachell, *This Was England*. Hodder and Stoughton, 1933.

286, 287. *Candlemas*

Yorkshire Dialect Poems (1673–1915), edited F. W. Moorman.

288. *Candlemas*

English Dialect Dictionary, edited Joseph Wright.

289. *Candlemas*

George Calvert–Stapylton manuscript book in possession of Mr J. Fairfax Blakeborough.

290. *Candlemas*

Brighouse News, 20 July 1889, quoted *English Dialect Dictionary*.

Compare:

On Valentine's Day will a good goose lay

and

If she be a good goose her dame well to pay,
She will lay two eggs before Valentine's Day.

and

Before St. Chad every goose lays both good and bad.

Ray.

291. *Good Friday*

Richard Blakeborough, *Yorkshire Wit, Character, Folk-lore, and Customs*, 1898, p. 79.

292. *Good Friday*

Compare:

One a penny, poker,
Two a penny, tongs,
Three a penny, fire irons,
Hot cross buns.
(Warwickshire folk-rhyme.)

and

One a penny, two a penny, hot-cross-buns:
Sugar 'em, and butter 'em, and stick 'em in your mums.
(Northamptonshire.)

G. F. Northall, *A Warwickshire Word-Book*, E.D.S., pp. 113, 154.

293. *March grows*

F. K. Robinson, *A Glossary of Yorkshire Words and Phrases collected in Whitby and the Neighbourhood*, 1855.

294. *A dry March*

C. Clough Robinson, *A Glossary of Words pertaining to the Dialect of Mid-Yorkshire*. E.D.S. 1876.

295. *Fogs in March*

Ripon Gazette and Observer, 4 March 1948, reporting local usage.

296. *April Noddy*

A Swaledale saying. Compare:

April Feul is past and gone,
An' thoo's a feul for thinking on.

Said to anyone who may attempt an April fool joke after mid-day.

W. Dickinson (Prevost), *A Glossary of Words and Phrases pertaining to the Dialect of Cumberland*, p. 6.

'Frisby Dike' in the B.B.C. Itma programme on April Fool's Day, 1948, gave this version:

April Noddy is past and gone
And you're a noddy for thinking on.

This is a better version than the Swaledale one, and it seems doubtful whether the saying is local to Swaledale.

297. *Tid, Mid, Miserae*

Rev. J. C. Atkinson, *A Glossary of the Cleveland Dialect*, 1868, p. 89.

Compare:

Tid, Mid, Miseray
Carlin, Paum an' Good-feeast day.

Frederick Ross, *A Glossary of Words used in Holderness*, p. 148.

Popular names for Sundays in Lent. Three of them are obviously from the old Latin service, Te Deum, Mi Deus, Miserere mei. The rest elucidate themselves.

John Trotter Brockett, *A Glossary of North Country Words*, vol. 2, p. 183.

Carlins: boiled peas eaten on Care Sunday, the Sunday before Palm Sunday.

Bamford's Tim Bobbin, p. 148.

In Richmond and other places in the district, the innkeepers give a feast of the peas to their customers on this Sunday morning.

Richmond Almanack, 1890.

Grey peas, first steeped a night in water and fried with butter.

A Dictionary of Swaledale Words, 1886.

They are eaten on the Fourth Sunday in Lent, which is called Carling Sunday. . . . The custom is still so far retained that bags of grey peas, specially provided to meet the demand, may be seen in the country shops as the day draws on. It is difficult to come to any conclusions with respect to the origin of this word. It is certain that the Fifth Sunday in Lent was called 'Care- or Carr-Sunday' from remote time.

Rev. J. C. Atkinson, *Cleveland Glossary*, p. 89.

In the North they are served at table, on the second Sunday before Easter . . . formerly denominated Care Sunday, as Care Friday and Care Week, were Good Friday and Holy Week—supposed to be so called from being a season of great religious care and anxiety. The peas appear to be a substitute for the beans of the heathens.

Brockett, *A Glossary of North Country Words*, vol. 1, p. 83.

Carlyngs: pease boiled on Care-Sunday; the first before Palm Sunday.

J. Sibbald, *Chronicles of Scottish Poetry*, vol. 4, 1802.

299. *May*

A Staithes fishermen's saying.

300. *Casting Clouts*

Compare:

Never think to cast a clout
Until the month of May be out.

Rev. J. C. Atkinson, *Cleveland Glossary.*

301. *Washing Blankets*

George Hardwick, *The Story of Flamborough*, p. 27.

302. *Royal Oak Day*

Altered from *Yorkshire Dialect Poems* (1672–1915), edited F. W. Moorman, and Richard Blakeborough's *Yorkshire Wit, Character, Folk-lore, and Customs.*

Compare:

Pancake-day, Pancake-day,
If you don't give us holiday,
We'll all run away.

G. F. Northall, *A Warwickshire Word-Book*, p. 167.

The restoration of King Charles II; in commemoration of which it is customary for the common people, in many parts of the North, to wear oak leaves in their hats, and also to place them on their horses' heads.

Brockett, *A Glossary of North-Country Words*, vol. 2, p. 103.

At Boroughbridge boys used to arm themselves with stinging nettles to inflict punishment upon the boys failing to wear oak leaves.

At night Mr Cook comes from London with letters, leaving all things there very gallant and joyful; and brought us word that the Parliament had ordered the 29th of May, the King's birthday, to be for ever kept as a day of thanksgiving for our redemption from tyranny, and the King's return to his Government, he entering London that day.

Pepys *Diary*, 1 June 1660.

How shall I speak of that triumphant day,
When you renew'd th' expiring pomp of May!
(A month that owns an interest in your name:
You and the flowers are its peculiar claim).

Dryden, *Astræa Redux*. A Poem on the Happy Restoration and Return of His Sacred Majesty Charles II, 1660, ll. 284–7.

303. *St Swithin's Day*

William Carr, *The Dialect of Craven*, 1828, vol. 1, p. 305.

304. *Harvest Home (We hev her)*

E. E. Taylor, *Wensleydale* (1921), p. 10; Frederick Ross, *Holderness Glossary*, p. 76.

305. *Harvest (John Metcalfe)*

E. E. Taylor, *Wensleydale*, 1921, p. 10; C. C. Robinson, *Mid-Yorkshire Glossary*, p. 82.

306. *Harvest (Blest be t'day)*

E. E. Taylor, *Wensleydale.*

307. *Harvest (Here we are)*

John Nicholson, *Folk Speech of East Yorkshire*, p. 12.

The bringing home of the last load of harvest is always a joyous time. At Bilton, when the harvest is safely gathered in, the whole village gives itself up to merriment and festivity. A half-holiday is given to all employees, and they, one and all, enter into sports and joyous holiday-making. But now one scarcely ever hears of the harvest song that used to be sung when the last load entered the well-filled 'stagga'th,' and when the younger people 'scram'led' for nuts and apples. Then the master, or foreman, entering the stack-garth at the horses' head, began,

Here we are, as tite as nip, etc.

Scrambling for nuts, apples, oranges and sweets, thrown by the shop-keepers was customary at Boroughbridge on New Year's Day fifty years ago.

308. *Harvest (Weel bun)*

Florence Tweddell, *Rhymes and Sketches* (1785), p. 4.

For an interesting chapter on the Mell-Supper and Shouting the Churn see p. 107 of *The Trial and Life of Eugene Aram, several of his letters and poems and his plan and specimens of an Anglo-Celtic Lexicon*, Richmond, 1832.

'Bonnin-awd-witch': an ancient custom still observed in many villages, particularly round Burlington, on the last day of harvest. A fire of stubble is made in the field, in which peas are parched and eaten with a plentiful allowance of ale; the lads and lasses dancing and romping round the fire, and deriving great fun from the blackening of each other's faces with burnt peas.

Frederick Ross, *Holderness Glossary*, p. 32.

Mell Supper note:

During haytime, the shoemakers and tailors would discard the lapstone and the goose, visit the neighbouring farmers, and give them valuable assistance in stacking, and when the crops were made secure, join in the mell supper, and to the merry notes of fiddle, give expression to the jolly rollicking spirit within by taking part in country dances.

'Northallerton Fifty Years Ago,' *Smithson's Northallerton Almanack*, 1889.

Sir Walter Scott has an account of a kirn supper that he attended on 26 October 1827:

The Fergusons dined; and we had the kirn Supper. I never saw a set of finer lads and lasses, and blithely did they ply their heels till five in the morning. It did me good to see them, poor things.

The Journal of Sir Walter Scott, 1825–32. Edinburgh, 1891, p. 469.

Dean Ramsey referred to the abolition of harvest homes in Scotland in his 'Reminiscences,' the first edition of which was published in 1857.

309. *September*

John Hartley's *Yorkshire Pudding*.

Compare Tusser's

September blowe softe
till fruite be in loft.

Five Hundred Points of Good Husbandrie, by Thomas Tusser: vide *Country Contentments, Courtesies, and Customs*. London: The Medici Society.

Thomas Tusser (1524?–1580), in his famous book (published 3 February 1557) originally entitled *A hundreth good Pointes of Husbandrie*, gives us many of the seasonal rhymes which we still repeat. 'Feb fill the dyke With what thou dost like,' 'Sweet April showers Do bring May flowers,' 'At Christmas play and make good cheer For Christmas comes but once a year,' etc. Many proverbs in current use are traceable to Tusser's work.

312. *Guy Fawkes' Day*

John Harland and T. T. Wilkinson, *Lancashire Folk-lore*, p. 252. See also No. 177.

PARKIN: Cakes made up of treacle and oatmeal; an article of common consumption by children. The great Parkin day, however, is the 5th of November, when the eating of it is general amongst the working classes. Enormous quantities are sold by the bakers and confectioners on this day.

C. C. Robinson, *The Dialect of Leeds*, 1862.

313. *Guy Fawkes' Day: A stick and a stake*

S. O. Addy, *Sheffield Glossary*, p. 239.

314. *Guy Fawkes' Day: Awd Grimey*

Richard Blakeborough, *Yorkshire Wit, Character, Folk-lore, and Customs*, 1898, p. 87.

315. *The Waits*

Boroughbridge, 1890.

Waits: musicians who parade and play by night in the streets about the time of Christmas and the new year; originally watchman or sentinels. One of the old towers, in Newcastle, was formerly called the Waits' Tower, and was the place of meeting of these itinerant musicians. They used to be the privileged minstrels at weddings and feasts.

Brockett, vol. 2, p. 202.

For fuller accounts of Waits see Thomas Newbigging, 'A Word for the Waits,' in *Love's Cradle and Other Papers* (J. M. Dent, 1902), and T. P. Cooper, *Christmas Waits and Minstrels of Bygone York* (York: Edwin Story, n.d.).

316. *A Merry Christmas*

The Chimney-Nook Original Almanack, by Sol Darrel, 1906.

There is a hint, in the humorous ending of this greeting, of a typical Yorkshire caution. The fates must not be tempted by assuming the appearance, already, of something that, strictly speaking, belongs to the future.

317. *Children's Christmas-Boxing Nominy*

John Nicholson, *Folk Speech of East Yorkshire*, p. 8.
Compare:

Ah wish ya a merry Kessimass,
An' a happy new year,
A pocket full o' money,
An' a cellar full o' beer,
An' a good fat pig
That'll last ya all t'year.

J. Fairfax Blakeborough, *Life in a Yorkshire Village*, 1912, p. 38.

And

I wish you a merry Christmas, and a happy New Year;
A pocketful of money, and a barrelful of beer;
Good luck to your feather-fowl, fere;
And please will you give me my Christmas-box!

C. C. Robinson, *Mid-Yorkshire Glossary*, p. 93.

318. *Cleveland Vessell Cups Song*

Mrs G. M. Tweddell (Florence Cleveland), *Rhymes and Sketches to illustrate the Cleveland Dialect*. Stokesley, 1875, p. 6.

A full version of this Christmas Carol appears in *Augustan Poets*, No. 74. Benn.

319. *Saying*

Bounce buckram, velvet's dear,
Christmas comes but once a year;
And when it comes it brings good cheer,
But when it's gone it's never the near.

Ray, p. 155.

NOTES ON FOLK-LORE RHYMES

320. *Wedding Rhymes*: *A weddin', a woo*

A. J. Brown, *Four Boon Fellows*, p. 228. J. M. Dent & Sons, Ltd.

At the sight of a wedding-party, children may be heard calling out: 'A weddin', a woo', etc., and (they) make a feint of taking off their shoes and throwing them at or after the couple.

C. C. Robinson, *The Dialect of Leeds*, 1862, p. 446.

The custom used to be known as 'trashing' . . . an old shoe is to this day called a trash.

N. and Q., vol. 8, p. 135.

321. *Wedding Rhymes*: *Green and white*

Yorkshire: green and white are unlucky colours in a wedding dress.

322. *Wedding Rhymes*: *Something old*

A. R. Wright, *English Folk-lore*, p. 17.

323. *Wedding Rhymes*: *The woman that changes her name*

Richmond Almanack, 1907.

324. *Wedding Rhymes: Happy is the bride*

N. and Q., vol. 6, p. 312.
William Carr, *Craven Glossary*, vol. 1, p. 211, adds 'Ridiculous as this distich is, many will give it full credence'.

'Happy is the corpse that the rain rains on,' a popular saying in Northumberland.

Brockett, vol. 2, p. 88.

325. *Wedding Rhymes: Marry in Lent*

N. and Q., vol. 2, p. 259.

326. *Wedding Rhymes: The bridegroom's health*

Richard Blakeborough, *Yorkshire Wit, Character, Folk-lore, and Customs*, 1898, p. 104.

The *Whitby Gazette*, 9 March 1934, has a note about this song.

Compare:

Oh, here's a good health to the bride of yond house
  That's provided us all this good cheer;
Lord send her her health.
Lord prosper her wealth,
  And may we be married next year.

It's fair to be seen he's drunk it off clean
  As any other man can,
And if that he please
Another at his ease
  And it shall be unto a good man.

Ella Pontefract and Marie Hartley, *Wensleydale*, p. 180. J. M. Dent & Sons, Ltd.

And

A Bacchanalian Verse

Drink up
Your cup,
But not spill wine;
For if you
Do,
'Tis an ill sign; . . .

Robert Herrick's, *The Hesperides*, vol. 2, p. 131. Lawrence & Bullen.

And

So drink, boys, drink,
And see you do not spill;
For if you do,
You shall drink two,
For 'tis your master's will.

William Hone, *The Every Day Book*, 1878, vol. 2, p. 584.

327. *Wedding-ring Mottoes*

Northallerton Almanack, 1880.

The *Richmond Almanack*, 1893, gave a list from the *New Academy of Compliments*, 1741.

328. *Babies' Teeth : Odd*

Publications of the Folk-lore Society, XLV, 1899.

329. *Babies' Teeth : Early*

A Northern proverb, when a child hath teeth too soon.

Ray, p. 16.

330. *Seean teeath, seean teeas.*

This means that if your baby's teeth begin to sprout early, you will soon have toes, i.e., another baby.

Specimens of Yorkshire Dialect. Richmond.

Compare:

Quickly too'd (i.e. toothed) and quickly go,
Quickly will thy mother have moe. (Yorkshire.)

Some have it quickly too'd, quickly with God, as if early breeding of teeth were a sign of a short life, whereas we read of some born with teeth in their heads, who yet have lived long enough to become famous men, as in the Roman History . . . and, among our English kings, Richard III.

Ray, p. 35.

331. *Babies' Teeth : Losing them*

John Nicholson, *Folk Speech of East Yorkshire*, p. 93.

When a child's tooth comes out, it must be dropped into the fire, and the rhyme repeated or the child will have to seek its tooth after death.

Compare:

Fire, fire, burn baan,
God send my tuthe again.

Specimens of Yorkshire Dialect. Richmond.

332. *Nursery Rhymes: Dressing Baby*

John Nicholson, *Folk Speech of East Yorkshire*, p. 15.

333. *Nursery Rhymes: Bonny Lass*

A manuscript note in a copy of C. C. Robinson, *The Dialect of Leeds.*

334. *Nursery Rhymes: The Baker's Man*

S. O. Addy, *Sheffield Glossary*, p. 44.

335. *Nursery Rhymes: The Cock-bird*

William Carr, *The Dialect of Craven*, vol. 1, p. 114.

336. *Nursery Rhymes: Cuckoo, Cherry Tree*

N. and Q., vol. 2, p. 164 (1850).

337. *Nursery Rhymes: The Daffodil*

William Carr, *The Craven Glossary*, vol. 1, p. 99; Grace Rhys, *Cradle Songs. N. and Q.*, vol. 3, p. 220 (1851)—from York.

338. *Nursery Rhymes: Diddle, Diddle, Dumpling*

S. O. Addy, *Sheffield Glossary*, p. 305.

339. *Nursery Rhymes: Little Miss Muffet*

S. O. Addy, *Sheffield Glossary*, p. 31; Grace Rhys, *Cradle Songs* (p. 117), gives 'tuffet' for 'buffet'.

340. *The Moon*

S. O. Addy, *Sheffield Glossary*, p. 322.

341. *The White Paternoster*

The Border Land in Olden Times, Carlisle, 1903; Grace Rhys, *Cradle Songs*, p. 75.

342. *Girls' Rhymes: The Peep Show. A pin a sight*

C. C. Robinson, *The Dialect of Leeds*, p. 398.

343. *Girls' Rhymes: A pin to look in*

C. C. Robinson, *The Dialect of Leeds*, p. 385.

344. *Girls' Rhymes: A pinnet a piece*

S. O. Addy, *Sheffield Glossary*, p. 325.

Pippy-show: a peep show. Pansies or other flowers are pressed beneath a piece of glass, which is laid upon a piece of paper, a hole or opening, which can be shut at pleasure, being cut in the paper. The charge for looking at the show is a pin. The children say 'a pin to look at a pippy-show.' They also say 'A pinnet apiece,' etc.

Ibid., p. 325.

345. *Boys' Rhymes: Barring-out*

S. O. Addy, *Sheffield Glossary*, p. 296. The custom was observed in other parts of Yorkshire, viz: Nidderdale and Teesdale within living memory.

School-boys barred the teacher out at Christmas and negotiated for holidays, before admitting him.

On Tuesday afternoon the scholars attending the Girls' School, Flimby, resorted to the old custom of 'Barring-Out,' the day being Shrove Tuesday (1895).

W. Dickinson, *A Glossary of the Words and phrases pertaining to the Dialect of Cumberland*, re-arranged by E. W. Prevost, p. 16.

This rude custom is still kept up in the country schools of the north. . . .

The Westmoreland and Cumberland Dialects, Dialogues, Poems, Songs and Ballads by various writers, 1839, p. 327.

A custom in some of the smaller schools in the north.

F. T. Dinsdale, *Teesdale Glossary*, 1873, p. 7.

The late Alderman Edwin Smith of Scarborough remembered singing the following verses at Lofthouse-in-Nidderdale:

Good Master, Good Master, be courteous and kind,
Remember your scholars and bear them in mind,
For when you was young you used to play,
So do your scholars this very day.

Pardon Master, pardon,
Pardon over a cheese,
If you don't pardon
Sit you down and freeze.

This verse was used if the day was cold, if not the alternative one on the next page.

Pardon Master, pardon,
Pardon over a churn,
If you don't pardon.
Sit you down and gurn.

Transactions of the Yorkshire Dialect Society, vol. 6, Pt. xxxix.

H. J. L. Bruff, *Barring-out Day*

346. *Counting-out: Holla, bolla*

Boroughbridge, 1890.

Richard Blakeborough, 1898 (p. 261) gives a North Riding counting-out rhyme:

Eary, ory, hickory, on,
Philson, Valson, Dickson, John,
Squeaby, Sqauby, Irishman,
Stiggerum, staggerum, buck. . . .

Staggerum buck, or Staggerer Staggera bobtail, is the name of a boy's game, very commonly played. 'Philson,' 'Valson,' and 'Dickson,' are examples of the elision of the possessive case, i.e., Phil's son, etc. (R. B.)

347. *Counting-out: Meny, meny*

John Nicholson, *Folk Speech of East Yorkshire*, p. 73.

348. *The Late Scholar*

Frederick Ross, *A Glossary of Words used in Holderness*, E.D.S., p. 53.

Compare:

Liggy-bed lollard,
Ten o'clock schollard.

Prevost, *A Glossary of the words and phrases pertaining to the Dialect of Cumberland*, 1899, p. 202.

349. *Boys' Rhymes: Bird-nesting*

John Nicholson, *Folk Speech of East Yorkshire*, p. 11.

Compare:

Rob a Robin
Go a-sobbing.

Richard Blakeborough, p. 278.

And

Wren and Robin
The robin and the red-breast,
The robin and the wren;
If ye take from their nest
Ye'll never thrive agen!

The robin and the red-breast,
The martin and the swallow;
If ye touch one o' their eggs,
Ill luck will surely follow.

Grace Rhys, *Cradle Songs*, p. 200

350. *Boys' Rhymes: Tom Plom*

S. O. Addy, *Sheffield Glossary*, p. 325.

351. *Boys' Rhymes: Whip Behind!*

John Nicholson, *Folk Speech of East Yorkshire*, 1889, p. 12; *Flamborough Village and Headland*, edited by Robert Fisher, 1894, p. 142.

Those who, in the course of a summer holiday, have journeyed from the direction of Bridlington to Flamborough—the 'Little Denmark' of Blackmore's *Mary Anerley*—will recall the above lines. As charabancs, wagonettes, flies, bicycles, pony-chaises, and weary pedestrians, after toiling along the dusty road from Dane's Dike, enter the Village of Flamborough, groups of bright-eyed, strong featured, comely urchins meet the welcome visitors and pour forth, in not unmelodious chorus, the above refrain.

Arthur H. Armytage, 'Flamborough Folk-Lore' in *Flamborough Village and Headland*.

The heading 'whip behind' may need explanation to younger readers. When boys ran after carts, wagonettes, or other vehicles, other boys and often grown-ups would call 'whip behind' to the driver as a direction to whip off the offenders.

352. *Children's Rhymes: Bell-horses*

The small horse in a team conveying lead to be smelted wore bells and was called the bell-horse.

S. O. Addy, *Sheffield Glossary*, p. 14.

Bell-horse: a familiar title bestowed on any one in the position of leader of a party, literally or figuratively. In the days of pack-horses, the horse that went first, and which wore bells, was called by this name.

C. C. Robinson, *Mid-Yorks Glossary*, E.D.S., p. 8.

See Samuel Smiles, *Lives of the Engineers, Metcalfe-Telford*, John Murray, 1904, for a full account of bell-horses, and an illustration of a pack-horse convoy.

He weeant' laak if he isn't t'bell-hoss.
As prood as a bell-hoss.

353. *Children's Rhymes: Cockelty Bread*

John Nicholson, *Folk Speech of East Yorkshire*, p. 90.

Compare:

My granny is sick and now is dead,
And we'll go mould some cocklety-bread;
Up with the heels and down with the head,
And that is the way to make cocklety-bread.

S. O. Addy, *Sheffield Glossary*, p. 47.

See *English Dialect Dictionary* for a full account of the game.

354. *Children's Rhyme: Dimples*

Richard Blakeborough, *Yorkshire Wit, Character, Folk-lore and Customs*, 1898, p. 115.

355. *Children's Rhymes: Gifts*

Frederic Ross, *Holderness Glossary*, p. 67; S. O. Addy, *Sheffield Glossary*, p. 88, says:

Gift: a white spot on a finger-nail, supposed to indicate a coming gift; but in Eastern Holderness the word GIFT is confined to the spots on the thumb, those on the fingers being called respectively 'friend,' 'foe,' 'lover,' 'journey to go.'

Holderness Glossary.

William Carr, *The Craven Glossary*, vol. 1, p. 182, and G. F. Northall, *A Warwickshire Word-Book*, give similar interpretations.

356. *Children's Rhymes: Handy-pandy*

Handy-pandy: A child's game, in which something is changed from one hand to the other, and guesses are made as to which hand contains it.

C. C. Robinson, *Dialect of Leeds*, p. 319.

Compare:

Handy-dandy, etc.

S. O. Addy, *Sheffield Glossary*, p. 101.

And

Handy-bandy, etc.

G. F. Northall, *A Warwickshire Word-Book*, p. 120.

And

Neevy neevy nack,
Whether hand will ta tack—
T'topmer or t'lowmer.

Cumberland Glossary, E.D.S., 1878, p. 66.

Neither cross and pile, nor ducks and drakes, are quite so ancient as handy-dandy.

Arbuthnot and Pope, quoted in Todd's *Johnson*.

I do not pretend to know the exact age of handy-dandy, but the sport of ducks and drakes is of high antiquity and elegantly described by Minutius Felix. . . .

Brockett, vol. 1, p. 147.

And

Pindy-pandy, which hand will you have.
Thomas Dekker, *Shoemakers' Holiday*, Act iv, sc. v.

357. *Children's Rhymes: Hickup-snickup*

The following couplet, thrice repeated, is a popular cure for this disagreeable convulsion.

Hickup-snickup, etc.

Major Moor gives a different version of the lines:

Hickup-snickup-look-up-right up—
Three drops in a cup—
Is good for the hiccup.

Brockett, vol. 1, p. 219.

Why, Gentlemen (says he) if there had been but a Snick-up in the Case, you'd have cry'd, *the Lord bless ye, Sir;* and there is more Danger in *Marrying*, I hope, than there is in *Sneezing*.

L'Estrange's *Fables of Several Authors*, Fab. 426.

358. *Children's Rhymes: Ifs and ands*

A Glossary of the Dialect of the Hundred of Lonsdale in the County of Lancashire, R. B. Peacock, edited by Rev. J. C. Atkinson. Philological Society, 1869, p. 87.

360. *Children's Rhymes: Raan, raan*

Richard Blakeborough (1898), p. 277.

361. *Sailors' Children's Rhyme*

Yorkshire Dialect Poems (1673–1915), ed. F. W. Moorman.

363. *Dent Knitters' Song*

Robert Southey, *The Doctor*, Longmans, Green & Co., 1874, p. 558. This occurs in 'A true story of the Terrible Knitters e' Dent. . . .'

For interesting correspondence between Robert Southey and Charlotte Brontë see *English Letters of the Nineteenth Century*. Pelican Books.

364. *Sweethearting*

Prevost, p. 363.

365. *Apple Pie*

Horace Annesley Vachell, *This was England*, 1933, p. 203.

366. *Singing Games*

A Fragment from Boroughbridge.

Compare:

Sally, Sally Slarter,
Sitting by the water,
Crying out and weeping
For a young man.
Rise, Sally, rise,
Dry up your eyes;
Turn to the east,
Turn to the west,
Turn to the young man
That you love the best.

S. O. Addy, *Sheffield Glossary*, p. 198.

367. *Singing Games: The Looby-Looby*

This seems to be the source of the HOKEY COKEY song which was recently so popular. It appears in Addy's *Sheffield Glossary*, E.D.S. 1888, p. 320.

A circle is formed by a number of children, who take hold of each other's hands and sing:

'Can you dance, looby, looby,' etc.

At the third line they put their right feet within the ring, then they take their feet out, and turn round. LOOBY is an old form of the modern word LUBBER, a clumsy fellow, dolt.

368. *Singing Games: The Jolly Miller*

In this game the following lines are sung to a pretty tune:

'There was a jolly miller', etc.

At the end of the game these lines are sung:

Sandy he belongs to the mill,
And the mill belongs to Sandy still,
And the mill belongs to Sandy.

S. O. Addy, *Sheffield Glossary*, p. 120.

Compare:

There was a jolly miller once,
Lived on the river Dee;
He work'd and sung from morn till night;
No lark more blithe than he.
And this the burthen of his song
For ever used to be:
I care for nobody, no, not I,
If no one cares for me. . . .

Isaac Bickerstaff: 'Love in a Village', Act i, sc. ii, *Everyman Dictionary of Quotations*, vol. 1, p. 15.

369. *Women, Geese and Hens: Tweea Mirricles*

East Riding. Heard at Wharram.

Compare:

Many women, many words,
Many geese, many turds!

1350 *Douce MS. Oxford Dictionary of English Proverbs.*

And

Three women and a goose make a market.

An Italian proverb quoted by Ray, p. 33.

370. *Women, Geese and Hens: Whistling Women*

Compare:

Than awn a crawing hen,
Ah seeaner wad t'au'd divil meet,
Hickity O, pickity O, pompolorum jig.
Or breed a whistling lass
Ah seeaner wad t'au'd divil treeat
Hickity O, pickity O, pompolorum jig.
Nowt bud ill-luck 'll fester wheear
Ther craws an' whistles sike a pair;
Maay hens an' wimin breed neea mair,
Pompolorum jig.

Richard Blakeborough, *Yorkshire Wit, Character, Folk-lore and Customs*, 1898, p 127.

And

A whistling woman and a crowing hen,
Are two of the unluckiest things under the sun.
(Cornwall.)

Choice Notes from *N. and Q.* (1859), p. 89.

And

A whistling woman and a crowing hen
Is neither fit for God nor men. (Northamptonshire.)

N. and Q., vol. 2, p. 164.

And

> A whusslin' lass an a bellerin cow
> An a crowin' hen 'll deu nea dow.

Prevost, *Cumberland Glossary*, p. 102.

And

> Whistlin' maids an' crawin' hens are no sonsie.

A. C. Gibson, *The Folk-Speech of Cumberland*, 1880, p. 199.

And

> That house doth every day more wretched grow,
> Where the Hen lowder than the Cock doth crow.

A French proverb, trans. by James Howell, *Familiar Letters*, 1705 edition, p. 160.

371. *Fire*

Heard in South Yorkshire.

372. *Horses*

A Yorkshire Dialogue (1697) and W. Dickinson, *Cumberland Glossary*, p. 110.

373. *Riding T' Stang*

From B. J. Harker's *Rambles in Upper Wharfedale*. Other versions, more or less similar to the above, are to be found in Richard Blakeborough's *Yorkshire Wit, Character, Folk-lore, and Customs*, 1898, p. 89; John Nicholson's *Folk Speech of East Yorkshire;* the *Richmond Almanack*, 1886; *Transactions of the Yorkshire Dialect Society*, vol. III, pt. xvi (an account in the Beverley dialect); *Old Yorkshire*, 1881.

According to an undated cutting from the *Yorkshire Evening Post*, a version similar to the one printed was used at Bedale.

On Monday there was a considerable commotion in the town of Bedale, the occasion being a revival of the ancient custom of riding the stang. The usual figure to represent the person who had offended against his wife was placed in a handcart and was drawn along the pavement, the bellman pronouncing at intervals the well-known doggerel:

> He tinkle, I tinkle, he tinkle tan,
> This is the first night that we ride the stang;
> It's neither for your cause, nor my cause, etc.

To ride stang : To take a kind of Lynch-law notice of the offences of an adulterous or brutal husband; in doing which the effigy of the offender—in rather more lawless times, it would be the offender himself—is carried about, astride, on a long pole, with the accompaniment of music (or clatter) of marrowbones and cleaver description, and with the frequent recitation of some doggerel—perhaps composed for the occasion—setting forth the offences of the culprit. Of frequent occurrence, even yet. Possibly the whole ceremony ends with a bonfire and the burning of the offender's effigy.

Rev. J. C. Atkinson's *Cleveland Glossary*, 1868, p. 491.

C. C. Robinson, *The Dialect of Leeds*, has a note stating:

It is commonly supposed that if the perpetrators go through the ceremony three nights successively—which they always do—and make the circuit of a church, that they are not amenable to law.

We are indebted here, as so often, to George Calvert's manuscript book for an account of a stang riding in 1669, at Castleton.

For God or ye Devil
June 17th 1669.

Suche a sighte was thys daye seen as purchance may neur be again let us pray God. Poe George Rodham, Will Hogget, Will Rowntree, and Mark Stapleton war alle stang ridden for that they war alle trew proven fornicators, and Eliza Parker was condemned to walk stripped to her sark from the high to the lowe end of Castleton and to be beaten with hazel switches on ye buttocks by any wedded dame on ye waye. Ye Town Cryer to go afront of her and ever like to publicklie bawl forth that she was a common drab and to publicklie expose her at both ends of ye Towne Street and thys was done.

George Calvert–M. Stapylton manuscript book in possession of Mr J. Fairfax Blakeborough.

Andrew Marvell in his Last Instructions to a Painter (*Satires of Andrew Marvell*, Muses Library, p. 33) also has an account of punishment to transgressing females:

The Court, as once of war, now fond of peace,
All to new sports their wonted fears release.
From Greenwich (where intelligence they hold)
Comes news of pastime martial and old.
A punishment invented first to awe
Masculine wives transgressing nature's law;
Where when the brawny female disobeys,
And beats the husband, till for peace he prays,
No concerned jury damage for him finds,
No partial justice her behaviour binds;
But the just street does the next house invade,
Mounting the neighbour couple on lean jade.

The distaff knocks, the grains from kettle fly,
And boys and girls in troops run hooting by.
Prudent antiquity! that knew by shame,
Better than law, domestic broils to tame;
And taught the youth by spectacle innocent.

According to Ray (p. 251), this word (STANG) is still used in some colleges in the University of Cambridge; to STANG scholars in Christmas time, being to cause them to ride on a colt-staff, or pole, for missing of chapel.

Marshall, *The Rural Economy of Yorkshire* (1788), vol. 2, p. 355, says, of Riding the Stang:

A custom, which few men, I hope, will censure, has prevailed in this country time immemorial, and is still, I find, prevalent. This custom . . . is used as a reproof to the man who beats his wife; or (when it happens) to the wife who beats her husband.

The ceremony is that of placing a man or a boy upon a long pole, borne on men's shoulders, and parading before the house of the delinquent; the rider repeating some rustic verses applicable to the occasion. If this be found ineffectual, the ceremony is repeated with stronger marks of disapprobation. In flagrant and obstinate cases, the door has been assailed, the offender seized, and the punishment of the ducking-stool added to the disgrace of the stang. Some inveterate cases, it seems have recently yielded to this admirable remedy.

Brockett saw a stang-riding. In an interesting note he states:

The person who has been thus treated, seldom recovers his character in the opinion of his neighbours. When they cannot lay hold of the culprit himself, a boy mounts the stang. . . . The proxy vociferously proclaims, that it is not on his own account that he is thus treated . . . I have been witness to processions of this kind myself. School boys are STANGED by other scholars, for breaking what they call, the rules or orders of the school. The ceremony is also resorted to when a woman has gained an improper ascendancy over her husband. . . . In Cumberland, it was a constant holiday custom, on Old Christmas Day, to carry every man they could catch, on a STANG, and every woman, in a SWILL, to a public-house, and fine them a pint of beer.

374. *Fishermen's Rhymes: A spraggy cod*

Whitby.

375–380. *Fishermen's Rhymes*

All these are Staithes fishermen's rhymes, and we are indebted for them to two Staithes fishermen, Messrs. Matthew and Richard Verrill of the 'Star of Hope.'

No. 375 means more hooks, more dog fish; No. 376, that the wind is against the coble and no help from the tide—hard rowing.

The Oxford Dictionary of English Proverbs has a version of No. 380.

381. *Fishermen's Rhymes: O the Boaty Row*

Staithes.

Compare:

I cast my line in Largo Bay,
And hauled up fishes nine.
They're three to boil and three to fry,
And three to bait the line.
(The Boatie rows: Auld Song.)

J. C. Wilcocks, *The Sea-Fisherman.* Longmans, Green, 1868.

SHEEP-SCORING NUMERALS

382. *Swaledale*

Joseph Lucas, *Studies in Nidderdale.*

383. *Wensleydale*

J. R. Witty, *Transactions of the Yorkshire Dialect Society*, vol. 4, pt. xxviii.

384. *Nidderdale*

Joseph Lucas, *Studies in Nidderdale.*

385. *Craven*

J. R. Witty (op. cit.); Joseph Lucas, *Studies in Nidderdale.*

386. *Knaresborough*

Lucas (*op. cit.*) gives also numerals from Kirkby Stephen (Westmorland), Middleton-in-Teesdale (Co. Durham), Coniston, Eskdale, and Wasdale Head (Cumberland), Epping (Essex), Maine, Hebron (Connecticut), and Cincinnati (Ohio).

From a linguistic point of view it is strange to find such an every day implement as a set of numerals persisting in the spoken speech of a people who hardly knew another word of the language of which these formed part, and who of course had their own numerals. It is perhaps not too romantic an explanation to suggest that among the few Celts who became subjects to the foreign invaders, were humble shepherds who had always tended sheep on the north country moors and fells. The new settlers would doubtless find it useful to keep them in their hereditary occupations, and in taking over the shepherd, they also took over his system of numeration which in his mind was indissolubly associated with the sheep under his care.

E. M. Wright, *Rustic Speech* (1913), p. 327.

387. *Masham*

Publications of the Folk-lore Society, XLV, 1899.

388. *The Miller: Mooter poke*

F. W. Moorman, *Yorkshire Dialect Poems* (1673–1915).

389. *The Miller: Down i' yon lum*

A miller near Rotherham acquired a reputation for taking a very liberal MOOTER or toll from the corn sent to be ground at his mill. First he tolled himself, then his son tolled, and lastly big Betty his wife tolled. After that the miller tolled it all over again. The miller having built a new parlour to his house, a local wit called it 'pinch-poke-parlour,' and wrote these lines on the subject.

S. O. Addy, *Sheffield Glossary*, p. 150.

390, 391. *The Thatcher*

John Nicholson, *Folk Speech of East Yorkshire*, p. 13.

392. *The Weaver*

Attributed to John Pearson, a Bramley character who could neither read nor write.

The domestic system, as they call it, sounds well enough, but that is all: every part except the weaving is performed at public mills.

Wm. Cookson in a letter to Wm. Wilberforce from Leeds, 5 February, 1805. *English Letters of the Nineteenth Century*, p. 29. Pelican Books.

It was not difficult to learn to work a hand-loom, and for a few years the profits were high. Agricultural labourers swarmed into it, and as they had been accustomed to low wages, the master spinners found them ready to work at an inferior price, and so discovered an outlet for their extra quantity of yarn.

J. L. Hammond and Barbara Hammond, *The Town Labourer, 1760–1832*, 1920, p. 12.

This at once led to a great depreciation in the price of hand-loom labour, and was the beginning of that train of disasters which has finally terminated in reducing those who have clung to it to a state of starvation.

P. Gaskell, *The Manufacturing Population of England*, 1833, p. 47, quoted J. L. Hammond and Barbara Hammond, op. cit., p. 13.

The Yorkshire weaver was a small master craftsman of the old type, himself buying and owning the raw material, and once or twice a week selling his cloth in the markets of Leeds or Wakefield

Sidney and Beatrice Webb, *The History of Trade Unionism, 1666–1920*, 1920, p. 35.

Most miserable of all were the handloom weavers, of whom several tens of thousands remained. It was common enough for the stockinger, in particular, to earn in a week what a miner earned in a day. Those who were independent were engaged in a crazy attempt to rival the speed of a power loom, and in this haste they lost even that care and accuracy which were the sole recommendation of a handmade product.

R. W. Postgate, *A Short History of the British Workers*. The Plebs League, 1926, p. 38.

(See Watson and Hobbs, *Great Farmers*, Selwyn Blount, 1937, for an account of the Yorkshire Weavers' contribution to the improvement of the pig.)

393. *The Chimney Sweep*

Samuel Dyer, *Dialect of the West Riding of Yorkshire*, 1891.

394. *The Bellman*

The Bellman was Dicky Fletcher of Bridlington (1748–1827).

The Bellman of Bridlington, who was killed in his 80th year, by falling down the steps of a cellar; famous for his facetious and rhyming announcements, delivered in the unadulturated Doric of his native tongue of which this is a specimen.

Frederick Ross, *Celebrities of the Yorkshire Wolds*, 1878, p. 66.

Compare with another bellman's cry (Ripon) which was often printed with the 'specimens' of Yorkshire dialect.

I is to gie notidge, that Joanie Pickersgill yeats yewn to neit, to moarn at moarn, an' to moarn at neit, an' nea langer as lang as storm hods, cause he can git na mair eldin.

Specimens of the Yorkshire Dialect. Otley, n.d.

This was printed by James O. Halliwell in his *Yorkshire*

Anthology, 1851, and in chapbooks printed at the Yorkshire market towns—e.g., Driffield (1899), Richmond, Kirby Moorside, Leeds, Otley, York.

A version appeared in the *Northallerton Almanack*, 1886.

395. *The Bird Tenter*

John Nicholson, *The Folk Speech of East Yorkshire*, p. 10.

396. *The Witch's Curse*

This is from Richard Blakeborough's poem *T'Hunt o' Yatton Brigg*, 2nd edition, 1899, p. 12.

Rev. J. C. Atkinson (*Forty Years in a Moorland Parish*. Macmillan, 1891) has much about witches and witch antidotes.

Roun-tree, or Rowan-tree, the quicken tree, mountain ash, or witch-wood, a tree of high consideration in the north, and considered by the superstitious peasantry of wonderful efficacy in depriving witches of their infernal power.

Brockett, vol. 2, p. 102.

Gad: a wooden rod, or handle; a story is told of a certain supposed witch, who stopped a lad's ploughing team, in the middle of a field. But the lad was amply prepared, having a whipstock of wickentree. With this, he touched his horses, in turn, and broke the spell, whereupon the old lady gave way to an angry rhythmical exclamation:

Damn the lad,
Wi' the roan-tree gad!

and disappeared.

C. C. Robinson, *Mid-Yorkshire Glossary*, p. 47.

If your whipstock's made of row'n
Your nag you may ride through any town.

Johnnie Gray, *Through Airedale from Goole to Malham*, Leeds, 1891.

Two notes from the George Calvert–M. Stapylton book in the possession of Mr J. Fairfax Blakeborough:

A love charm worn by Martha Willson . . . (a design of the charm). . . .

It was inchanted by Molly Milburn of Danby. Yt was worked on skinne with silken thread and worne over the heart. Molly mayde manny suche. She was deeply versed in suche like matters and allsoe the warding off of evil spells, and witchcraft, and the evil eye. Molly was greatly skilled in the curing of divers ailments, and wrought she many exceeding winderfull cures such as war nuer heeard on afore her days.

Oct ye 5 1663 Molly Milburn was thys daye whipped for that she been a witch and worke greate evil amang Thomas Turners cattel, so that a grevious scab dyd brek out . . . amang yem. At ye same tyme was whipped Jane Nailer for that she having now her fourth bastard, was adjudged woman drab. Both war beaten at Castleton high end.

Another 'Evil Eye' note from Yorkshire:

Ye gang out ov a night—ivery night while ye find nine toads —an when ye've gitten t'nine toads, ye hang 'em up ov a string, an' ye make a hole and buries t'toads i' t'hole—and as t'toads pines away, so t'person pines away at you've looked upon wiv a yevil eye, an' they pine and pine away while they die without ony disease at all!

Choice Notes from Notes and Queries, 1859, p. 130.

397. *A Charm*

Richard Blakeborough, *Yorkshire Wit, Character, Folk-lore, and Customs*, 1898, p. 151.

I had this from the Wise Man as a charm again the ill will of witches or the like other inchantment to be tyed rownd the necke and then yt to wander freely. Promise when ye tie yt on that ye will give the same to ye Lord within a twelvemonth from that time, and alle schalle be well. No witch with evil eye spell inchantment whatsoever schalle come nigh your flocke, but be ye sure to keep your promise with ye Lord, or evil days schalle follow you even as your shaddow. I have tried thys for many yeares and no evil ever came nigh my flocks save when the charm one strayed from ye flocke.

George Calvert-M. Stapylton manuscript book in possession of Mr J. Fairfax Blakeborough.

See also Michael Drayton's *Nymphidia* for a charm (*A Sixteenth-century Anthology*, edited by Arthur Symonds), and George Borrow, *The Bible in Spain*, chap. iii, for a remarkable Portuguese one.

398. *A Fairy Rhyme*

Nanny Button-cap, the name of a fairy. The lines are repeated by children. In the Norse mythology the goddess Nanna was the wife of Balder. She was a moon-dis, or moon goddess, and was 'the daughter of the ruler of the moon.'

Rydberg's Teutonic Myth., trans. by Anderson, p. 463.
Supplement to the S. O. Addy, *Sheffield Glossary*, p. 30.

Maye ye 7th 1650.

Veri earlie in ye morning Ralph Blackburn, George Pickersgill Anthony Thompson, and Marn hys wife, having to go to Whitby, and when they cam nigh unto Agar Barker . . . close, they ane and alle espied manny fairies disporting themselves righte merriely in their sprightly midnight revels. They watched them closely for some time until one dancing a little space from ye rynge, discovered yem, when gyving a signal, they departed on ye instant, and not one of them kennd wither. Alle ye witnesses are of good report. Thys pleaseth ye townsfolk mightlie, nane been seen hereabout sin Dan Outhwaite war murdered eight year come next cannelmas. The fairies war oft seen after thys, even mysen as stated a week syn. T. R.

George Calvert–M. Stapylton manuscript book in possession of Mr J. Fairfax Blakeborough.

399. *A Fairy Rhyme*

Near Flamborough is a circular pit where a girl named Jenny Gallows is said to have committed suicide. It is a common belief along the coast that anyone running nine times round the hole can hear the fairies. Another legend connected with the spot is that the spirit of Jenny, dressed in white, rises when the eighth circuit is completed, and cries out:

'Ah'll tee on me bonnet,' etc.

Flamborough : Village and Headland, edited by Robert Fisher, 1894, p. 147.

400. *Hob Rhymes : Hob-hole Hob !*

Rev. J. C. Atkinson, *A Glossary of the Cleveland Dialect*.

This was said by mothers who took their children who had whooping-cough to the cave at Runswick Bay known as Hob Hole. Hob was the spirit who lived in the cave, and he was popularly supposed to be able to cure this malady.

The fishermen of the neighbourhood still regard the place with superstitious dread, and are unwilling to pass it at night.

N. and Q., vol. 6, p. 447 (1852).

401. *Hob Rhymes : Hob trush Hob !*

Hobtrush: a word occurring in the designations Hobtrush or Obtrush Rook (a tumulus on the Farndale Moors) and Hobtrush Hob, a being once held to frequent a certain cave in Mulgrave Woods, and wont to be addressed, and to reply as above.

Rev. J. C. Atkinson, *A Glossary of the Cleveland Dialect*, 1868, p. 263.

402. *Hob Rhymes : Gin Hob mun hae*

Hob at Hart Hall, in Glaisdale, was, as the legend bears, a farm-spirit 'of all work, thrashing, winnowing, STAMPING the bigg, leading,' etc. Like the rest of the tribe who ever came under mortal eye, he was without clothes—nakt—and having had a HARDING-SMOCK made and placed for him, after a few moments of—it would seem, ill-pleased—inspection, he was heard to say the above lines.

Rev. J. C. Atkinson, *A Glossary of the Cleveland Dialect.*

See *Yorkshire Dialect Society's Transactions*, vol. vii, pt. xliii, for a paper 'Yorkshire Hobs' by Professor Bruce Dickins, M.A.

May 15th 1669.

Nathan Warner of Castleton thys daye had speech of the Hob Nydy that hanth ye Hob Garth from hys nid whither he had that daye been. Thys he sweare on oath, and he is a man of good report, and not given to vain talk. Methought I once had sighte of hym mysen, but not been over certyne ont, I held my peace: but after what Warner declareth on oath, I holde no doubt but that yt war hym I spyed mysen: but I doe not declare yt to be certayne. The Lord knoweth.

George Calvert-M. Stapylton manuscript book, in possession of Mr J. Fairfax Blakeborough.

See Rev. J. C. Atkinson's *Forty Years in a Moorland Parish*, 1891, p. 51.

403. *Churning Rhyme*

Publications of the Folk-lore Society, XLV, 1899.

404. *The Sun*

A Staithes fishermen's rhyme.

405. *The Moon : A Setterda's meean*

Compare:

A Saturday's Moon
If it comes once in seven years
it comes too soon. (Sussex.)

N. and Q., vol. 2, p. 515.

And

Friday's moon
Come when it will, it comes too soon.

Brockett, vol. i, p. 178.

406. *The Moon: Saturday's moon*

Compare:

Saturday new and Sunday full
Never was fine and never wool. (Devon.)
N. and Q., vol. 2, p. 515.

407. *Clear moon*

Kimble's preface to *The Shepherd of Banbury's Observations.* Sylvan Press.

408. *I see t'mean*

Yorkshire Dialect Poems (1672–1915), edited F. W. Moorman, p. 127; *Publications of the Folk-lore Society*, XLV, 1899, p. 43 (in St English).

Compare:

I see the moon and the moon sees me
God bless the parson that baptized me.
C. C. Robinson, *Dialect of Leeds*, p. 301.

409. *A far-off brough*

Whitby District.

Brough: a halo round the moon.
Brockett, vol. i, p. 67.

Compare:

A far-off burgh tells of a near hand storm.
Prevost, p. 48.

When t'burr's far, t'rain's nar.

If t'bur o' t'muin be far away
Mek heaste an' house yer cworn an' hay;
Bit if t'bur be nar t'muin
We'll hev a clash bit nit sae suin.
Prevost, p. 48.

410. *Mair rain*

General. Hazlitt gives a Cornish addition 'more water will suit the ducks best.'

411. *Raan afoor seven*

If it begins to rain an hour or two before sun-rising, it is likely to be fair before noon, and so continue that day, but if the rain begins an hour or two after sun rising, it is likely to rain all that day, except the rainbow be seen before it rains.

'Shepherd of Banbury,' *N. and Q.*, vol. 8, p. 512.

412. *If the rain comes*

Northallerton Almanack, 1912.

413. *Snow*

Yorkshire Dialect Poems (1673–1915), edited by F. W. Moorman, p. 130.

Compare:

Snaw, snaw, faster;
Bull, bull, faster;
Owd women picking geese,
Sending feathers down to Leeds.

C. C. Robinson, *Dialect of Leeds*, p. 259.

Bull: A word in use amongst children, and this only during a fall of snow when they cry in concert . . . (above lines). It may possibly be a corruption of 'burl' to pour.

Ibid.

And

The old woman's a-pickin' her geese.

Word-Lists from the South: American Dialect Society. Publication 2: *A Word-List from the Southern Highlands.* Josiah Combs. Texas Christian University.

And

In Borrowdale they have a saying that 'when it rains on Maudlin (Magdalen) day, Jenny Maudlin is bleaching her brat.' This is the 2nd of August.

Dickinson, *Cumberland Glossary*, p. 10.

414. *Frost*

A Staithes fishermen's saying.

Compare:

Three white frosts, and then rain.

F. W. Dowson, *Goathland in History and Folk-lore.*

And

Frost and fraud have always foul ends.

Camden, *Remains Concerning Britain.*

415. *Fog*

Whitby District.

Brockett, vol. i, p. 208. HAR: A mist or thick fog.

See also number 295.

416. *Mist: A moorn hag-mist*

Whitby District.

417. *Mist: When the mist comes from the hill*

Compare with numbers 234 and 238, and Ray's:

When the clouds are upon the hills,
They'll come down by the mills (p. 28).

418. *Mist: An awd meean mist*

F. W. Dowson, *Goathland in History and Folk-lore.*

Hazlitt gives Denham's version which adds, 'but a new moon's mist will never lack thrist (thirst).

419. *Clouds and Sky: When it gangs up i' sops*

Sops: Small detached clouds hanging on the sides of a mountain, which prognosticate rain, agreeably to the Craven proverb (above) which is equivalent to Ray's (quoted above).

William Carr, *Craven Glossary*, vol. ii, p. 147.

420. *If woolly fleeces*

Northallerton Almanack, 1912. Denham (1846) Hazlitt.

421. *A mackerel sky*

S. O. Addy, *Sheffield Glossary*, p. 36; G. F. Northall, *A Warwickshire Word-Book*, p. 140; *Supp. to Vocabulary of East Anglia* (E.D.S.), p. 71.

Hazlitt, *English Proverbs and Proverbial Phrases*, 1869, has an astonishing version: 'The mackerel's cry is never long dry.'

422. *Hen scrats an' filly tails*

Compare:

Whene'er ye spy hen-scrats and filly tails
Be sure ye mind to lower your topsails.

William Carr, *Craven Glossary*, vol. i, p. 149.

423. *A red sky at night*

S. O. Addy, *Sheffield Glossary*, p. 188.
Compare:

Evening red and morning grey,
are unfailing signs of a genial day.
Bohn, *A Handbook of Proverbs*, 1855, p. 348.

And

If the evening's red, and the morning gray,
It is a sign of a bonnie day;
If the evening's gray and the morning red,
The lamb and the ewe will go wet to bed.
Grace Rhys, *Cradle Songs*, p. 191.

And

Sky red in the morning
Is a sailor's warning;
Sky red at night
Is the sailor's delight.

And

A dog at night
Is the farmer's delight.

Dog: a partial rainbow. *Lonsdale Glossary*.

424. *When the days lengthen*

Ray, p. 28; *N. and Q.*, vol. 2, p. 515.

425. *As monny haws*

As many haws, so many cold toes (*Whitby Glossary*, p. 22).
Compare:

Monny haws.
Monny snaws.
F. T. Dinsdale, *Teesdale Glossary*, p. 20.

And

A haw year
A snaw year. (Scotland.)

And

Many haws
Many cold toes.

Thomas Gibson, *Legends and Historical Notes on Places in the East and West Wards, Westmorland*. Manchester, 1877.

426. *Winter's thunder*

Winter's thunder makes summer's wonder.

Camden, *Remains concerning Britain*, 1870 edition, p. 336.

Winter's thunder is the world's wonder.

Cradle Songs.

427. *The Onion*

Northallerton Almanack, 1912.

428. *The Seasons*

Attributed to Sydney Smith (1771–1845), one-time vicar of Heslington and of Foston. He was a noted wit, essayist, and reviewer.

Sydney Smith said he liked Grote because he was so ladylike and Mrs Grote because she was such a gentleman.

Lucie Duff Gordon, *Gordon Waterfield*, p. 36. Murray.

Thursday, November 25th 1824.—We breakfasted at Thirsk on our way to Mr Sydney Smith, at Foston; arrived by a very good cross-road, without going to York. We found at the Smith's, besides their two daughters, Mr Vernon, one of the innumerable sons of the Archbishop of York, and Mr Beverley, a young Yorkshireman of very good mind and manners. We passed the evening very agreeably with music, and with the inexhaustible conversation of our host.

Extracts of the Journals and Correspondence of Miss Berry, vol. 3, p. 357. Longmans, Green & Co., 1865.

As a county magistrate he was concerned in erecting the modern walls round York Castle which were known as 'Smith's hardest joke.'

K. E. T. Wilkinson, *York.*

429. *Birds: The Bat*

Frederick Ross, *Holderness Glossary*, p. 30.

430. *The Bat*

Staithes, 'Backbearaway: the bat.' E.D.S. xxii, *Supp. to East Yorkshire Words.*

Compare:

Bat! bat! bear away,
Here-away, there-away
Inta my hat.

Rev. J. C. Atkinson, *Lonsdale Glossary.*

431. *The Crow*

C. C. Robinson, *Dialect of Leeds*, p. 300.

Compare:

> Craw, craw, flee oot o' seet,
> Or else Ah'll eat yer liver an' leet.

Richard Blakeborough, *Yorkshire Wit, Character, Folk-lore, and Customs*, 1898, p. 277.

And

> Crow, crow, get out of my sight,
> Or else I'll eat thy liver and lights.

John Harland and T. T. Wilkinson, *Lancashire Folk-lore*, 1867, p. 70; and *N. and Q.*, vol. 4, p. 53.

432. *The Crow*

Northallerton Almanack, 1913.

If you see Two Crows you'll have good luck after it, but if you should chance to spy one crow single 'tis a Bad Omen and some ill will betide you.

L'Estrange, *Life of Æsop*.

433 and 434. *The Cuckoo*

Grace Rhys' *Cradle Songs* includes both these under the heading 'The Cuckoo in Yorkshire,' p. 177.

Compare:

> In the month of Averil,
> The gawk comes o'er the hill,
> In a shower of rain;
> And on the — of June,
> He turns his tune again.

William Carr, *Craven Glossary*, vol. i, p. 14.

435. *The Cuckoo*

Northallerton Almanack, 1913.

436. *The Cuckoo*

Farndale, from *A Bo'ddin o' Cowls.* Arthur Stanley Umpleby, 1937, p. 10.

Compare:

> In April
> The cuckoo shows his bill.
> In May
> He is singing all day;

In June
He changes his tune;
In July
He prepares to fly;
In August
Fly he must.

Northallerton Almanack, 1913.

437. *The Lapwing*

Brockett, vol. 2, p. 71.

The common people in the North Riding of Yorkshire believe that at one period the cushat, or ringdove, laid its eggs upon the ground, and that the peewit *e contra* made its nest on high. They further believe that an amicable exchange took place between the two birds and that at the present day they respectively sing out their feelings upon the subject. A local rhyme will have it that the pee-wit sings,

Pee-wit, pee-wit,
I coup'd my nest and I rue it.

And that the cushat's note implies

Coo, coo, come now,
Little lad with thy gad,
Come not thou.

See note 396 for explanation of 'gad.'

We like C. J. F. Atkinson's description of a poor pasture:

It wod nobbut carry twea geese and a tewit ti t'acre.

Recollections from a Yorkshire Dale, p. 189.

438. *The Magpie*

Richmond Almanack, 1907.

439. *The Magpie*

North Country Lore and Legend, 1887, p. 375.

440. *The Magpie*

Whitby District. However by making as many crosses upon the ground as there are birds, you may avert these indications.

441. *The Magpie*

Richmond Almanack, 1907.

442. *The Magpie*

Yorkshire Dialect Poems 1673–1915, edited by F. W. Moorman; S. O. Addy, *Sheffield Glossary*, p. 183.

443. *The Magpie*

John Nicholson, *The Folk Speech of East Yorkshire*, p. 11; C. C. Robinson, *Mid-Yorks Glossary*, p. 142; and S. O. Addy, *Supplement to Sheffield Glossary*, p. 58.

444. *The Magpie*

Compare:

Tell tale tit,
Thy tongue shall split,
And every little dog
Shall have a little bit.

S. O. Addy, *Sheffield Glossary*, p. 253.

And

Tell-pie-tit,
Thy tongue'll slit,
An' every dog i' t'town'll get a bit!

C. C. Robinson, *Mid-Yorkshire Glossary*, p. 142.

And

A pleean-pie tit
Thy tongue sal be slit
An' iv'ry dog i' th'town
Sal hev abit.

William Carr, *Craven Glossary*, vol. ii, p. 49.

445. *The Peacock*

Northallerton Almanack, 1912.

446. *The Seagull*

Bogg, *History of Richmondshire*, p. 673.

Compare:

Sea-gull, sea-gull, sit on the sand,
It's never good weather while you're on the land.

Smithson, *Northallerton Almanack*, 1912; Grace Rhys, *Cradle Songs*.

Horace Annesley Vachell, *This Was England*, 1933, gives:

Sea-gull, sea-gull, get thee on't sand,
'Twill never be fine while thou'rt on land.

The Gull comes against the rain.
Oxford Dictionary of English Proverbs.

447. *The Seagull*

A Staithes fishermen's rhyme.

449. *The Sparrow*

Rev. J. C. Atkinson, *Lonsdale Glossary*, p. 54.

450. *Ladslove*

William Carr, *Craven Glossary*, vol. i, p. 273.

451. *The Docken*

Richard Blakeborough, *Yorkshire Wit, Character, Folk-lore, and Customs*, 1898, pp. 276–7.

Compare:

Out 'ettle in dock
Dock zhall ha' a new smock,
'Ettle shall ha' nar-run (ne'er a one)
Britton, *Beauties of Wiltshire* (1825). E.D.S.

And

In dock, out nettle,
Nettle have a sting' me.
James Jennings, *The Dialect of the West of England*, 1869.

And

Out nettle in dock.
Camden.

And

Thow biddest me I sholde love another
Al freshly newe, and lat Criseyde go!
It lyth not in my power, leve brother.
And though I mighte, I wolde not do so.
But canstow pleyen raket, to and fro,
Netle in, dokke out, now this, now that,
Pandare?

Chaucer: Troilus and Criseyde, Bk. iv, v. 66, *The Complete Works of Geoffrey Chaucer*, edited Rev. Walter W. Skeat. Clarendon Press.

In Dock out Nettle upon the change of Places, when one is no sooner out, but another is in his place.

A New Dictionary of the Terms Ancient and Modern of the Canting Crew in its Several Tribes of Gypsies, Beggars, Thieves, Cheats, etc., n.d. [1700].

When a labourer or child has been severely stung with nettles, some good matron collects the dock-leaves, spits upon them, and begins to rub with them all the parts affected, repeatedly pronouncing the following words of incantation, 'In docken, out nettle.' This operation is continued till the violent smarting and inflammation subside: the time seldom exceeds ten minutes.

A List of Ancient Words at present used in the Mountainous District of the West Riding of Yorkshire, by Robert Willan, M.D., F.R.S., 1811. (E.D.S., 1873.)

452. *The Docken*

Richard Blakeborough, *Yorkshire Wit, Character, Folk-lore, and Customs.*

William Barnes in his *Poems of Rural Life* alludes to the custom in the poem 'Dock-leaves.'

How we, when nettles had a-stung
Our little hands when we wer young,
Did rub 'em wi' a dock, an' zing
'Out nettl', in dock. In dock, out sting.'

453. *Quaking Grass*

Richard Blakeborough, *Yorkshire Wit, Character, Folk-lore, and Customs.*

Quaking-grass: Briza media.

English Dialect Dictionary, edited by Joseph Wright.

454. *The Ash Tree*

S. O. Addy, *Sheffield Glossary*, p. 6; George Borrow, *Lavengro*, gives another 'ash' rhyme:

Ash when green,
Is fire for a Queen.

455. *Bees*

This is from the Diary of Francis Mewburn of Darlington (*The Larchfield Diary*). He was the last Chief Bailiff of Darlington, and the first railway solicitor in the world. He corresponded with Lingard, the historian, on dialect.

Britton's *Beauties of Wiltshire* has an interesting note about Bees under Tang:

> To make a noise with a key and shovel at the time of swarming of a hive, not, as is supposed, to induce them to settle, but to give notice of the rising of the swarm, which could not be followed if they went on a neighbour's premises, unless this warning was given; so that this kind of rough music was called Tanging, it being an imitation of a bell.
>
> E.D.S. 1879 reprint of Britton's *Beauties of Wilts* (1825).

Ray (p. 26) gives the first two lines, but omits the June couplet, as does the Shepherd of Banbury.

456. *The Ladybird*

Yorkshire Dialect Poems (1673–1915), edited by F. W. Moorman; William Carr, *Craven Glossary*, vol. i, p. 89 (with second line reading 'your children do roam').

457. *The Snail*

Frederick Ross, *Holderness Glossary*, p. 132.
Compare:

> Sneel, sneel, put oot yer hoan
> Or Ah'll kill yer fayther and muther te moan.
>
> John Nicholson, *The Folk Speech of East Yorkshire*, p. 14.

458. *The Church Bell*

According to Mary A. Boultree (*Gleanings from an Iron Chest*, Darlington, 1901), this was the inscription on the church bell of St. Mary's Hornby at the time of Henry VII.

Mark Pattison, the scholar and biographer, was born at Hornby, and spent much of his early life there. According to A. Blythe Webster's *A Biographical Memoir*, *George Saintsbury*, The Memorial Volume (Methuen, 1945), Mark was the only person for whom Saintsbury had a harsh word.

> Many people still believe that the tolling of the parish church bell at the time of death or funeral, commonly called the passing bell, the dead bell, or the soul bell, is for the purpose of driving away the evil spirits, which dare not, it is imagined, come within hearing of the solemn sound. It used formerly to call good Christians to pray for the soul of the deceased person. Hence the old couplet:
>
> When the bell begins to toll,
> Lord, have mercy on the soul. . . .

Bede is the first who mentions the custom.

William Brockie, *Legends and Superstitions of the County of Durham*. Sunderland, 1886.

Compare:

When thou dost hear a toll or knell
Then think upon thy passing bell.

Ray, 156, and Ingledew, *The History and Antiquities of Northallerton*, 1858.

Passing bell, nine knells for a man, six for a woman, three for a child.

When the bell begins to toll
Lord have mercy on the soul.

Christopher Clarkson, *History of Richmond*, 1821.

Compare:

I rang for the living, I tolled for the dead,
I gave the first greetings to those who were wed;
And still in God's house I stand by the door,
To open the portals to rich and to poor.

At Norton, Sheffield. Arthur Mee, *King's England, The West Riding*, p. 270.

The Passing Bell.

The Bell is tolled when an inhabitant dies, giving nine knells for a man, six for a woman, and three for a child—so not one of Richmond's community, even the humblest, lives anonymous or dies unknown. Just before the Bell is tolled, a card with the full name inscribed is affixed to the Town Hall door that all may read the record of the death which has set tolling the Bell.

Souvenir Programme in Commemoration of the 850th Anniversary of the Enfranchisement of Richmond, 1st to 7th August 1943.

'GANGIN TO TH'PASSING.' The passing bell was formerly tolled to warn the neighbourhood to pray for the departing soul, but now it only indicates death, and gives the signal for the neighbours to lay out the dead body.

Is there any man in his chamber hears a bell toll for another man, and does not kneel down to pray for that dying man? and when his charity breathes out upon another man, does he not also reflect upon himself, and dispose himself as if he were in a state of that dying man? We begin to hear Christ's Bell toll now, and is not our bell in the chime? We must be in his grave before we come to his resurrection, and we must be in his death, before we come to his grave.

Dr. Donne's *Sermons*, vide William Carr, *Craven Glossary*, vol. 2, p. 34.

APPENDIX I

On Ilkla Moor Baht 'at

Parent. Wheer wer' ta bahn w'en Aw saw thee,
On Ilkla Moor baht 'at?

Son. Aw wor a-coortin' Mary Jane,
On Ilkla Moor baht 'at.

P. Aw'll tell thi father w'en he comes whoam,
On Ilkla Moor baht 'at.

S. Nay, nay, owd lad, don't tak on soa,
On Ilkla Moor baht 'at.

P. Tha'll sewerly ketch thi deeath o' cowd,
On Ilkla Moor baht 'at.

S. Aw'm sewer it wor as warrm as toast,
On Ilkla Moor baht 'at.

P. Tha'll get a bonny month i' bed,
On Ilkla Moor baht 'at.

S. Then yo can coom an' berry me,
On Ilkla Moor baht 'at.

P. Then wurrms'll coom an' ate thee oop,
On Ilkla Moor baht 'at.

S. Ahr ducks'll gobble up t'wurrms,
On Ilkla Moor baht 'at.

P. Tha feearly maks mi bluid rin cowd,
On Ilkla Moor baht 'at.

S. An' yo can gobble oop t'ducks
An' so get back yor awn ;
An' 'appen they will pizen ye,
An' 'appen they will pizen ye,
An' then yo'll keep me company,
On Ilkla Moor baht 'at.

Solo to ' me an' all,' or
All in unison to ' me an' all,' and Chorus as before.

So let us all together goa,
On Ilkla Moor baht 'at,
Wi' Peg and Kate, John Willie an' Jo,
Wi' Dodd o' Bill's an' ahr Sam Poll,
Wi' Ben's lil lass an' me an' all,
On Ilkla Moor baht 'at.

All in unison lines 1–5, with Chorus, lines 6–8.

O, Ilkla Moor's both broad and fair,
Its air so sweet and fine!
But long t'days sin' we ran there:
Ay, long t'days sin' we ran there:
The days, the days of Auld Lang Syne!
A cup o' kindness yet,
A cup o' kindness yet,
We'll tak' for Auld Lang Syne!

APPENDIX 2

Cleveland Lyke-Wake Dirge

(Sir Walter Scott's version)

This ae nighte, this ae nighte,
  Every nighte and alle;
Fire and sleete and candle lighte,
  And Christe receive thye saule.

When thou from hence away art paste,
  Every nighte and alle;
To Whinny-muir thou comest at laste;
  And Christe receive thye saule.

If ever thou gavest hosen and shoon,
  Every nighte and alle;
Sit thee down, and put them on;
  And Christe receive thye saule.

If hosen and shoon thou ne'er gavest nane,
  Every nighte and alle;
The whinnes shall pricke thee to the bare bane,
  And Christe receive thye saule.

From Whinny-muir when thou mayst passe,
  Every nighte and alle;
To Brigg o' Dread thou comest at laste,
  And Christe receive thye saule.

(A stanza wanting)

From Brigg o' Dread when thou mayst passe,
  Every nighte and alle;
To purgatory fire thou comest at laste;
  And Christ receive thye saule.

If ever thou gavest meat or drinke,
  Every nighte and alle;
The fire shall never make thee shrinke;
  And Christe receive thye saule.

If meate or drinke thou never gavest nane,
  Every nighte and alle;
The fire will burn thee to the bare bane;
  And Christe receive thye saule.

This ae nighte, this ae nighte,
  Every nighte and alle;
Fire and sleete and candle lighte,
  And Christe receive thye saule.

Cleveland Lyke-Wake Dirge
(Richard Blakeborough's version)

This yah neeght, this yah neeght,
  Ivvery neeght an' awl,
Fire an' fleet an' cann'l leeght,
  An' Christ tak up thi sowl.

When thoo fra hither gans awaay,
  Ivvery neeght an' awl,
Ti Whinny Moor thoo cum'st at last,
  An' Christ tak up thi sowl.

If ivver tho gav' owther hosen or shoon,
  Ivvery neeght an' awl,
Clap tha doon an' put 'em on,
  An' Christ tak up thi sowl.

Bud if hosen or shoon thoo nivver ga' neean,
  Ivvery neeght an' awl,
T'whinnies'll prick tha sair ti t'beean,
  An' Christ tak up thi sowl.

Fra Whinny Moor that thoo mayst pass,
  Ivvery neeght an' awl,
Ti t'Brigg o' Dreead thoo'll cum at last,
  An' Christ tak up thi sowl.

If ivver thoo gav' o' thi siller an' gawd,
  Ivvery neeght an' awl,
At t'Brigg o' Dreead thoo'll finnd footho'd,
  An' Christ tak up thi sowl.

Bud if o' siller an' gawd thoo nivver ga' neean,
  Ivvery neeght an' awl,
Thoo'll doon, doon tumm'l tiwards Hell fleeams,
  An' Christ tak up thi sowl.

Fra t'Brigg o' Dreead 'at thoo mayst pass,
  Ivvery neeght an' awl,
To t'fleeams o' Hell thoo'll cum at last,
  An' Christ tak up thi sowl.

If ivver thoo gav' owther bite or sup,
 Ivvery neeght an' awl,
T'fleeams'll nivver catch tha up,
 An' Christ tak up thi sowl.

But if bite or sup thoo nivver ga' neean,
 Ivvery neeght an' awl,
T'fleeams'll bo'n tha sair ti t'beean,
 An' Christ tak up thi sowl.

From *Yorkshire Wit, Character, Folk-lore and Customs*, 1911, p. 119.

APPENDIX 3

George Calvert–M. Stapylton Manuscript Book

Readers will have noticed the many references to the George Calvert–M. Stapylton manuscript book. This valuable dialect and folk-lore material was collected by George Calvert under the direction of Martin Stapylton in the early years of the 19th century. Fortunately it passed into the possession of Richard Blakeborough, and then later into the hands of his son, Mr. J. Fairfax Blakeborough, who kindly lent the manuscript to the Yorkshire Dialect Society for exhibition on their stand at the Yorkshire Agricultural Society's 99th Annual Show at Beverley, May, 1936.

We give below the characteristic and interesting dedication of the work by George Calvert to Martin Stapylton.

To Martin Stapylton, Esq.

The following bits I have gotten together according to your wish at the cost of much time and great trouble. The matter herein wrote do make a true account of those things which I have gotten both first hand from trusty folk and from the writings of their forelders: these latter I did oft find beyond my schooling so that they were past my reading. I then got me to our parson Mr. Smyth and he on your behalf did always give me the same in the writing of our time. I have also had the like good help from the Pickering parson who hath always done into English all I ever took him which I did find past my schooling for to decipher.

So now after a space of nine years my labours on your behalf do now come to an end.

To you, Sir, I do leave the task of setting all I have gotten together in that order in which you will doubtless desire to have them but the which is altogether past me to set about the doing of.

I therefore subscribe myself your Humble and Obedient servant.

George Calvert.

1823.

GLOSSARY

Aence: ounce.
addle: earn.
agate: busy.
ahint: behind.
aibles: perhaps.
als: as.
amell: among.
anent: beside.
arvall: funeral.
ass: ash.
assin': asking.
atstead: instead.
awmers: gift, small portion.

Baan: bone.
baat, baht: without.
bain, bane: near.
barghams: horse-collars.
barguest: a ghost commonly appearing near gates or stiles; often took the form of a mastiff, a pig, a donkey, etc.; considered a harbinger of death.
barm: yeast.
bastile: work-house.
bauks: swells.
beals: bellows.
beeak: (1) book; (2) bake.
behont: behind.
belive: soon.
bettermy: superior, best.
bield: shelter, house.
blaze: bleat.
boamin': trailing along.
bodle: one sixth of a penny.
boss: kiss.
bou't: bolt, arrow.
brast: burst.
brat: (1) apron; (2) turbot.
breeadin': making twine covering of a crab-pot.
breeak: become bankrupt.
breckons: bracken.
broach: church steeple.
brossen-gutted: burst-bellied, greedy.
brough: halo round the sun or moon.
browden: fond.
buffet: stool.
bull-segg: castrated bull.
bun: bound.
bunch: kick.
burn: water.

Caar: sit.
cameril-hough: bend of hind leg.
capt: surprised.
cauf'd: calfed.
causey: raised road across a moor, highway.
cess: toll.
chimley: chimney.
chunther: grumble.
clame: heap.
clam: pinched, seized.
clamm'd: starved.
claumin': hanging about a person caressingly.
clems: daubs, sticks to.
clep: gaff for hauling fish aboard.
cletch: a brood of young birds.
cletchin' straws: straws indicating number and sex of children wished for.
clew-stick: the stick that holds the twine (clew) that controls the kite.
clocks: beetles.
clog: log of wood.
close: field.
cluthered: heaped up.
coit: coat.
cockelty-bread: a game played by children.
connies: an expletive like 'Bless me!'
coulpress: rough sea across harbour mouth.
coup: exchange.
cowl: rake.
crammle: hobble along.
crammly: tottery.
cratch: arm-chair.
culler'd: coloured, blushing.

Daffled: confused, stupid.
dainshed: made fastidious.
daytalman: farm-labourer hired by the day.
deagh: dough.
deeased: dazed.
deed: doings.
deid: death.
donn'd: dressed.
doonkessen: downcast.
dow: recover, thrive.
dowly: dismal.
doy: darling.
drab: slut.

draugh : draff.
dree : sad, weary.
driblets : small, inconsiderable things.

Egh : eye.
eldin : fuel.
esins : eaves.

Fahl : foul.
fain : glad, happy.
faldered : worn-out, exhausted.
farm-pleeacin' : service.
fauf : fallow.
feart : afraid.
feat : lively.
feck : great part.
feg : fig.
felted : hidden.
fend : mak a fend means to return to one's daily task.
fet : fit, suit.
fettle : clean, put in order.
feul : fool.
flackered : fluttered.
flags : flakes.
flaid : frightened, timid.
flannin : flannel.
flat-back : knife.
flay : frighten.
flay-kreeake : scare-crow.
flaysome : frightening.
fleead : flayed, skinned.
fleet : floor.
fligged : fledged, grown-up.
flittermoos : bat.
floats : ends or picks not properly stitched in weave.
flooer : flour.
floss-docken : foxglove.
fog : aftermath after hay-harvest, coarse grass.
fowd-garth : farm-yard.
frame : prepare.
frames : pretends.
frugan : curved iron rake for stirring the ashes in an oven.
frundel : handful.
fruzzins : short ends of yarn.
futtered : bustled.

Gaan : gown.
gad : wander aimlessly.
gainest : nearest.
gain-hand : near at hand.
galluses : straps.
galt : boar.
gam : sport.
garne : yarn.
gate : road, way.
gaum : notice.
gauvin' time : twilight, dusk.
gawk : cuckoo.
gear : possessions.
gen : grin.
Gerston : Grassington.
gif : if.
gilt : sow.
gimmer : young female lamb.
gin : grin.
gliff : glance.
glinck and glime : look cunningly.
gom : grandmother.
goodies : sweetmeats.
gowk : fool.
gradely : true, genuine.
graith : substance, wealth.
green fowk : fairies.
greet : weep.
gresins : stairs.
grou : sullen.

Haas : Hawes.
haggle : hail.
hag-mist : a thick white mist or fog.
hag-rid : bewitched.
ham-sam : in disorder.
handsel : use for the first time.
hap : cover.
happings : wrappings.
hardlins : scarcely.
harns : brains.
havver-ceeak : oat-cake.
heart aboon : cheerful, elated.
helter-full : halter-full.
hike : gore.
hime : hoar-frost.
hine : away.
hoan : horn.
hoast : cough.
hod : hold.
hodden-grey : grey homespun.
hopper : basket containing the seed-corn when sowing, usually suspended with a strap over the shoulder.
hoppit : hive.
hough-band : band on a cow's leg to prevent her from kicking.
hull : pig-sty.
hurn : corner.

Intak : that portion (of a farm) taken in from moor.

Jawther : mixture, mess.

Kale for kale : turn and turn about.

keeak : cake.
keffal : an old horse.
kelter : money.
kenspack : oddity, conspicuous sight.
kesting : swarming.
kill : kiln.
kimlin : tub.
kirne : churn.
kirne milk : butter milk.
kist : coffin.
kittle : tricky, difficult.
kreatchy : feeble.

Laate : seek.
lahl : little.
lahtle : little.
laikin' : playing.
lall : amble leisurely.
lall-dabber : cuff.
larock : lark.
lat : late.
lay : scythe.
leear : scythe.
leap-stang : long pole used for leaping over dykes.
lear-deers : barn-doors.
licks : beats, surpasses.
lig : lie.
ligs away : stops work.
lisk : flank.
lithin : thickening, flour and water used to thicken broth, gravy, etc.
livver : deliver.
lollard : a lazy person.
looance : allowance, wage.
lurry : feast.
loused : set free.
low : light.
lownd : calm.
lowsing-time : time to quit work and go home.
Maccaroni : dandified.
madlin : fool.
mall : mallet.
mally-mawk : slut.
mannishment : manure.
marrowed : matched.
maulin-shaft : handle of oven mop.
maut-hearted : maggot-hearted.
mawmetry : idolatrous, magical.
meer : mare.
mell : harvest-supper.
mell : mallet.
menseful : decent, fit.
mistal : cow-shed.
moother : take toll for grinding corn.
moot(h)er : toll for grinding corn.
mort : great deal, abundance.
muin : moon.

Nae : now.
nanpie : magpie.
needle : a short time (the time required to knit the stitches off one knitting needle).
neevy : fist.
neist : next.
neive : fist.
nestle : bustle about.
niber : neighbour.
nim : walk quickly.
nippins : wasted weft.
nowt : ox.

Ooined : worn out, depressed.
oond : hound.
ore : over, too.
oute'en : unless.
owmer : shade.
owmerin' : overshadowing.
owsen : oxen.

Paar : power.
pannierman : hawker who carries his goods in panniers slung over a horse's back.
pate : part.
pavors : paving-stones.
perch : pole over which pieces of cloth are pulled to be examined.
phiz : face.
pienannie : magpie.
pike : stack.
pleeaf : plough.
pleean : complaining.
plet : arrange in order.
plod : labourer.
ploo : plough.
poak : bag.
pobs : bread and milk.
pollaneeses : a dress for young boys, an old-fashioned long, tight-fitting overcoat.
poodther : powder.
pool : pull.
pranked : decked out, dressed.
pronsy : over-dressed.
put : gore.

Quarted : quarrelled.

Ram : forward.
randiboo : associate.
ratchets : sounds heard overhead during the night, resembling the yelping of dogs. An omen of death.
rannel-bauk : chimney cross-beam.
reckans : iron chains for pot-hooks.
recks : cares.

rist: rest.
rood: cross.
rowts: snorts.
rubbin'-steeans: scouring stones.
runty: thick-set.

Sackless: innocent.
sack-poke: corn sack.
sad-keeak: fatty cake, pastry cake.
sam: pick.
sannut: shall not.
sark: shirt.
sarrow: serve, supply with food.
sarten: certain.
scaumin': scowling.
scaup: scalp.
scrat: the devil.
scraumin': scribbling on.
scrawmy-cauf'd: having a badly-shaped calf (of the leg).
scruffle: weed turnips.
seaun: quickly.
seck: sack.
seeam: fat, lard.
seeat: soot.
seeght: lot (of).
seeght: sight.
seemin-glass: looking-glass.
seet: sight.
sell: self.
sen: say.
shap: shape.
shaumin': to warm the knees and feet by sitting close to the fire.
sheeanless: shoeless.
sheddler: swindler.
shill: howl, whine, whistle.
shun: shoes.
shuts: shutters.
side up: tidy.
sike: such.
sind: rinse.
skeeal: pail.
skelpin: huge.
skep: large basket.
slaaper: slippery.
slant: bent down.
slap: at great speed.
sleck: dust.
slope: impostor.
sluffened: disheartened.
sluppered: done in a slovenly, slip-shod way.
smedy: smithy.
smoke: discover.
snickle: snare.
snod: smooth, neat, snug.
snoutband: to be angry and hasty with.

L

spornin': spurring.
sprent: sprinkling.
staggarth: stack-yard.
stall: tire, weary.
stand-hecks: stalls.
stang: sting, throb, ache.
stark at the rent: very dear at the rent.
statis: annual fair at which farm servants were hired.
staup: walk.
steck: shut.
steeal: stool.
steg: gander.
stickle but haste: very great haste or speed.
stiddy: anvil.
stoor: value.
spraggy: young, lean.
stot: bullock.
stown: stolen.
stritch: strut about.
strum: stick.
swat: squat, sit.
swattin': hammering.
sweal: melt.
swill: bucket.
swill gullets: heavy drinkers.
swipple: flap-end.

Tack: piece-rate.
tail: pigtail or queue of a wig.
takker-in: the man who inspects the woven goods as he receives them from the weaver.
tane: one (the one).
tee: tie.
teeals: tools, also tales.
team: full.
teem: pour.
temm'd: poured.
temple: a piece of wood with brass pins at each end to keep the piece its proper width.
tent: look after.
tew: toil.
theeak: thatch.
theet: water-tight.
then: than.
thod: third.
thoddy: third man on the farm.
thir: those.
thivel: porridge stick.
thoil: endure, bear.
threng: busy.
tippy-teease: tip-toes.
tit: nag.
tite: quickly.
toltherin': hobbling.

touch: a small amount.
traake: wander aimlessly.
traipse: tramp.
trig: fill.
trod: footpath.
trouts: curds.
tucker: piece of linen formerly worn by women, folded across the breast.
tute: to it, get on with it.
tweea: two.

Ullot: owl.
uncouth: strange.
unscaape: to disclose, materialise, become apparent.
uphod: warrant, vouch for.

Vast: great deal, great number.

Wa': wall.
waintly: strangely.
wait: know.
walsh: insipid.
wame: stomach.
wammely: shaky, unsteady.
wankle: weak, tottery.
war: worse.
war-day: weekday.
warp: threads running lengthwise in a fabric, and crossed by the weft.
wath: ford.
wave: wove.
weam-tow: belly-band.
weazen-pipe: wind-pipe.
weean: female.
weaud: mad.
weft: threads interwoven with the warp.
wellanerin: alas!
whimly: soft.
whishon: cushion.
wharn: hand-mill, quern.
wick: living, alive.
wick: gather couch grass.
wick-set: quick-set, hedge.
wick-siller: quick-silver.
winder: winnow.
winner: window.
wisht: silent.
wooad: wold.
wom: home.
worsed: worsted.
wots: oats.
wrowt: worked.
wuther'd: roared.
wyes: heifer calves.

Yacker: acre.
yaeiver: however.
yakron: acorn.
yal: ale.
yal-hoose: ale-house.
yam: home.
yan: one.
yarmin': whining.
yat: gate.
yats: heats.
yeats: eat.
yeauke: itch.
yed: head.
yerd: heard.
yewn: oven.
yeth: earth.
yode: horse.
yowes: ewes.
yuen: oven.
yune: oven.
yune-head: oven top.

BIOGRAPHICAL NOTES

ABBAY, REV. RICHARD, M.A.

Born at Aldborough, near Boroughbridge, 11 February 1844. Lecturer and Demonstrator in Natural Science, King's College, London, 1868. Elected to Fellowship in Natural Science, Wadham College, Oxford, 1868.

Abbay wrote much poetry in standard English, his principal poem being one entitled 'The Castle of Knaresbrough,' a narrative poem in octosyllabic verse occupying 270 pages. (See Wm Andrews' *North Country Poets.*)

J. Horsfall Turner included Abbay's 'Barnaby of Boroughbridge' in his *Yorkshire Anthology*, 1901.

BINNALL, MRS GERALDINE B.

Second daughter of the late Hugh Pearson, solicitor, Malton, where she was born. Married the Rev. R. G. Binnall, who was vicar of Bransdale-cum-Farndale for four years. Later lived in Lincolnshire, and now resides at Chalford, Stroud. Mrs Binnall has written more verse in standard English than in dialect.

BLACKAH, THOMAS (1828–95)

Born at Hardcastle, near Greenhow Hill. A lead-miner in the Kell Houses area. Wrote and published at Pateley Bridge for many years *T'Nidderdale Olminac* under the pseudonym of Natty Nydds. Published *Songs and Poems*, 1867.

BLAKEBOROUGH, RICHARD (1850–1918)

Born at Ripon 24 January 1850, educated St Agnesgate Grammar School there. Later resided at Guisborough, which town he left in 1893. Died at Norton-on-Tees.

Richard Blakeborough was a gifted and versatile man who did excellent work in many fields. Besides being a painstaking collector and recorder of both folk-lore and dialect, he wrote two dramatic poems in the Cleveland Dialect, 'T'Hunt o' Yatton Brigg' and 'Aud Nan o' Sexhow,' which are without equal in this dialect. He also wrote many dialect prose sketches which achieved great popularity.

Blakeborough's *Wit, Character, Folk-lore, and Customs of the North Riding* is as indispensable to any student or lover of the Cleveland Dialect as it is to students of folk-lore. These pages bear ample witness to the value of Richard Blakeborough's work and our indebtedness to it.

BROWN, FRED

Born at Keighley. Moved to Huddersfield at the age of seven. Textile worker, who (in his own words) 'would like to see workers more craft conscious.' Author of *Songs of the Factory and the Loom*, 1943; *More Songs of the Factory and the Loom*, 1947.

BROWNE, REV. THOMAS (1771–98)

Born at Lastingham. First a schoolmaster at Yedingham, and then at Bridlington. For a time editor of the *Hull Advertiser*, and whilst a journalist took Holy Orders. Poems (standard English and dialect) published posthumously at Hull in 1800 under the title *Poems on Several Occasions*. A pioneer Yorkshire dialect poet whose dialect poems were often reprinted in the chap-books published in the first half of the nineteenth century.

BRUFTON, H. P. (1871–1947)

Born at Crookes, Sheffield. First worked as a grinder, and then with a firm of carpenters' brace-bit manufacturers. Contributed dialect verse to local journals under the pseudonym of 'T'Owd Hammer.' Published *Sheffield Dialect Poems*, 1932; *Sheffield Dialect and Other Poems*, 1937.

BURNLEY, James (1842–1919)

Born at Shipley. Studied law for a time, but devoted himself later to writing. Author of many works—poems, sketches, travel books—in standard English. Contributed much to Yorkshire journals, and was editor of *The Yorkshire Magazine* and *The Yorkshireman*. Produced a dialect annual, *Saunterer's Satchel*, 1874.

BYWATER, ABEL (1795–1873)

Born at Sheffield. At one time an awl-blade maker, and later a druggist. His Annuals set the fashion for this type of publication, but they were more serious in outlook than their successors. A man of strong convictions in religion, politics, and temperance reform, who wrote with passion on all these subjects. His writings, apart from the Annuals, appeared in the *Sheffield Courant*, the *Sheffield Examiner* and the *Iris*. His main single published work was *The Sheffield Dialect*, 1834.

CARLILL, JOHN ALBERT (1865–1947)

Born at Hull. Lived first forty-eight years of his life at Cottingham. Chartered accountant. Author of *Wo'zls*, 1909.

CARTER, F. A.

Born at Kirkburton, near Huddersfield. Regular dialect contributor to local journals. Founder member of Huddersfield Thespians and Yorkshire Comedy Players. Published many dialect plays. These include *Neighbourly Love*, 1930; *A Turn for t'Better*, 1932; *Mary's Black Eye*, 1938; *A Fine Romance*. Most of these plays have been broadcast.

CASTILLO, JOHN (1792–1845)

Born at Rathfarnum, near Dublin, about 1792. In his second or third year was brought by his parents to England. Spent childhood at Lealholm Bridge.

Castillo's first and best-known poem, 'Awd Isaac,' was first published under the title *A Specimen of the Bilsdale Dialect, or two poems on Isaac Telltruth, and Sammy Standfast* (with a six-page preface by John Nelson) by J. Metcalfe, at Northallerton, in 1832.

Awd Isaac, The Steeple Chase and other Poems was published at Whitby in 1843.

Castillo died at Pickering.

'Awd Isaac' had a very wide circulation, as it was included, indeed was the principal item, in the many *Specimens of Yorkshire Dialect* that were published (see also note 38).

CHARLESWORTH, DOUGLAS (1884–1941)

Born at Cawthorne, near Barnsley. Farmer, scholar, and sportsman, with a great love of the countryside and country folk. Published many dialect poems in the *Yorkshire Weekly Post, Poetry Review*, and the *Transactions of the Yorkshire Dialect Society*.

COOKSON, HENRY (1855–1943)

Born at Mirfield. By trade a plasterer. A prominent Methodist, and President of the dialect section of the Spen Valley Literary and Scientific Society. Contributed many dialect poems and sketches to the local press.

COWLEY, WILLIAM

Born at Middlesbrough 1915. Founded Cambridge University Yorkshire Society. Indian Civil Service 1939–48. Now farming at Over Silton, Thirsk. Author *Tara Devi and other Verses* (Lahore, Punjab, 1945).

COWLING, GEORGE H. (1886–1946)

Born at Leeds. Reader in English Language and Literature, Leeds University, 1923–7. Joint Editorial Secretary of the Yorkshire Dialect Society, 1919–27. Professor of English at Melbourne University, 1927–46. His publications include *A Yorkshire Tyke*, 1914; *The Dialect of Hackness*, 1915; *A Preface to Shakespeare*, 1925; *Chaucer*, 1926; *The Use of English*, 1934.

CUDWORTH, WILLIAM (1830–1906)

Born at Bradford. Began in the printing department of the *Yorkshire Observer*, later transferred to the editorial side. Wrote many books dealing with the history of Bradford and neighbourhood. Among his published works are *Round about Bradford*, 1876; *Yorkshire Dialect and Character Sketches*, 1884; *Yorkshire Speyks*, 1906.

DARREL, SOL (JAMES SHIRES, 1867–1946)

Born at Leeds. A director of the Bright Steel Co., Malton, where he died. Produced *The Chimney-Nook Original Almanack* from 1901 to 1916.

DIXON, JAMES HENRY (1803–1876)

Although Forshaw (*Holroyd's Collection of Yorkshire Ballads*) states Dixon was a native of Craven, William Andrews (*Modern Yorkshire Poets*) states he was born in London in 1803, and was sent to Skipton at an early age. He lived for a time at Grassington and in County Durham. In 1846 the Percy Society issued to its members a volume entitled *Ancient Poems, Ballads and Songs of the Peasantry of England*, edited by James Henry Dixon. Dixon also published an edition of *The Felon Sewe of Rokeby and The Freeres of Richmond.*

He died at Lausanne.

DOWSON, FRANCIS WRIGHTSON (1880–1947)

Born at Goathland 1880, died there 1947. Mr Dowson revived the Goathland Plough Stots some years ago. He was a great lover of dialect and folk-lore and was a member of the Council of the Yorkshire Dialect Society for many years.

Goathland in History and Folk-Lore, including original Dialect Verses (limited edition, posthumously, A. Brown & Sons, 1947).

ECCLES, JOSEPH H. (1824–1883)

Born at Ripponden, near Halifax. A self-taught man, he moved to Leeds in 1845, where he engaged in business. Contributed to local periodicals, and produced one or two dialect annuals, *Tommy Toddles*, *Tommy's Annual*, and *The Leeds Loiner*. Published *Yorkshire Songs*, 1872.

ELGEE, FRANK (1880–1944)

Born at North Ormesby. Late Curator of the Dorman Memorial and Stewart Park Museums, Middlesbrough.

Author of *The Moorlands of North-east Yorkshire*, 1912; *Romans in Cleveland*, 1923; *Early Man in North-east Yorkshire*, 1930; *Archaeology of Yorkshire* (with wife), 1933; *Scarth Wood Moor*, 1936, etc.

ENGLISH, BRENDA H. (DR BRENDA H. RIDDOLLS)

Born at Netherby, Sleights. Joint author (with Miss Irene Sutcliffe) of three volumes of *Rhymes of a Yorkshire Village* (Whitby, 1932, 1933, 1934).

GRASSBY, ELSIE A.

Born at Leavening, near Malton. Daughter of schoolmaster there. Entered service of G.P.O. at Hull at sixteen, and is still there as overseer, although, happily, she has maintained contact with the Wolds, and writes with intimate knowledge of them and their people.

GREGSON, JAMES R.

Born at Brighouse. Actor, producer, dramatist, and until recently Director of Drama, Northern Region, B.B.C. Author of many plays and stories, including *Young Imeson*, *Sar' Alice*, *T'Marsdens*, and *A Family Fugue*. His dialect plays represent the highest achievement in this branch of drama, and won wide recognition.

HALLIDAY, W. J.

Born at Pudsey. Editor of the *Transactions of the Yorkshire Dialect Society*, 1919–46, of *The York Minster Screen* (Yorkshire Dialect Reprints, No. 1), 1938, and of two collections of Yorkshire dialect prose, and one of verse, 1942–5. Contributor in and on Yorkshire dialect to various journals. Publications include *Refining Fires*, *Pro Patria*, and editions of English classics.

HAMPSON, WALTER (1864–1932)

Born at Rothwell, near Leeds. Started work at eight in a rope-walk. Moved early to Normanton, where he spent the rest of his life. Worked first with a colliery (as surfaceman), and then on the railway as cleaner, fireman, and engine-driver. Published *Songs of the Line and Other Poems*, 1905; *Tykes Abrooad*, 1911; *Private Job Muggleston*, 1915. Edited the *Clock Almanack* from 1918 to 1932.

HARDWICK, GEORGE

Born at Driffield. Has resided at Bridlington for many years. Publications: *Random Rhymes*, *Stories in Dialect*, *The Story of Flamborough* and several one-act plays. Has frequently broadcast dialect.

HARLAND, CAPTAIN JOHN

Compiled a Glossary of Words used in Swaledale (Trübner: London, 1873).

HARTLEY, John (1839–1915)

Born at Halifax. The most prolific of all Yorkshire dialect writers. Poet, story-writer, and essayist. Famous as the editor of the *Halifax Original Illuminated Clock Almanack* from 1867 until his death, with two short gaps when he lived in America. His publications include *Yorkshire Ditties*, 1868, 1873; *Yorkshire Tales*; *Yorkshire Puddin'*, 1876; *Seets i'London*, 1876; *Grimes' Trip To America*, 1877; *Seets i'Paris*, 1878.

HATTON, EDMUND (1844–93)

Born at Bradford. Cashier with a textile firm. His dialect verses appeared in *The Yorkshire Christmas Annual*, which he edited in 1871, and in the *Clock Almanack*, which he edited in 1873 and 1874, when John Hartley was in America.

HEATON, WILLIAM (1805–71)

Born at Luddenden, near Halifax. A carpet weaver, and later a park-keeper. Regular contributor to the local press. Published *The Flowers of Calderdale*, 1847; *The Old Soldier, Wandering Lover, and Other Poems*, 1857.

HEDGER, RUTH

Born at Fulford, York. Resided at Coxwold, where her father was vicar for many years. First dialect appeared in *The Countryman*, illustrated by her own engraving. Has written children's stories (one of which has been broadcast) and many short stories. Was in A.T.S. two years.

HOPPER, FLORENCE M.

Born at Driffield. Free-lance journalist and script writer for B.B.C. Has done much broadcasting.

HORSPOOL, ROBERT

Midlander by birth. Artist and craftsman by profession. Many years Art Master at Bridlington School. Publications: *The Wreckers of Auburnswick, The Silver Plate, Camborough Folk, The Price, The Bayle at Bridlington*, etc.

HYDE, FRANCIS AUSTIN

Born at Driffield, 1889. Headmaster Lady Lumley's Grammar School, Pickering. Publications (one-act dialect plays): *Wireless and Such Like, The Ship Comes In, First Aid, The Tyrant, Honest Folk, Safe Custody, After Marston Moor, Maker of Highways, Four White Socks*, and *Spanish Wine*.

LANCASTER, GEORGE

Born at North Ferriby, near Hull, 1846. Spent most of his boyhood at Welton. Went to Ontario. Returned to England 1879. Edited *Hull Bellman*. Published *Lays and Lyrics*, 1879. In 1883 joined staff of *Eastern Morning News*. In 1888 published *Legends of Lowgate*.

LANGSTAFF, LETITIA A.

Born at Middleton-in-Teesdale, married William Langstaff, a Mickleton farmer who is also a dialect poet. Mrs. Langstaff has composed words and music of songs and hymns which have been broadcast.

LAYCOCK, SAMUEL (1826–93)

Born at Marsden. Worked at a very early age in the woollen trade, and 'a sufferer from the evils that existed in the days preceding the Factory Acts' (Holroyd). Most of his verses are in the Lancashire dialect, and were contributed to Lancashire periodicals. He published *Lancashire Rhymes*, 1864; *Lancashire Songs*, 1866; *Lancashire Poems, Tales and Recitations*, 1875.

LEWIS, DAVID

Native of Knaresborough or immediate neighbourhood. At one time he was occupier of Belmont Farm near that town; but, according to William Grainge, with little success. He was afterwards book-keeper and a schoolmaster, but generally in poor circumstances. He died at Knaresborough in 1858.

The Landscape and Other Poems. York, 1815.

MALHAM-DEMBLEBY, JOHN

Author of *Original Tales and Ballads in the Yorkshire Dialect*, 1912.

MIDGLEY, WILSON

Born at Bingley. Journalist in England and America. Now Editor of *John o' London's Weekly*. Author of *Possible Presidents*, 1924; *From my Corner Bed*, 1946; *Cookery for Men Only*, 1948; *The Terrible Turk* (for children), 1948.

MILLIGAN, JAMES

Lived at Great Ayton a short time, and for a period at Stockton-on-Tees. The 4th edition of his *Hills and Vale of Cleveland*, 1885, was issued from Sheepscombe, near Stroud, where he was then living.

MOORMAN, F. W. (1872–1919)

Born at Ashburton. Professor of English Language, Leeds University, 1909–19. Editorial Secretary of the Yorkshire Dialect Society, 1911–16, and editor of *An Anthology of Yorkshire Dialect Poems*, 1916. Published in the Yorkshire dialect *Songs of the Ridings*, 1918; *Plays of the Ridings*, 1919; *Tales of the Ridings*, 1920. Author of *Robert Herrick: a Biography*, *Interpretation of Nature in English Poetry from Beowulf to Shakespeare*, and *Place-names of the West Riding*, etc.

MYERS, E. IRENE

Born at Yeadon. Interest in dialect began while teaching at Boroughbridge. Schoolmistress at Horton-in-Ribblesdale twelve years.

NEWBOULT, F. J.

Born at Bradford. Early life spent in the Bradford trade. Later entered journalism and became leader writer on the *Yorkshire Observer* and editor of the *Yorkshire Observer Budget*. Publications include *Summat an' Nowt*, *Abe Clegg in War-time*, and *The Upstroke*.

NICHOLAS, Q.

This is the pseudonym of an East Riding man who 'whether from shyness or shame' prefers to remain anonymous. May have spoken dialect as a boy, but no longer does so and blames his university education for this.

His lyrics appeared in the *Yorkshire Evening Post*.

NORTH, GORDON ALLEN

Born 7 February 1904, at Scholes, Thongsbridge. Has contributed short stories to various magazines, periodicals, and book collections, including *John o' London's Weekly*, *Northern Review*, *New Short Stories*, *Story*, etc. His stories have been broadcast by the B.B.C. Contributor to *Yorkshire Dialect Prose* (Second Series).

PARKE, A. IRVING

Born at Malton, 10 January 1881. Bank clerk at Whitby until he entered father's business at Amotherby Mill, January 1900.

Published *T'Awd Apple Tree*, 1927.

PETCH, IRENE

Born at Kirbymoorside. Has contributed non-dialect verse to many periodicals and appeared in *Some Yorkshire Poets*, 1924–5, and *The Best Poets of* 1928.

Publication: *The Waiting-Room*, Basil Blackwell, 1931.

PRESTON, BENJAMIN (1819–1902)

Born at Bradford. A worker in the woollen trade. Lived for a time at Bingley, and then at Eldwick. Many of his poems show his sympathies for the underpaid workers of his day, particularly in the textile industry. Published *Dialect Poems*, 1872; *Dialect and Other Poems*, 1881.

RATCLIFFE, DOROTHY UNA (MRS MCGRIGOR PHILLIPS)

Yachtswoman, traveller, lecturer, playwright, poetess, author of children's travel books, and of many Yorkshire character sketches. Is widely known for her dialect, drama, folk-lore, folk-dancing and many other interests. A generous patron of a wide range of North Country and National Cultural Institutions.

Publications for Children: *Nightlights*; *The Smuggling Hob*. Plays: *Dale Dramas*; *Nathaniel Baddely*; *Bookman*; *Hazelthwaite Hall*; *The Gone Away*; *Gypsy Dorelia*. Verse: *From all the Airts*; *Romany Joker*; *The Shooting of Jerry-go-Nimble*; *Dale Courtin'*; *Dale Lyrics*; *Singing Rivers*. Character Sketches: *Lapwings and Laverocks*; *What do they know of Yorkshire?* *Mrs Buffey in War Time*; *Fairings, Lillilows*; *Dale Folk*. Travel: *News of Persephone*; *Swallow of the Sea*; *Equatorial Dawn*; *South African Summer*.

SOWERSBY, MOSES (1846–1916)

Born at Wetwang. Lost his sight when twelve years of age. He continued to attend Wetwang school until he entered the Yorkshire School for the Blind, York, in 1859. He was admitted to the workshops of the Institution in 1867, married in 1870.

Published *Recitations in the Folk-Speech of East Yorkshire and Other Poems* with an introductory preface by the Very Rev. A. P. Purey-Cust, D.D., Dean of York (Leeds, 1914).

SUTCLIFFE, IRENE

Native of Whitby. Joint author (with Brenda English) of three volumes of *Rhymes of a Yorkshire Village*, Whitby, 1932, 1933, and 1934. The three volumes are illustrated by Miss Sutcliffe.

THWAITE, JOHN (1873–1941)

Born at West Burton, near Aysgarth, 26 January 1873. Died at Hawes, 1941. Served his apprenticeship as a grocer at Manchester. Eventually went into business at Hawes but with no great success. Had a deep love of his native fells, woods, gills, birds, and flowers, which is revealed in his *Wensleydale Dialect Rhymes*, published posthumously by Dalesman Publishing Co., 1946.

TURNER, BEN (1863–1942)

Born at Holmfirth. From textile worker became President of National Union of Dyers and Bleachers, 1922. M.P. for Batley, 1922–31. Minister of Mines, 1929. Chairman of Trades Union Congress, 1928. Mayor of Batley, 1914–16 and 1934. Knighted 1931. Regular contributor in dialect to local journals. Published *Pieces from a Yorkshire Loom*, 1909; *About Myself*, 1929; *Collected Rhymes and Verse*, 1934.

TURNER, REV. WALTER F. (–1916)

This author is best known for his character sketches published under the title *Goodies*. His father, the Rev. W. N. Turner, was vicar of Middleton, near Pickering, 1870–1902, and Walter F. acted as curate to his father from about 1897 to 1901. Previously he was assistant curate of St Matthew's, Westtown, Dewsbury. The Rev. Walter F. Turner died at Fridaythorpe.

TWEDDELL, FLORENCE (ELIZABETH COLE) (1824–1899)

Born at Stokesley. Married George Markham Tweddell in 1843. They were master and matron of Bury Industrial and Ragged Schools for some years. George Tweddell published his wife's *Rhymes and Sketches to illustrate the Cleveland Dialect* in 1875.

TWISLETON, TOM (1845–1917)

Born at Winskill. His father was a Craven farmer. He published *Poems in the Craven Dialect*, 1869.

UMPLEBY, ARTHUR STANLEY

Born at Boroughbridge 21 April 1887. Removed with parents to Birstwith, 1898. Entered North-Eastern Railway service 1901, and afterwards lived at Ripley, Flamborough,

Hawes, York, Moss, Staithes, Newham Bridge in Cleveland, Haverton Hill, Billingham, West Hartlepool, and Darlington. Now resides at Masham. Was drawn to dialect writing by the late Professor Moorman's Anthology. Publication: *A Bo'ddin o' Cowls*, 1937. Edited John Thwaite's *Wensleydale Dialect Rhymes*, 1946.

WALTER, ETHEL

Born at Bradford. Married to Walter Holroyd. Contributor to *Poetry Review*, *Poetry Quarterly*, *Woman's Magazine*, *Catholic Gazette*, and to two anthologies, *This Living Stone* and *The Greenwood Anthology of New Verse*. Published *Twenty-three Poems*.

WILLIAMSON, REV. T. P.

Was vicar of Little Brickhill, Bucks, when 'Jilted' appeared in *Tweddell's North of England Illustrated Annual*, 1878. He contributed another longer dialect poem on the St. Leger. Williamson lived in Cleveland.

WRIGHT, WILLIAM (1836–97)

Born in a house which was one of a group known as Hoylus End in Hermit Hole, a small village between Keighley and Haworth. In his early days was in turn a warp-dresser, a strolling player, and a soldier. Settled down as a warp-dresser. Wrote under the pseudonym of 'Bill o' th' Hoylus End,' and published *The Haworth, Cowenheead and Bogthorne Original Almanack*, 1873–79; *Random Rhymes and Rambles*, 1876; and a play *The Wreck of the Bella*.

WRIGLEY, AMMON (1861–1946)

Born at Saddleworth. Began work in the mill at the age of nine. Poet, dialect writer, artist, and archaeologist. The Ammon Wrigley Fellowship was founded in honour of his literary work in 1931. Published *Annals of Saddleworth*, 1901; *Songs of the Saddleworth Dales*, 1903; *Saddleworth: its Prehistoric Remains*, 1911; *Songs of a Moorland Parish*, 1912; *At the Sign of the Three Bonnie Lasses*, 1925; *Those were the Days*, 1937; *Songs of the Pennine Hills*, 1938, and numerous other works.

YORKE, MAY

Born at Scarborough, and has lived most of her life in Yorkshire. Her childhood was spent in Craven by the Ribble, then she lived by the Nidd at Bewerley for many years, and for the last twenty-five years by the Ure. Miss Yorke is a great lover of dialect, and has contributed many dialect poems to local journals and to the Transactions of the Yorkshire Dialect Society.

SELECT BIBLIOGRAPHY

BOOKS OF REFERENCE

A Bibliographical List of the Works that have been published or are known to exist in MS., illustrative of the various Dialects of English. Edited by Rev. Walter W. Skeat and J. H. Nodal. English Dialect Society, 1877.

Bibliographical account of nearly Fifteen Hundred Curious and Rare Books, Tracts, MSS. and Engravings relating to the History and Topography of Yorkshire. Collected by John Camden Hotten.

Folk-Lore Society Publications, 1881 and 1899.

History, Directory, and Gazetteer of the County of York. Edward Baines, 1823.

Notes and Queries, Vols. 1–8 (1849–53).

Rustic Speech and Folk-Lore. Elizabeth Mary Wright. O.U.P., 1913.

The Book of Days. W. and R. Chambers, 1863.

The Every Day Book. William Hone, 1878.

The New Yorkshire Gazetteer or Topographical Dictionary. S. R. Clarke, 1828.

The Yorkshire Library. William Boyne, 1869.

Transactions of the Yorkshire Dialect Society, 1897–1947.

Wit, Character, Folk-lore and Customs of the North Riding of Yorkshire. Richard Blakeborough. London: Henry Frowde, 1898. 2nd ed. Saltburn: W. Rapp & Sons, 1911.

Yorkshire Folk Talk. Rev. M. C. F. Morris. Henry Frowde, 1892.

GLOSSARIES

A Collection of English Words by John Ray, to which is appended Thoresby's Letter to Ray (1703), re-arranged and edited by Rev. Walter W. Skeat. E.D.S., 1874.

A Dictionary of Lowland Scotch. Charles Mackay, 1888.

A Dictionary of Swaledale Words. 1886.

A Dictionary of the Dialect of the North Riding of Yorkshire. Sir Alfred Edward Pease, Bt., M.A., with notes and comments by Major John Fairfax Blakeborough, M.C. Whitby, 1928.

A Glossary of Dialectal Place-Nomenclature. Robert Charles Hope. 2nd ed., 1883.

A Glossary of North Country Words. John Trotter Brockett. Newcastle, 1846.

A Glossary of Provincial Words used in Teesdale. [F. T. Dinsdale], 1873.

A Glossary of the Cleveland Dialect. Rev J. C. Atkinson, 1868.

A Glossary of the Dialect of the Hundred of Lonsdale. Robert Backhouse Peacock. Edited by Rev. J. C. Atkinson. Asher & Co., 1869.

A Glossary of Words and Phrases pertaining to the Dialect of Cumberland. William Dickinson. E.D.S., 1878.

A Glossary of Words and Phrases pertaining to the Dialect of Cumberland. Re-arranged by E. W. Prevost. Carlisle, 1899.

A Glossary of Words pertaining to the Dialect of Mid-Yorkshire with others peculiar to Lower Nidderdale. C. Clough Robinson. E.D.S., 1876.

A Glossary of Words used in Holderness. Frederick Ross, Richard Stead, and Thomas Holderness. E.D.S., 1877.

A Glossary of Words used in the Neighbourhood of Sheffield. Sidney Oldall Addy. E.D.S., 1888.

A Glossary of Words used in Swaledale, Yorkshire. Captain John Harland of Reeth, Richmond. Trübner & Co. for E.D.S., 1873.

A Glossary of Yorkshire Words and Phrases collected in Whitby and the Neighbourhood by An Inhabitant. [F. K. Robinson], 1855.
A List of Provincial Words in use at Wakefield. William Stott Banks, 1865.
American Dialect Society Publication, No. 2.
A Provincial Glossary with a collection of Local Proverbs and Popular Superstitions. Francis Grose. 1st ed., 1787; 2nd ed., 1790.
A Warwickshire Word-Book. G. F. Northall. E.D.S., 1896.
Beauties of Wiltshire (Britton, 1825). Compared with Akerman's Glossary. E.D.S., 1879.
Dialectal Words from Kennett's Parochial Antiquities (1695). E.D.S., 1879.
Dialect of the West Riding of Yorkshire. Samuel Dyer, 1891.
East Yorkshire Words (Supplement). Mr Marshall (1796). E.D.S., 1879.
English Dialect Words of the Eighteenth Century as shown in the Dictionary of Nathaniel Bailey. Edited by W. E. A. Axon. E.D.S., 1883.
Rustic Studies in the Westmorland Dialect. 1868.
The Dialect of Craven in the West Riding, by a native of Craven. [Rev. Wm Carr, B.D.], 2 vols., 1828.
The Dialect of Cumberland. Robert Ferguson. Williams & Norgate.
The Dialect of Leeds and its Neighbourhood. C. C. Robinson, 1862.
The Dialect of the West of England. James Jennings, 1869.
The English Dialect Dictionary. Edited by Joseph Wright, 1898–1905.
The Folk-Speech of Cumberland. Alex. Craig Gibson. Carlisle, 1880.
The Folk-Speech of East Yorkshire. John Nicholson, 1889.
The Hallamshire Glossary. Rev. Joseph Hunter, 1829.
The Rural Economy of Yorkshire. Mr Marshall. T. Cadell, 1788.
The Slang Dictionary. Hotten. 3rd ed., 1864.
The Speech of Holderness and East Yorkshire. W. H. Thompson. Hull, 1890.
Vocabulary of East Anglia. E.D.S., 1879.
Westmorland and Cumberland Dialects. 1839.

BOOKS OF PROVERBS

A Collection of English Proverbs. J. R(ay). Cambridge, 1670.
A Complete Collection of English Proverbs. J. Ray. London, 1817.
A Dictionary of Phrase and Fable. Rev. E. Cobham Brewer. Cassell.
A Dictionary of Quotations from Authors Old and New together with an Alphabet of Proverbs. J. M. Dent & Sons. Everyman ed.
A Hand-Book of Proverbs. Henry G. Bohn, 1855.
English Proverbs and Proverbial Phrases. W. Carew Hazlitt, 1869.
Yorkshire Toasts, Proverbs, Similes and Sayings. Richard Blakeborough. London: E. T. W. Dennis, 1907.

YORKSHIRE DIALECT VERSE

A Bo'ddin o' Cowls. Arthur Stanley Umpleby. C.U.Y.S., 1937.
A Specimen of the Bilsdale Dialect. Northallerton, 1832.
A Yorkshire Dialogue in its pure Natural Dialect as it is now commonly spoken in the North Parts of Yorkshire. York. 1683, 1685, 1697.
A Yorkshire Tyke. George H. Cowling. Grant Richards, Ltd, 1914.
Collected Rhymes and Verse, 1884–1934. Sir Ben Turner.
Dale Courtin'. Songs in the Dialect of the Yorkshire Dales. Dorothy Una Ratcliffe. John Lane, 1933.
Leet Livvy. J. S. Fletcher. Sidgwick & Jackson, Ltd., 1919.

More Rhymes of a Yorkshire Village. Irene Sutcliffe and Brenda H. English. Whitby, 1933.
More Songs of the Factory and the Loom. Fred Brown. Huddersfield, 1947.
Musings of Field and Hearth. Sherwin. Bradford.
Poems in the Craven Dialect. Tom Twisleton. Settle, 1893. 5th ed.
Poems in the North Yorkshire Dialect by the late John Castillo. Edited by George Markham Tweddell. Stokesley, 1878.
Quaaint Owd Knayesborough and Other Poems in the Dialect of the West Riding of Yorkshire. C. W. Eastwood. Folk Press.
Random Rhymes. E. Yorks. Dialect. George Hardwick.
Recitations in the Folk Speech of East Yorkshire and other Poems. Moses Sowersby. Leeds, 1914.
Rhymes and Sketches to illustrate the Cleveland Dialect. Mrs G. M. Tweddell (Florence Cleveland). Stokesley, 1875.
Rhymes of a Yorkshire Village. Irene Sutcliffe and Brenda H. English. Whitby, 1932.
Rhymes, Verses and Poems from a Yorkshire Loom. Sir Ben Turner. Pontefract, 1934.
Sheffield Dialect and other Poems. T'Owd Hammer (H. P. Brufton). Sheffield, 1937.
Songs of the Factory and the Loom. Fred Brown. Huddersfield.
Songs of the Ridings. F. W. Moorman. Elkin Mathews, 1918.
Still More Rhymes from a Yorkshire Village. Irene Sutcliffe and Brenda H. English. Whitby, 1934.
T'Band Contest and other Poems and Parodies. Aaron Calder (George Todd).
The Dialect Poems of Benjamin Preston. Saltaire, 1872.
T'Hunt o' Yatton Brigg. Richard Blakeborough, 1896. 2nd ed., 1899.
Under T'Hawthorn. Dorothy Una Ratcliffe. Frederick Muller, Ltd, 1946.
Wensleydale Dialect Rhymes. John Thwaite. Dalesman Publishing Co., 1946.
Woz'ls. J. A. Carlill. Hull, 1909.
York Minster Screen. Y.D.S. Reprint, No. 1, 1937. Edited by W. J. Halliday and Bruce Dickins.
Yorkshire Ditties. John Hartley. W. Nicholson & Sons.
Yorkshire Ditties. John Hartley. Edited by William Deardon. John Camden Hotten, 1868.
Yorkshire Ditties (Second Series). Wakefield: William Nicholson.
Yorkshire Songs. J. H. Eccles. Leeds: Hirst, Brooke, and Hirst, 1862.

YORKSHIRE DIALECT PROSE

Adventures of a Yorkshire Farmer and his Scapegrace Nevvy in London. Timothy Goorkrodger. F. M. Fetherston, Huddersfield.
Brazzock or Sketches of some humourous characters of a Holderness Parish. Rev. William Smith. A. Brown & Sons, Ltd, 1905.
Chuckle with Chickweed. John Lyth. Henry Walker, Ltd, Leeds, n.d. (1947).
Goodies and other Stories in a Yorkshire Dialect. Walter F. Turner. E. T. W. Dennis & Sons, Ltd, n.d.
Grimes's Trip to America. John Hartley. Wakefield: Wm. Nicholson & Sons, 1877.
Lizzie Leckonby. J. Fairfax Blakeborough.
Oops an' Doons an' Sayin's an' Doin's o' Timothy Goorkrodger. Knaresborough, n.d.

Rattleham Feast or t'Adventures o' Nicholas Gravy, and John Rushforth his man, with other tales. Henry Constantine, Senr. Carlton-in-Coverdale. Beverley, 1858.
Stories in Dialect. George Hardwick.
The Sheffield Dialect. Abel Bywater, 1834.
Yorkshire Dialect and Character Sketches. W. Cudworth, 1884.
Yorkshire Dialect Prose. Henry Walker, Ltd, Leeds, for Y.D.S., 1944.
Yorkshire Dialect Prose (Second Series). Henry Walker, Ltd. for Y.D.S., 1945.
Yorkshire Dialect Readings. Richard Blakeborough.
Yorkshire Pudding. John Hartley.
Yorkshire Speyks. W. Cudworth, 1906.

YORKSHIRE DIALECT VERSE AND PROSE

(Individual Authors.)

Dialect Poems and Prose of Thomas Blackah. Edited by H. J. L. Bruff. York, 1937.
Original Tales and Ballads in the Yorkshire Dialect. John Malham-Dembleby. The Walter Scott Publishing Co., 1912.
Rural Poetry and Prose. Henry Constantine of Carlton, the Coverdale Bard. Beverley, 1867.
T'Awd Apple Tree and some verses in the Yorkshire Dialect. A. Irving Parke. Malton, 1927.

ANTHOLOGIES OF YORKSHIRE DIALECT

A Little Book of Yorkshire Dialect. *Y.D.S. Transactions.* Extra number, No. 1, 1921.
A Yorkshire Dialect Reciter compiled by George H. Cowling. Folk Press.
Broad Yorkshire, being Poems and Sketches from the writings of Castillo, Tweddell, Reed, Brown, Lewis and others. Edited by W. H. Burnett. Middlesbrough, 2nd ed., 1885.
Specimens of the Yorkshire Dialect. Leeds.
" " " " York.
" " " " Richmond, 1887.
" " " " Knaresborough.
" " " " Driffield, 1899.
" " " " Otley.
The Yorkshire Dialect exemplified in various Dialogues, Tales and Songs. London: William Cole, 10 Newgate St.
The Yorkshireman's Book. Edited by Charles Ireton. Ripon: W. Harrison.
Yorkshire Dialect Poems (1673–1915). Compiled by F. W. Moorman. 3rd impression, 1919.
Yorkshire Dialect Poems (1914–43). Henry Walker, Ltd., for Y.D.S., 1943.

OTHER ANTHOLOGIES WHICH INCLUDE YORKSHIRE DIALECT

A Garland of Poetry by Yorkshire Authors. Selected by Abraham Holroyd. Saltaire, 1873.
Ancient Poems, Ballads, and Songs of the Peasantry of England. Edited by Robert Bell. London: Griffin Bohn & Co., 1862.

Country Ballads, Preserved by Tradition, and never before Printed. Pateley Bridge, 1869.

Early Ballads illustrative of History, Traditions and Customs. Edited with notes by Robert Bell. London: Charles Griffin & Co.

Holroyd's Collection of Yorkshire Ballads. Edited by Chas. F. Forshaw. London: George Bell & Sons, 1892.

Modern Yorkshire Poets. Edited by William Andrews. Hull, 1885.

North Country Poets. Edited by William Andrews. Hull, 1889.

Some Yorkshire Poets (1924–25). Edited by S. Fowler Wright. Merton Press.

The Ballads and Songs of Yorkshire. Edited by C. J. Davison Ingledew Bell and Daldy, 1860.

The Book of the Microcosm. Edited by Dorothy Una Ratcliffe.

The County Anthologies, No. 1, Yorkshire. Edited by G. F. Wilson, 1929.

The Northern Minstrel or Tyne Songster. Gateshead, 1806.

The Poets and Poetry of Yorkshire. William Grainge. Wakefield, 1868.

The Poets of Yorkshire. William Cartwright Newsam and John Holland. London, 1845.

The Yorkshire Anthology, a Collection of Ancient and Modern Ballads, Poems, and Songs, relating to the County of Yorkshire. Collected by J. O. Halliwell. London, 1851. Printed for private circulation.

The Yorkshire Garland and Specimens of the Yorkshire Dialect. Northallerton, 1825.

York Poets and Poetry. (Manuscript—not published.) By T. P. Cooper.

Yorkshire Garland. Northallerton, 1826.

OTHER WORKS INCLUDING YORKSHIRE DIALECT

A few Specimen Poems and Aphorisms. W. H. Burnett. Blackburn, 1907.

Awd Isaac, The Steeple Chase and Other Poems. John Castillo. Whitby.

Collected Rhymes and Prose 1884–1934. Sir Ben Turner (1843).

Earning a Living. Harry Brearley. Mexborough, n.d. (1947).

Memoirs of Samuel Hick, the Village Blacksmith (Aberford). Wm Nicholson & Sons, n.d.

Poems on Several Occasions. Rev. Thomas Browne, 1800.

Random Rhymes and Rambles. Bill o' th' Hoylus End, 1876.

Songs of the Line and Other Poems. Walter Hampson, 1905.

The Bard of the Dales or Poems and Miscellaneous Pieces with a Life of the Author written by himself, by John Castillo. Stokesley: W. F. Pratt, 1858.

Ditto Windermere, 1902.

The Bards and Authors of Cleveland and South Durham and the Vicinage. George Markham Tweddell. Stokesley, 1872.

The Doctor. Robert Southey. Longmans, Green & Co., 1874.

The Hand of Glory. Collected by the late R. Blakeborough and edited by J. Fairfax Blakeborough, M.C. Grant Richards, n.d.

The Hills and Vale of Cleveland and other Poems. James Milligan. Middlesbrough. 3rd ed., 1881.

The Landscape and Other Poems. David Lewis. York, 1815.

Northern Garlands. Edited by Joseph Ritson, 1810.

Yorkshire Legends and Traditions. Rev. Thomas Parkinson, 1889.

Yorkshire Oddities. S. Baring Gould. John Hodges, 1874.

ALMANACKS

Hiscock's Wensleydale and Swaledale Almanack. 1910–15.
Poet Close's Chronicles of Westmoreland. 1871–81.
Smithson's Northallerton Almanack. 1880–1913.
Spencer's Richmond Almanack. 1886–1907.
The Bairnsla Foak's Annual an Pogmoor Olmenack, 1887 (for memoir of Charles Rogers—Tom Treddlehoyle).
The Chimney Nook Original Almanac in the Yorkshire Dialect by Sol Darrel. 1903–15. (Leeds.)
The Nidderdill Olminac. 1886.
The Halifax Original Clock Almanack. 1867–1947.
Tweddell's North of England Illustrated Annual. 1878.
Tyke's Own Almanack. 1923. (York.)

YORKSHIRE AND NORTHERN MAGAZINES

Northern Lights. 1939.
Northern Review. 1946 to date.
The Country Words of the West Riding. Price 1*d.* Monthly. Vol. 1, 1870.
The County Monthly, Vol. 1, 1901–2.
The Dalesman. 1939 to date.
The Northern Counties' Magazine, Vol. 1, 1900–1.
The Yorkshire Monthly. 1934–5.
Yorkshire County Magazine. 1871–91.
Yorkshire Notes and Queries, Vol. 1.

DIALECT OTHER THAN YORKSHIRE

Chronicles of Scottish Poetry. Edited by J. Sibbald. Edinburgh, 1802.
Cummerland Talk. John Richardson. Carlisle, 1886.
Dialect of South Lancashire. Samuel Bamford. Manchester, 1850.
Lancashire Rhymes. Samuel Laycock. J. Heywood, n.d.
Legends and Historical Notes on Places in the East and West Wards of Westmorland. Thomas Gibson. 1877.
Miscellaneous Poems. John Stagg. Wigton, 1808.
Oor Mak o' Talk. An Anthology of Lakeland Dialect Poems. Carlisle, 1946.
Poetical Works of Richard Watson (The Teesdale Poet). Darlington, 1884.
The Folk-Speech of Cumberland. A. C. Gibson. Bemrose & Sons, 1880.
The Poetical Works of Robert Anderson. Carlisle, 1820.
The Songs and Ballads of Cumberland. Edited by Sidney Gilpin. Carlisle, 1866.
The Songs of the Tyne. Newcastle. John Ross, n.d.
The Westmoreland and Cumberland Dialects. Dialogues, Poems, Songs, and Ballads by various writers. London: John Russell Smith, 1839.
Tim Bobbin's Toy-Shop Open'd. Manchester, 1763.
Tyneside Dialect Poems. J. E. Smith. Newcastle, 1923.

BOOKS WITH YORKSHIRE DIALECT OR NORTH COUNTRY FOLK-LORE INTEREST

About Yorkshire. Thomas and Katharine Macquoid. 1883.
A Compendious account of the Antient and Present State of the Northern Circuit. Samuel Tymms. London, 1837.
A Guide to Cotherstone and Neighbourhood. Allan Ramsden. 1911.
A Month in Yorkshire. Walter White. 3rd ed., 1859.
A Picture of Whitby and its Environs. Rev. George Young. Whitby, 1840.
A Yorkshire Man's Coat of Arms. London: O. Hodgson, Maiden Lane.
Celebrities of the Yorkshire Wolds. Frederick Ross. 1878.
Choice Notes from Notes and Queries (Folk Lore). 1859.
Christmas Waits and Minstrels of Bygone York. T. P. Cooper.
Country Contentments, Courtesies and Customs. Moira Meighn. Medici Society.
County Folk-lore. Vol. 2 (N. Riding, York and the Ainsty). Edited by Mrs. Gutch (Nutt), 1901.
Cradle Songs and Nursery Rhymes. Edited by Grace Rhys. Canterbury Poets.
Croft Spaw: Yorkshire. A Brief Address with digressions. 3rd ed., 1822.
Drunken Barnaby's Four Journeys to the North of England. 1805 ed.
East Yorkshire. A. N. Cooper. 1913.
English Folklore. Christina A. Hole. 1940.
English Folklore. A. R. Wright. Benn's Sixpenny Library.
Flamborough Village and Headland. Edited by Robert Fisher. Hull, 1894.
Forty Years in a Moorland Parish. Rev. J. C. Atkinson. 1891.
Four Boon Fellows. Alfred J. Brown. J. M. Dent & Sons, Ltd, 1930.
From Eden Vale to the Plains of York. Edmund Bogg, Leeds.
Gleanings from an Iron Chest. Mary A. Boultree. Darlington, 1901.
Goathland in History and Folk-lore. F. W. Dowson. (Privately printed.) 1947.
Guide to Ryedale. George Frank. 3rd ed., 1875.
Guide to Wensleydale (John Routh). 2nd ed., 1879.
Higher Wharfeland. Edmund Bogg. Leeds, 1904.
History and Topography of the Wapentake of Claro. Beverley, 1871.
History, Directory and Gazetteer of the County of York. 1823.
History of Knaresborough. E. Hargrove. 1828.
History of Richmond. Christopher Clarkson. 1821.
Humours of Village Life. J. Fairfax Blakeborough, M.C. 1933.
In and Around Darlington. C. P. Nicholson.
John Hartley, Memoir of. J. H. Waddington. (Privately printed.) 1939.
John Hartley. W. J. Halliday. Trans. Y. D. S. 1939.
Lancashire Folk-lore. John Harland and T. T. Wilkinson. 1867.
Legends and Superstitions of the County of Durham. William Brockie. Sunderland, 1886.
Letters of Laurence Sterne. 1794.
Let us now praise Famous Men. A. W. M. Close (unpublished).
Life and Legends of Saint Chad. R. Hyett Warner. Bell & Daldy.
Life in a Yorkshire Village. J. Fairfax Blakeborough. Stockton, 1912.
Lights o' York. T. P. Cooper.
Love's Cradle and Other Papers. Thomas Newbigging. J. M. Dent & Co., 1902.
Moorland Tramping in West Yorkshire. Alfred J. Brown. 1931.
Mrs Buffy in Wartime. Dorothy Una Ratcliffe. 1942.
My Moorland Patients. R. W. S. Bishop. John Murray, 1922.
Nidderdale. William Grainge. 1863.

Nooks and Corners of Yorkshire. J. S. Fletcher. Eveleigh Nash.
North Country Lore and Legend. 1887.
Northern Garlands. Edited by Joseph Ritson. London: R. Triphook, 1810.
Old Cleveland: a collection of papers on Local Writers and Local Worthies. Middlesbrough, 1886.
Old Time Local Quips and Quirks collected by A. W. M. Close. (Not published.)
Old Yorkshire. William Smith. 8 vols. 1881–91.
Original Readings. William Myers, Wetwang. (Manuscript.)
Pennine Ways from Skipton. The Saint Catherine Press, Ltd.
Picturesque Yorkshire (York and North Riding). W. Andrews. Valentine & Sons.
Publications of the Folk-lore Society, XLV. 1899.
Rambles in Cleveland. M. Heavisides. Stockton, 3rd ed., 1909.
Rambles in Swaledale. John Routh. Hawes, 1880.
Rambles in Upper Wharfedale. B. J. Harker.
Rambles in Wensleydale and Swaledale. J. Routh. Leyburn, n.d.
Recollections from a Yorkshire Dale. C. J. F. Atkinson. Heath Cranton, 1934.
Records of a Yorkshire Manor. Sir Thomas Lawson-Tancred. Edwin Arnold & Co.
Regal Richmond. Edmund Bogg. Leeds, 1909.
Reminiscences of Scottish Life and Character. E. B. Ramsay, Dean of Edinburgh. 15th ed., 1867.
Richmondshire. Edmund Bogg.
Richmondshire, its Ancient Lords and Edifices. W. H. D. Longstaffe.
Robin Hood: Ballads and Songs relating to. Bell & Daldy, 1865.
Romantic Richmondshire. H. Speight. 1897.
Roseberry Topping, A Poem by Thomas Pierson, with notes by John Walker Ord. Stockton, 1847.
Round about Leeds. Edmund Bogg. Leeds, 1904.
Scarborough. Ernest E. Taylor. 'Handy' Guide Series. 1921.
Scenery of the Whitby and Pickering Railway. 1836.
Stokesley and District Past and Present, with a chapter on Bilsdale and its Hunt. J. Fairfax Blakeborough.
Studies in Nidderdale. Joseph Lucas. Pateley Bridge, n.d.
Summer Holidays in North East England. Walter Scott, n.d.
Swaledale. Ella Pontefract and Marie Hartley. J. M. Dent & Sons.
Sydall's Charity. Knaresborough: W. Parr.
Teesdale. C. P. Nicholson. 'Handy' Guide Series. 1921.
The Annals of Stockton-on-Tees. Henry Heavisides. Stockton, 1865.
The Border Land in Old Time. Carlisle, 1903.
The Bridges of the County of Durham. H. D. Pritchett.
The Cleveland Hounds as a Trencher Fed Pack. Sir Alfred E. Pease. 1887.
The Common Bellman of the City of York. T. P. Cooper.
The County of the White Rose. A. C. Price. 1915.
The County Palatine of Durham. Gaillard Thomas Lapley. 1900.
The Crosses on the North York Moors. T. H. Woodwark. Whitby, 1926.
The Enchanting North. J. S. Fletcher. 1908.
The Evolution of an English Town. Gordon Home. J. M. Dent & Sons, Ltd., 1915.
The Golden Vale of Mowbray. Edmund Bogg. Leeds, 1909.
The Hermit in York. Mrs Sidney. 1823.
The History and Antiquities of Cleveland. Rev John Graves. Carlisle, 1808.
The History and Antiquities of the Parish of Darlington in the Bishoprick. W. Hylton Dyer Longstaffe. Darlington, 1854.

The History and Antiquities of Masham and Mashamshire. John Fisher. Ripon: W. Harrison, 1865.
The History and Antiquities of Northallerton. C. J. Davison Ingledew. 1858.
The History of Northallerton. 1791.
The History and Antiquities of Scarborough. Thomas Hinderwell. 2nd ed., 1811.
The History and Antiquities of the Deanery of Craven. 3rd ed.
The History of the Castle, Town and Forest of Knaresborough. E. Hargrove. 1798.
The Honest Yorkshire-Man. A Ballad Farce acted with great Applause at the Theatre Royal in Drury Lane and Covent Garden, written by Mr Harry Carey. London: Printed for T. Lownds at his Circulating Library in Fleet Street, MDCCLXIII.
The Larchfield Diary (Francis Mewburn, First Railway Solicitor). 1876.
The Life and Adventures of that most eccentric character James Hirst (of Rawcliffe). Knottingley, n.d.
The Literary Shrines of Yorkshire. J. A. Erskine Stuart. 1892.
The Lower Vale of Wharfe and York. Edmund Bogg. 1923.
The Middle Valley of the Wharfe. Edmund Bogg. 1923.
The New Yorkshire Gazetteer. 1828.
The North Riding of Yorkshire. Joseph E. Morris. Methuen.
The Rivers, Mountains and Sea-Coast of Yorkshire. John Phillips. 2nd ed., 1855.
The Road to the North. Frank J. Nash. North-Eastern Railway Co., 1903.
The Sea Fisherman. J. C. Wilcocks. 1868.
The Shepherd of Banbury's Observations. Sylvan Press.
The Spell of Yorkshire. J. Cumming Walters. Methuen, 1931.
The Story of Flamborough. George Hardwick. (Privately printed.)
The Tourist's Guide, being a concise History and description of Ripon. 1838.
The Trial and Life of Eugene Aram, Several of his Letters and Poems, and his Plan and Specimens of an Anglo-Celtic Lexicon. Richmond, 1832.
The Watering Places of Cleveland. Samuel Gordon. Redcar, 1869.
The Yorkshire Coast and the Cleveland Hills and Dales. John Leyland. 1892.
The Yorkshire Garland. York, 1788.
Tramping in Yorkshire (North and East). Alfred J. Brown. 1932.
Vallis Eboracensis, comprising The History and Antiquities of Easingwold. Thomas Gill. 1852.
Waifs and Strays of North-Humber History. Rev. Scott F. Surtees. 1864.
Walks and Talks on the North Yorkshire Moors. W. Ridley-Makepeace. 1931.
Walks Through Leeds, or the Strangers Companion. John Heaton. 1835.
Walks in Yorkshire. W. S. Banks. 1866.
Walks Through the City of York. Robert Davies. 1880.
Weardale Past and Present. J. J. Graham. Northumberland Press, Gateshead.
Wensleydale. Ella Pontefract and Marie Hartley. J. M. Dent & Sons, Ltd., 1936.
Wensleydale. Ernest E. Taylor. 'Handy' Guide Series. 1921.
Whitby. F. K. Robinson. 1860.
Whitby Lore and Legend. Shaw Jeffrey.
York. K. E. T. Wilkinson. 'Handy' Guide Series, No. 12.
York. The Titles 'Lord Mayor' and 'Right Honourable.' T. P. Cooper. Corporation of the City of York, 1935.
Yorkshire Anecdotes. R. V. Taylor. 1883.
Yorkshire Dales and Fells. Gordon Home. 1906.
Yorkshire Days and Yorkshire Ways. J. Fairfax Blakeborough, M.C. 1935.

Yorkshire Illustrations of English History. J. G. Miall. 1865.
Yorkshire North Riding Footpath Guides. The Saint Catherine Press.
Yorkshire Rivers: (1) The Wharfe; (2) The Nidd; (3) The Ure; (4) The Swale. Tom Bradley. Yorkshire Post.
Yorkshire Tour. Ella Pontefract and Marie Hartley. J. M. Dent & Sons, Ltd.
Yorkshire Treasure. R. Wilfrid Crosland. 1947.
Yorkshire Legends and Traditions. Thomas Parkinson. Stock, 1889.

INDEX OF PERSONS

INDEX OF PLACES IN YORKSHIRE

INDEX OF PLACES OUTSIDE YORKSHIRE

GENERAL INDEX

INDEX OF FIRST LINES